## PUNCTUATION



## DICTION



## SPELLING



## MECHANICS



## LIBRARY AND RESEARCH PAPER



## CORRESPONDENCE




THE COMPOSITION AS A WHOLE

THE PARAGRAPH

ANALYSIS OF THE SENTENCE

GOOD SENTENCES

GRAMMATICAL USAGE

PUNCTUATION

DICTION

SPELLING

MECHANICS

LIBRARY AND RESEARCH PAPER

CORRESPONDENCE

scrupulous - 230
beneficent
empirical } 231
discrimination
vulnerable } 232
predominant
simultaneously } 233
intuitive
entities } 235
procrastination
amiability } 236
perversity 239
sublimate 240
apocalyptical 241
potent
despicable - 271
nicety - 272
ingenuous
Cynical }
dexterity 274
stoical 275

frugality
parsimonious
flagrant } 36[illegible]

Prodigal 369

circumspect
punctilious

rigorously
meticulous } 3[illegible]

Probity
malevolent
mitigated } 3[illegible]

376

moralizing 63
stimulus 64
pseudo 64
analogous
[illegible]
categorical

COLLEGE HANDBOOK

OF

COMPOSITION

CT analysis by classification by division

8T. what does [illegible] scientific Revolution

Monday
SEMANTIC, PARABLE
Page 123 CT

Fri WRITE THEME
out of class

voc. wed.
words to too two

SIXTH EDITION

# COLLEGE HANDBOOK OF COMPOSITION

EDWIN C. WOOLLEY FRANKLIN W. SCOTT FREDERICK BRACHER

D. C. HEATH AND COMPANY Boston

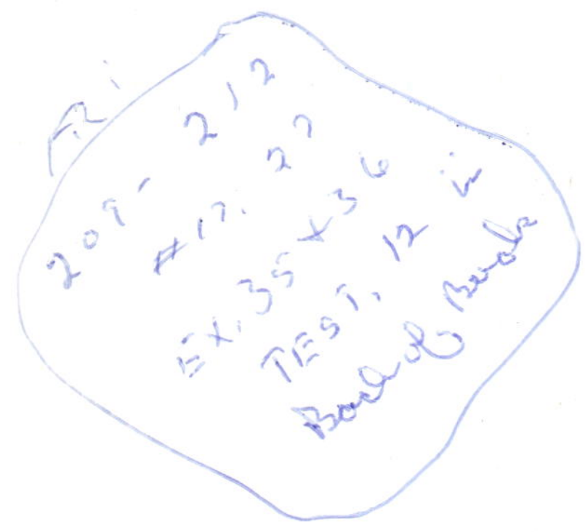



*Printed in the United States of America* 5 B 9

*Library of Congress Catalog Card Number 58–5894*

# PREFACE

The Sixth Edition of the *College Handbook of Composition* has been reorganized and renumbered in order to make material more easily available to students. In place of the 100 numbered divisions of the Fifth Edition, there are now 50 major reference sections, plus sections on The Library, The Research Paper, and Correspondence. Most of the sections have been rewritten to include a concise explanation of each rule as well as illustrative sentences. Exercises have been reworked, expanded, and placed immediately after the explanation of the points under discussion. A good many general review exercises have been added. The principal aims of this revision have been to simplify the organization of material, to clarify explanations, and to expand and modernize the exercises.

In its approach to the problems of usage, the Sixth Edition recognizes that English varies with time and circumstance. However, it assumes that the user of a handbook will want the reassurance of plain answers to simple questions: Is it all right to use this construction? How should this sentence be punctuated? An answer which merely hands back to the questioner the responsibility for making a choice defeats the purpose of a handbook.

The Sixth Edition discusses the existence of levels of usage and attempts throughout to increase the student's sensitivity to the tremendous potential of the English language. But an earnest attempt has also been made to give unequivocal answers to common questions on current usage.

FREDERICK BRACHER

# CONTENTS

# COLLEGE HANDBOOK OF COMPOSITION

# The Composition as a Whole

## 1. PURPOSE AND PLAN IN WRITING

- **a.** Choosing and limiting a subject
- **b.** Planning a paper
- **c.** Unity
- **d.** Organizing material
- **e.** Order of material
- **f.** Emphasis

## 2. OUTLINING

- **a.** Topic and sentence outlines
- **b.** Logical subdivisions
- **c.** Overlapping subdivision
- **d.** Single subdivision
- **e.** Specimen outlines and student theme

## 3. WRITING THE PAPER

- **a.** Coherence
- **b.** Beginning a composition
- **c.** Ending a composition

## 1 PURPOSE AND PLAN IN WRITING

The purpose of most writing is practical: to give clear directions for operating an adding machine, to explain why a certain clause should be inserted in a contract, to complain about trash pickup service, to summarize a patient's symptoms and the laboratory reports, to present the results of a research project. Composition courses in college are supposed to teach the student how to say, clearly and effectively, what he may need to say, and a major part of such a course is the writing of "themes." These are artificial exercises: once past freshman English, a student will probably never have to write a theme again. But if he is planning a professional or executive career, he will have to do a good deal of writing of a more practical kind. Themes are only a means to an end, and writing themes is a useful exercise only if it improves one's ability to express himself in the practical situations which he will eventually be confronted with.

A realistic attitude is needed, and too often a student's attitude toward theme writing is unrealistic. "A 500-word theme is due next Monday. What shall I write about? If I write about my job last summer, can I get 500 words?" This kind of thinking exactly inverts the real problem. In practical writing situations, the subject is determined by the occasion, and the writer does not worry about multiplying words until he reaches the magic number, 500. On the contrary, he sweats over the problem of boiling his material down to the briefest and clearest statement he can manage. It may be folklore that no executive reads beyond the first page of any report, but it is a good warning to keep in the back of one's mind. The problem is not how many words can I get, but how briefly and effectively can I say something. Ideally, theme assignments should encourage such a practical approach to writing.

## 1a Choosing and Limiting a Subject

Choose something you know about or can find out about. Your material, for any piece of writing, will have to come either from your own experience — what you have seen, or done, or thought — or from reading what other people have seen, or done, or thought. Don't try to write over your head. If you have had little mathematics and physics, don't try to explain the principles of cybernetics or guided missiles.

If you are given complete freedom of choice, pick a topic that interests you: jobs, people, places, opinions, favorite studies, hobbies, the content of courses you have taken or are taking. Ordinary, unsensational topics are likely to be best. What may seem familiar and commonplace to you may be novel and fresh to a reader. There are no inherently dull subjects; there are only dull ways of seeing and writing about material. Use your imagination, not to invent strange and exotic situations, but to see the interesting possibilities in the ordinary and familiar.

When your instructor says "A 500-word theme," he is giving an approximate indication. He does not have time to count the words and then penalize the student who has 490 or 510. But common sense suggests that one page will probably be not enough, and ten pages will certainly be too long. The problem is not really one of words at all; it is rather a matter of adapting the subject to the space at your disposal. If the subject is too large, it cannot be boiled down to 500 words without sacrificing the detail which gives it weight and point. It is even worse to try to pad out a small subject to meet an assigned length. If the material can be adequately covered in 200 words, you must add more material, not just verbal padding.

The physical properties of oxygen can be described in a very few words, and this would probably not be a good topic for a 500-word theme. But "Some Commercial Uses of Oxygen" takes in a good deal more territory, and this expanded subject could be made to fit the space at your disposal.

Conversely, a topic like "The American Character" is far too large for a 500-word theme, or even a 5,000-word paper. But it can be cut down to size. What are some of the traits of the American character? Most foreign observers mention optimism, preoccupation with technical skills, generosity, and tolerance. Concentrating on any one of these would represent a limitation, and thus be a step in the right direction.

Suppose you choose tolerance. You may well find, when you start to jot down ideas on the subject, that it is still too large. On the whole, Americans are tolerant of widely divergent religious beliefs. But are they equally tolerant of unorthodox economic ideas? What about their tolerance of racial minorities? And what do you really know about these matters? Well, the block you live in may be fairly typical, and it contains Presbyterians, Roman Catholics, Baptists, Jews, a number of nonbelievers, and one elderly bachelor who is a militant atheist. How do they get along? Is social prestige, or the lack of it, influenced by religious beliefs? Do these people belong to the same clubs and organizations? Do they cooperate in civic enterprises like the Red Cross and Community Chest? Do they take part in semireligious observances like a joint Thanksgiving service? Do they intermarry? Such questions as these may suggest usable material, as well as possibilities for further limitation of the subject.

### EXERCISE

List subdivisions of the following general subjects that would be suitable for (a) 10-page papers, (b) 500-word themes.

**Example.** General topic — The automobile industry.

10-page paper topics:

1. Foreign cars and their effect on the American automobile industry
2. Real changes vs. "new models"
3. The used car market — or racket

500-word theme topics:

1. Automatic gear shifts
2. Hot rods and drag races
3. Check points in buying a used car

1. Amateur athletics
2. Chain newspapers and public opinion
3. The Atomic Age
4. Air transportation
5. Popular music
6. The modern house
7. East Asia in the 20th century
8. Television
9. The United Nations
10. Outdoor sports

## 1b Planning a Paper

Planning before writing is necessary for even experienced writers. It is not always necessary to make a detailed outline; a few jottings on a scratch pad may serve. But material does not organize itself; you will have to survey your material and put it into some recognizable and useful order.

If you jot down your ideas on a subject just as they occur to you, you will see why planning in advance is essential. When undisciplined by a controlling purpose, ideas follow each other by random association. You start thinking, let us say, about possible careers after graduation. This reminds you of some vocational interest tests your friend Green took last spring. They showed that he was suited for medicine, law, and engineering. But since these were the only three choices he was considering, the tests did not help much. You remember your psychology professor saying that such tests were of negative value, primarily: they tell you what you shouldn't do, not what you should. Green was in that psychology class, and you used to argue with him about the value of tests in general. Green's father, a successful lawyer, had laughed at them. He had studied law at night school because he was tired of clerking in a hardware store. That must have been in Minnesota, where Green was born. You remember their summer cottage on the lake. You met a girl there . . . and so on — a medley of irrelevancies and random associations.

Even if you stick to the subject, ideas are apt to come to you haphazard, in no logical order. Everyone has heard a bungling storyteller getting things mixed up, interrupting himself with "Oh, I forgot to say . . . ," spoiling the point of his story by repetitions and the omission of essentials. If you try to write without planning beforehand what you want to say and how you will say it, your paper will probably be just as rambling and disorganized.

## 1c Unity

Notice that even in the random reverie on careers given above, all the ideas are connected in some fashion. If they were not, the result would resemble the disturbed incoherencies of a madman or the babbling of an idiot. But the fact that ideas have some relation to each other in your mind is not enough to insure unity. For effective writing they must be evidently relevant to a purpose. Your writing is supposed to *do* something: to prove a point, explain a principle, present some facts. To accomplish this purpose successfully, everything in the paper must bear on the main point. If all irrelevant matter is eliminated and all important details are included, the paper will have unity. If, in addition, the material is put together in some recognizable pattern, the paper will be organized.

### Thesis Sentence

A good way to begin is to write out, in a single declarative sentence, the purpose of your paper: "This paper will describe the limitations of vocational interest tests," or "This paper will explain the principle on which vocational interest tests are constructed." This *thesis sentence* need not appear in the completed theme; it is for your own use — to help you determine whether a particular fact or idea should be included. Test every point that occurs to you: does it contribute in some way to the purpose you have defined in the thesis sentence? If not, no matter how interesting it seems, it should be omitted.

#### EXERCISE

I. Thesis sentence: This paper will describe the purposes and organization of the Lewis and Clark expedition.

Which of the details listed on the next page are relevant to the purpose? Mark them with an *x*.

II. Thesis sentence: This paper will discuss the personalities and backgrounds of Lewis and Clark.

Which of the details listed on the next page are relevant to the purpose? Mark them with a *y*. Note that some details may be relevant to both papers.

## LEWIS AND CLARK

1. Expedition planned by President Jefferson and Meriwether Lewis in 1802.
2. Jefferson wanted to explore the Louisiana territory, which he hoped to buy.
3. Expedition might establish trade route from headwaters of the Missouri to St. Louis.
4. Lewis hoped to find route across the Rockies from the upper Missouri.
5. If they could hit the headwaters of the Columbia, they could go all the way to the Pacific.
6. Lewis at the time was Jefferson's private secretary.
7. Poorly qualified in spelling and grammar.
8. Clark was even worse.
9. Sample of Clark's writing: "verry insolent both in words and justures."
10. Lewis had been Paymaster of the 1st U.S. Infantry.
11. Had served in Pennsylvania during the Whiskey Rebellion.
12. Born on a Virginia plantation.
13. Looked something like Napoleon.
14. Clark had grown up on a neighboring plantation.
15. Invited by Lewis to join expedition.
16. Problem of joint commanders:
17. Lewis was senior officer, since Clark did not get a promotion.
18. Orders were signed "The Commanding Officers."
19. Clark an experienced army officer with scientific interests.
20. Youngest brother of General George Rogers Clark.
21. General Clark, famous for conquests in Northwest Territory, later took to drink and amateur science.
22. William Clark inherited the family red hair.
23. Serious and responsible even as a boy of 16.
24. Lewis tried to keep real purpose of the expedition a secret.

25. Clark attempted to start false rumors.
26. One was that they planned to explore the source of the Mississippi.
27. Soldiers and experienced hunters recruited for expedition.
28. On the way, expedition ate "four deer, an Elk and a deer, or one buffaloe" daily.
29. Lewis carried a fast-firing airgun, which fascinated the Indians.
30. Expedition made preparations near mouth of the Missouri.
31. Lewis, a ladies' man, popular with the girls at St. Louis.
32. Clark supervised the construction of boats.
33. A 22-oar keelboat and two pirogues started up river.
34. Cargo included 34 barrels of parchmeal and flour, and seven barrels of salt.

## 1d Organizing Material

Having defined his purpose, a writer begins to collect and organize material. For a short theme, a student might begin by jotting down all the relevant points he can think of. Later these can be selected, expanded, or eliminated. Here is an example.

Purpose: To explain how to resurface a kitchen floor.

1. Anyone can do it with modern materials
2. Must have a smooth surface to work on
3. Plastic tile is an ideal covering material
4. It is impervious to water and most stains
5. Wood must be continually painted or varnished
6. Cork absorbs grease too easily
7. Sheet linoleum is too hard to handle
8. Plastic tile comes in various colors and patterns
9. Important to lay adjacent tiles with pattern at right angles

10. Purpose: to break up straight lines and give all-over effect
11. If covering a wooden floor, sand it smooth and coat with sealer
12. Wood should not absorb adhesive
13. Waterproof cement should be used
14. Tiles applied when cement is tacky
15. Do not slide tiles into place or cement will ooze up in cracks
16. Extra cement can be removed with wood alcohol
17. Put felt lining over wood as base for tile
18. Use same cement as for tile
19. Apply cement with notched trowel
20. Start from center and work toward walls
21. Reason: no room is perfectly square
22. Lay first tiles along guide lines
23. These are drawn on felt, at right angles, from room center

There's more material, of course, but this will do for an illustration. Probably all of these details are relevant, but they have not yet been organized. At present, the situation is similar to that of a hardware dealer who has received an order of various sizes of nails, screws, nuts, and bolts all dumped together into one barrel. Before he can use them, they must be sorted out — that is, organized.

The principle is simple: put like things together. First do a rough sorting: all nails in one box, nuts and bolts in another, screws in another. Then each box can be resorted, by size. These boxes correspond to categories, or main headings, in writing. Once you have decided on the main headings, you can arrange the material under them, subordinating the less important and eliminating the unnecessary.

Normally, two or three main headings are enough for a theme or article. If on a first try you come out with six or eight main headings, look at the material again to see if some of your eight headings are not, in reality, subordinate parts of a larger heading. A short theme built on a framework of eight main headings will almost certainly seem scrappy and disjointed.

The details listed above fall naturally under three main headings:

I. Materials
II. Preparation
III. Laying the tile

But there are other possibilities. Various methods produce different effects and emphases, and the writer tries to find the method of organization best adapted to his purpose. What is important is that the material be organized in some fashion.

Sorting out the details under the three headings suggested above produces an orderly pattern:

I. Materials
    Waterproof cement
    Felt lining
    Floor-covering material
        Wood needs paint or varnish
        Cork is too absorbent
        Sheet linoleum too awkward
        Plastic tile is ideal
            Available in various colors and patterns
            Impervious to water and most stains

II. Preparation
    Sand wooden flooring
    Seal to prevent adhesive soaking in
    Apply cement with notched trowel
    Put on felt lining as base for tile

III. Laying the tile
    Draw guide lines on felt, at right angles from center of room
    Always start tiles at center and work toward walls
        Reason: no room is perfectly square
        Following guide lines keeps tile square with axis
    Wait until cement is tacky before applying tile
    Lay adjacent tiles with design at right angles to give all-over effect
    Do not slide tiles into place or cement will ooze up
    Excess cement can be removed with wood alcohol

Remember that this preliminary organizing is temporary scaffolding and can be torn down or changed at any time. Don't take your categories too seriously, so that they become a strait jacket instead of a support. The actual writing of a composition may suggest new material, or reveal a lack of material, and thus force you to modify your original plan. Don't make the error of the historian who, in planning an elaborate work on Iceland, left room for a chapter entitled "The Snakes of Iceland." His chapter finally consisted of one sentence: "There are no snakes in Iceland."

## 1e Order of Material

There is one further problem to consider. In what order will you put the material? One of your headings must come first; another must be last. Don't leave it to chance. Plan it. Often the material determines what order is best. In the plan given above, chronological, or time, order is clearly indicated: first, materials needed; second, preparation of surface; third, the operation itself. If you were discussing the relation between climate and agriculture in California, chronology would not be a useful ordering principle. There are, let us say, three main climatic divisions in California: the interior valleys, the coast, and the desert. Which comes first? You might put them in order of geographic location, west to east: the coast, the interior valleys, the desert. Or you might put them in order of importance, disposing of the less important areas first and leading up to the most important so far as agriculture is concerned: the desert, the coast, the interior valleys.

The same principle of order is illustrated within the first main heading in the plan for covering a kitchen floor. The less important materials (cement and lining) are discussed first, and the writer leads up to the real question: wood, linoleum, cork, or plastic? This list of possible materials is also in climactic order. The writer will first discuss the least promising material, wood, and lead up to the plastic tile which he recommends and which he will write about at length.

Inductive order and deductive order are widely used in argumentation, explanation, and description. Using inductive order means giving first the evidence or details on which a conclusion is based and then leading up to the conclusion:

1. Scanty and irregular rainfall produces marginal farm lands
2. If such land is tilled, a prolonged drought will cause serious dust storms
3. Dust storms ruin the land for any purpose
4. Therefore, such land should be utilized for grazing and not cultivated

Deductive order is just the opposite: beginning with the conclusion or main point and supporting it with specific evidence and detail:

1. Marginal farm lands should be utilized for grazing and not cultivated
2. Marginal land determined by scanty and irregular rainfall

3. If such land is tilled, a prolonged drought will cause serious dust storms
4. Dust storms ruin the land for any purpose

In longer pieces of writing, one is likely to use a combination of these methods: to state the main point, at least briefly, in the introduction even though the order is primarily inductive; and to conclude with a short summary even if deductive order is used. The important thing is to leave nothing to chance in organizing a paper. Careful planning makes for easier writing, and much easier reading.

## 1f Emphasis

Emphasis is not achieved merely by intensification. If every note in a tune is played fortissimo, no one of them is emphasized. An emphatic note is one that stands out prominently from the rest, and loudness is only one way of producing this differentiation.

In writing, it is of course desirable to express oneself forcefully. A strong and vivid phrase is better than a weak and colorless one, and ways of making words and sentences more forceful will be discussed later. But it is also important to give proper emphasis to the main points in a paper, so that they will not be lost in a mass of subordinate detail. In speech it is possible to emphasize important points by tone of voice, by speed of utterance, by loudness, by facial expression, or by gesture. The writer lacks all these aids, and must depend for emphasis mainly on proportion and arrangement.

### Proportion

Other things being equal, a reader will assume that the more space you give an idea, the more important it is. Do not deceive him by elaborating minor points at disproportionate length.

Suppose part of your working outline looks like this:

Reasons for juvenile delinquency

1. Poverty
2. Racial discrimination
3. Unhappy family life

Suppose further that you do not consider points 1 and 2 very significant. (Racial discrimination is a factor in only a few parts of the country, and poverty is a doubtful cause, since delinquency occurs on all economic levels.) The point you want to stress is the connection between unhappy or broken homes and delinquent children. Under these circumstances, it is misleading to go into a long discussion of pachuco gangs in the Southwest, or tenement life in urban slum areas. Instead, dispose of 1 and 2 in a short paragraph, and give the bulk of your space to point 3.

Do not be misled by your own outline. Coordinate items in an outline need not be given equal weight and space in the composition itself. Condense or telescope your minor points, so that you will have room left to elaborate the points you want to emphasize.

### Arrangement

Put important material at the beginning and at the end of your composition. The end is especially important, since climactic order is a very common means of securing emphasis, and a reader will normally assume that you are saving your main points for the last. If you begin your composition, for example, with a full discussion of family life as a factor in juvenile delinquency and then add brief and qualified references to poverty and racial discrimination at the end, you throw away the possibility of emphasis inherent in climactic order, and the composition will trail off into thin air.

The beginning of a composition is the place to announce your main theme, and a good introduction is often just such a preliminary sounding of the keynote. Then clear away the lesser points, make any concessions or allowances that truth requires — "it must be admitted that conclusive evidence is hard to obtain," etc. — and lead up to your main point. The pattern just described may be diagramed as follows:

| Introductory statement of main theme. |
|---|

| Minor points: definitions, explanations, background material, less important reasons, necessary concessions. |
|---|

| Development of main theme. |
|---|

This arrangement is used very frequently in expository writing, to give emphatic structure either to a single paragraph or to the composition as a whole. Keep it in mind.

# 2 OUTLINING

A visual representation of the plan and structure of an essay is called an outline. Even professional writers make some kind of informal outline before beginning to write, and college students should do no less. How detailed it should be depends on one's working habits, the kind of material, the length of the assignment. Since no one else will see it, you need not worry about form, so long as the outline helps you to organize your material. An informal outline should be, above everything else, useful to the writer.

Formal outlines are sometimes required, either as a part of a long written assignment or as an exercise in the comprehension of reading. Since formal outlines are meant to be read by others they should follow conventional form and style.

## 2a Topic and Sentence Outlines

Two types of formal outline are common: the topic outline and the sentence outline. The topic outline uses no complete sentences; each item is a brief phrase or single word. An example may be found on page 22. Because of its brevity, however, a topic outline may not be clear to a reader. Hence the sentence outline, with its more complete statements, is often preferable. It has the further advantage of compelling you to formulate more explicitly the material you intend to use. An example may be found on page 23.

Both forms of outline indicate by numbering and indention which are the main points and which are the subordinate points. The following system of numbering and lettering has become almost universal:

I.<br>
    A.<br>
    B.<br>
        1.<br>
        2.<br>
            a.<br>
            b.<br>
                (1)<br>
                (2)<br>
                    (a)<br>
                    (b)<br>
II.<br>
    A.<br>
    B.<br>
        1. etc.

Note that coordinate points are indented the same distance from the left margin.

## 2b Logical Subdivisions

It is important that the headings and subordinate items in a formal outline correspond to logical divisions and subdivisions of the material. The indention and numbering of items in the outline should indicate the parallelism or subordination of ideas. When one sees a pattern like the following:

I.<br>
    A.<br>
    B.<br>
II.

he expects to find two parallel ideas (A and B) under I, and a larger division (II) parallel in content with I. He would *not* expect to find material like the following:

I. Advantages of outboard motors
  A. Relatively inexpensive
  B. Attachable to any small boat
II. Easily transportable

"Easily transportable" is logically a subtopic under I, and it should be made parallel with A and B. II should introduce a larger division, parallel with I.

I. Advantages of outboard motors
  A. Relatively inexpensive
  B. Attachable to any small boat
  C. Easily transportable
II. Disadvantages

Subdivisions which do not, taken together, cover all the material implied by a main heading are logically, though not always practically, an error.

I. Literature in the United States
  A. New England
  B. The South

This is illogical since New England and the South do not constitute the United States. It can be made logical by limiting the main heading, by adding more subdivisions, or both.

I. Literature in the American colonies (Limitation)
  A. New England
  B. The Middle Colonies (Addition)
  C. The South

In actual writing, however, such rigid logical requirements do not always applv. In an essay on Outdoor Recreation, one might have the following heading and subdivisions:

I. Field sports
  A. Hunting
  B. Fishing

without being compelled to add C. Steeplechase riding, D. Bird watching, and E. Other, or Miscellaneous, just for the sake of logical consistency.

## 2c Overlapping Subdivision

When one subheading includes material covered in parallel headings, the subdivisions are said to overlap. Overlapping subdivisions are a sign that you have not properly analyzed your material.

I. Organized welfare groups
  A. Early history of relief organizations
  B. Red Cross
  C. Community Chest
  D. Relief organizations today

"Relief organizations today" includes the Red Cross and Community Chest. If you begin subdividing on a chronological basis, stick to it consistently, and make a sub-subdivision for Red Cross and Community Chest:

I. Organized welfare groups
  A. Early history of relief organizations
  B. Relief organizations today
    1. Red Cross
    2. Community Chest

If the Red Cross goes back in time to what you would call "early history," then another method of subdivision may be necessary to prevent overlapping:

I. Organized welfare groups
   A. The Red Cross
      1. Predecessors
      2. Early history
      3. Present activities
   B. The Community Chest

## 2d Single Subdivision

It is sometimes argued that each topic that is subdivided must have at least two subheads. The argument is that dividing something produces at least two parts: a lone subtopic is not really a subdivision, but rather an amplification or illustration of the point preceding. This is logically sound, and an outline like the following does seem overelaborate:

I. Ancestry
   A. German
II. Birthplace
   A. Farm in Indiana

There are really only two points here, and the subtopics should be combined with them or omitted altogether:

I. German ancestry
II. Birthplace (or Birthplace: an Indiana farm)

Sometimes, however, a lone subhead is a useful means of indicating in the outline an example, illustration, or reference:

I. Extension of Mohammedan power under the early caliphs
   A. Eastward and northward
      1. For example, Persian and Greek lands
   B. Westward
      1. For example, Syria, Egypt, and northern Africa

## 2e Specimen Outlines and Student Theme

Following are examples of two formal outlines, the first a topic outline and the second a more complete sentence outline. These are followed by a student theme.

### Topic Outline

Three-Dimension in the Motion Picture Industry

I. Revolution in motion picture industry
   A. Need to meet competition of TV
   B. Early box-office success of 3-D
   C. Problems
      1. Fickleness of public interest in fads
      2. Choice of available systems

II. Methods of producing 3-D illusion
   A. Cinerama
      1. Three-lens camera
      2. Wide, curved screen
      3. No need of glasses for audience
   B. Stereoscopic photography
      1. Two-lens stereoscopic camera and projector
      2. Polaroid glasses for audience
      3. Ordinary screen

III. Evaluation
   A. Advantages
      1. To audience
      2. To producer
      3. To exhibitor
   B. Disadvantages
      1. To producer
         a. Limited appeal of trick shots
         b. Backlog of standard films
      2. To the exhibitor
         a. High cost of some equipment
         b. Uncertainty as to popular choice

### Sentence Outline

Three-Dimension in the Motion Picture Industry

I. In 1952 motion picture industry was being revolutionized by 3-D.
   A. 3-D was developed to meet the threat of TV competition.
   B. Early showings had huge box-office success.
   C. But 3-D presented problems to the industry.
      1. Public interest in fads is usually short-lived.
      2. The industry must gamble in its choice of systems.

II. There are various methods of producing the illusion of 3-D.
   A. Cinerama tries to give the full scope of normal vision.
      1. It uses a 3-lens camera.
      2. It requires a wide, curved screen.
      3. The audience does not need to wear special glasses.
   B. Other systems use true three-dimension photography.
      1. Stereoscopic camera and projector have two lenses.
      2. Polaroid glasses must be worn by the audience.
      3. An ordinary screen can be used.

III. It is difficult to make an overall evaluation of 3-D.
   A. It has some advantages over standard two-dimension films.
      1. It looks real to the audience.
      2. It saves the producer time and money in lighting and camera angles.
      3. It pleases the exhibitor by bringing in customers.
   B. 3-D also has serious disadvantages.
      1. The producer is faced with new problems.

a. Trick shots have only a limited audience.
b. The backlog of standard films on hand might be made obsolete.

2. To the exhibitor, 3-D has disadvantages.
   a. Equipment for some systems is very expensive.
   b. No one can be sure what system will become standard.

## Student Theme

Three-Dimension in the Motion Picture Industry

In 1952 the world of the motion picture, from the research laboratories and studios of Hollywood to the many thousands of theaters across the country, found itself in what the industry likes to call "the throes of a revolution." Realizing the threat of television, Hollywood had been looking for a new attraction to lure back into the theater the millions of potential customers who preferred sitting cheaply and comfortably in darkened living rooms to walking down to the neighborhood movie theater.

The unexpected public interest in "depth" pictures suggested that some form of three-dimensional picture, or approximation to it, might be the answer to TV. Reports of big box-office returns from the early, experimental 3-D films started a rush to warehouses and laboratories in search of old equipment and new improvements. The basic principles of 3-D had been known for more than twenty-five years; back in 1937, audiences put on red and green glasses to watch Pete Smith's "Audioscopics." Now that there seemed to be a market for such productions, it was argued, serious research would undoubtedly improve the processes of making and showing them. To many observers, it seemed likely that the changes in the industry would be as revolutionary as those in the early thirties, when the screen found its voice and public enthusiasm prodded Hollywood into adopting sound as a standard addition to films.

The industry was not as happy about the situation as one might think. There were problems. In the first place, producers wondered whether the public's interest would last. If 3-D was just a fad, like Peewee golf or flagpole sitting, it would have been foolish to invest large sums in new equipment. On the whole, the producers made a calculated gamble that the public interest would last, but they were not very happy about it. The second problem was the kind of equipment to adopt. There were several systems of producing the illusion of three dimensions on a screen, but no one knew which the public would ultimately choose. And there was always the prospect that some hard-working engineer would invent a true stereoscope which required no viewing-glasses, and would thus make other systems obsolete.

Several 3-D systems were available to the industry, each with its own advantages and disadvantages. Cinerama is distinguished by the fact that no glasses are needed to achieve the illusion. But the illusion is not complete, despite the stereophonic sound which accompanies the showing. Cinerama makes use of a three-lens camera. The center lens points straight ahead, and the other two are pointed at angles across it. For showing the film, three separate projectors are required, as well as a specially built screen. The screen, 51 feet in length, curves across the front of the auditorium. It is constructed of vertical strips of perforated tape, set like a Venetian blind on its side. If a curved screen were made solid, reflections from the edges would cause distortions elsewhere. The wide curved screen affords the audience almost the area which the human eye normally sees, and the brain produces the illusion of depth. But it is only a partial illusion.

An alternative method makes use of true stereoscopic photography, and several companies have manufactured equipment based on the old principle of the stereopticon. Two horizontally separated lenses focus slightly different images of the same object on two films, each film recording the vision of one "eye." At the theater, the two films are projected simultaneously and in strict synchronization. But in order to fuse the two images and get the illusion of an extra dimension, the audience must wear Polaroid glasses. An advantage to the exhibitor is that an ordinary screen will serve; no elaborate remodeling is required to show the pictures.

An overall evaluation of 3-D is difficult; as is so often the case, there is much to be said on both sides. No matter which system is used, 3-D has, for the mass audience, the great advantage of looking real. You can see the roundness of a tree, or an actress. You can gasp as a speedboat seems to leap out of the screen at you; you can feel depth and distance in scenic shots. For the producer, there are advantages, too. He doesn't have to worry about elaborate space lighting to give the illusion of depth; the depth illusion is built in. There is less necessity to shift camera angles for the sake of variety. Both of these save time and money. For the exhibitor there is only one advantage, but it is crucial: 3-D brings in the customers.

3-D has no disadvantages for the mass audience, except perhaps the inescapable fact that any novelty soon loses its appeal. In 1952 the producers were worried about this. If they overplayed sensational trick shots, they might soon bore a fickle public. But unless 3-D offered something new and different, the potential audience would continue to crouch before its TV sets. Another major problem was the huge investment represented by the backlog of two-dimension films already on hand. If the whole industry should swing over to 3-D, these would become as obsolete as silent pictures after the introduction of sound.

Today the exhibitor still has plenty of worries. 3-D seems to bring in the customers, but it costs money to bring in 3-D. Cinerama is especially expensive to set up, in some cases requiring actual alterations in the theater building. Normal cost of Cinerama projectors and screen

```
is estimated at between $40,000 and $70,000.  Other
3-D systems are not so expensive to install, but
their existence raises new questions.  Which system
will win out and become standard?  Which should
the exhibitor bet on?  Or should he wait and see if
a new method will supersede all others?  The
trouble with revolutions is that it's so difficult
to tell how they're going to come out.
```

### EXERCISE

1. For one of the following subjects, write a thesis sentence and make a topic outline suitable for a composition of about 1,000 words.

The change from school to college
Compulsory military training
Science fiction
Television programs
City life vs. country life
Trends in popular music

2. Read the following selection carefully. Write a thesis sentence for the selection. Make a formal topic or sentence outline of the selection.

Sympathy for wild animals, sympathy that is intellectual as much as emotional, has not been a strong element in the traditional American way of life. "I was wrathy to kill a bear," David Crockett said, and that is essentially all one learns about bears from the mightiest of frontier bear-hunters — except that he killed a hundred and five in one season and immediately thereafter got elected to the Tennessee legislature on his reputation. How familiar the iterated remark: "I thought I might see something and so took . . . along my gun" — as if no enjoyment or other good could come from seeing a wild animal without killing it. Buffalo Bill derived his name from the fact that he excelled in killing buffaloes, not from knowing anything about them except as targets or from conveying any interest in them as a part of nature. While Zebulon Pike and two of his explorers were lying in the grass on the plains of Kansas, November 1, 1806, a band of "cabrie" (antelopes), he records, "came up among our horses to satisfy their curiosity. We could not resist the temptation of killing two, although we had plenty of meat." Any restraint put upon killing was from motives other than sympathy. On one occasion Pike prevented his men from shooting at game "not merely because of the scarcity of ammunition but, as I conceived, the law of morality forbade it also. . . ."

In *The Texan Ranger*, published in London, 1866, Captain Flack, fresh from the sporting fields of the Southwest, describes the game of slaughtering thus: The men of one community lined up against those of another to see which group could kill the most game during a day's shooting. A squirrel and a rabbit counted one point each, a wild turkey five points, a deer ten points. The number of points scored in the particular contest described by Captain Flack totaled 3,470.

These are not instances of eccentricity but of the representative American way, until only yesterday, of looking at wild animals. Often while reading the chronicles of frontiersmen one does come upon an interesting observation concerning wildlife, but it is likely to be prefaced by some such statement as, "I didn't have a gun, and so I thought I might as well see what happened." The majority of country-dwellers in western America today would consider it necessary to apologize for not killing a coyote they happened to see doing something unusual. This traditional killer attitude is part of the traditional exploitation of the land. A few early farmers conserved the soil — George Washington was one — but they were stray oddities. A few pioneers had naturalistic interests, but any revelation of such interests branded the holder of them as being peculiar or even undemocratic. The mass rule then, as now, was: Conform and be dull.

In 1846 a young Englishman named George Frederick Ruxton landed at Vera Cruz, equipped himself with pack mules, rode to Mexico City, then up through "the Republic" to El Paso, across New Mexico into Colorado, where he spent the winter. . . . He carried home a chronicle that remains one of the most delightful and illuminating books of travel that North America has occasioned — *Adventures in Mexico and the Rocky Mountains*.

In Colorado, as Ruxton tells in the book, he made acquaintance with a large gray wolf. . . . For days he followed Ruxton. At camp every evening, he would "squat down quietly at a little distance." . . . In the morning, as soon as the men broke camp, the lobo, in Ruxton's words, "took possession and quickly ate up the remnants of supper and some little extras I always took care to leave him. Then he would trot after us. . . . But when I killed an antelope and was in the act of butchering it, he gravely looked on, or loped round and round, licking his jaws in a state of evident self-gratulation. I had him twenty times a day within reach of my rifle, but we became such old friends that I never dreamed of molesting him."

No American contemporary of Ruxton's on the frontier would have resisted killing that wolf. He would have said that he was killing it because the wolf killed; he would have said that the wolf was cruel, sneaking, cowardly. Actually, he would have killed it because he was "wrathy to kill." It did not strike Ruxton that the wolf was cruel — at least not more cruel than man. It struck Ruxton that the wolf was interesting; he had towards it the sympathy that comes from civilized perspective.

This sympathy is found in the two extremes of society — savages and people with cultivated minds and sensibilities. . . . "We be of one blood, ye and I," is the call of the jungle folk. "And what is man that he should not run with his brothers?" asked Mowgli of *The Jungle Book*. "Surely the wolves are my brothers." The American Indian's sympathy for fellow animals was not sentiment or superstition; . . . it was a part of his harmony with nature.

Mary Austin, who perhaps more than any other interpreter of the Southwest has sensed the spiritual values in nature, said: ". . . The best thing we get out of any study of animal life is the feel of it." This feel, this sympathy, reaches its climax among the civilized in such diverse natures as tart Thoreau of Walden, sweet St. Francis of Assisi, patrician Grey of Fallodon, . . . scientific Jefferson, and plain William Wright of the bears, who, watching a great grizzly looking out for long whiles from the top of a snowy mountain, concluded that he was "enjoying the scenery." Among the wise, this civilized sympathy infuses knowledge. It is a kind of cultivated gentleness. It is foreign to harsh and boisterous frontiers and comes after many of the wild creatures to which it is directed have been destroyed.[1]

[1] From *The Voice of the Coyote*, by J. Frank Dobie. Copyright, 1949, by J. Frank Dobie. By permission of Little, Brown and Company.

# 3 WRITING THE PAPER

The way you write up your material will depend on the people who are expected to read it. Ordinarily, writing is not merely a form of self-expression; it is a means of communication. If your audience cannot understand what you have written, there's no point in writing at all. Recent discoveries in physics can be most accurately described in the language of mathematics. For specialists, this is an ideal medium. But if the average, educated reader is to understand it, the writing must be much less technical, even though the simplification distorts the content somewhat.

If you are aiming at the widest possible audience, the language and syntax must be very simple indeed. A classic example is the bulletin *Infant Care* published by the U.S. Department of Labor. Thousands of copies of this manual are circulated every year to people of every degree of intelligence and education, and the instructions must be clear to all persons who have babies. Furthermore, there must be no omissions which permit misunderstanding: it is just as important *not* to do certain things to infants as it is to do others. The writing of such a manual, aimed at so wide an audience, is a formidable task. The author cannot be satisfied with making himself understandable; he must, so far as it is humanly possible, make sure that he cannot be misunderstood.

This is not a bad standard to set for any serious writing. Make sure that you have actually said what you want to say, but don't stop there; it is deceptively easy for you to understand the paper, since you know what you're trying to say in it. Try to see it through the eyes of a reader who doesn't already know what you want to say, who may be honestly baffled by phrases which to you seem crystal clear, or who may even be trying to twist your words and read another meaning into them.

Getting this kind of outside, objective view of your own writing is sometimes extremely difficult, but it is nevertheless indispensable. The habit of permitting yourself no weak compromises in phrasing will do much to remove the marginal comments "Vague" and "Not clear," which appear so frequently on corrected themes.

For the writing you do in composition courses, you can usually assume an audience of reasonably well-educated people — like your classmates or your instructor — who have a normal fund of general information but who have no specialized knowledge in the field you are writing about. A phrase like "the plane of the ecliptic" is accurate, concise, and useful, but you cannot assume that the general reader will understand it. In writing on technical subjects, you may need to use technical terms, but you will have to define them so that they can be understood by the nontechnical reader.

### EXERCISE

1. Write a 300-word theme utilizing material taken from some fairly technical college course. Pick a small topic that can be covered fully in so short a space — one point, say, from a lecture in physics, or economics, or government, or psychology. Assume that the audience will be the instructor in the course, and concentrate on exactness of expression and completeness of statement.

2. Rewrite the same material so that any literate person can understand it. This may require more than 300 words, but keep it as concise as possible. Almost certainly it will

involve some sacrifice of technical accuracy and completeness in the interest of clarity. If you must use technical terms, explain them whenever there is any doubt of their being intelligible.

### 3a Coherence

Coherence means, literally, sticking together. As applied to writing, it means that the connections between parts of an essay are clear. Now the relationship of ideas in your own writing will very likely seem clear enough to you. After all, you put the essay together. The question is: Will it be clear to a reader? If not, the paper will seem to lack coherence.

To achieve coherence, you must make sure that the reader will not hesitate, wondering or being forced to guess why one part of a paper follows another. You know where the paper is going, but the reader may need signposts. Are you still talking about the first point, or does the new paragraph begin the discussion of the second? Write "In the second place," and there is no further question. Does the next paragraph contain an example of what you have just been talking about, or does it introduce new material? Begin with "For example," and the question never arises.

Another means of achieving coherence is the repetition of a word or phrase, or the use of a pronoun which refers to a word in an earlier sentence. Sentences in parallel structure serve the same purpose. The italicized words in the following passage help to give it coherence by tying the sentences together.

> *People* living in the seventeenth century had a different conception of *history* from *ours*. *We* tend to think of *history as a record of* man's progress from a less civilized to a more civilized state. The *people* of *the seventeenth century* regarded *history as the record of* a steady decline from an original perfection. Whether *they* accepted the Biblical story of the Gar-

> den of Eden and man's fall from grace, or the classic Greek account of the Golden Age, followed by lesser Ages of Silver and Iron, *they took it for granted that man gets* worse *as time goes on. Our* picture of the past has been conditioned by the theory of evolution, which *we* apply to social and moral, as well as biological, changes. *We*—or at least most of us—*take it for granted that man gets* better *as time goes on.*

Such sentence links are not usually sufficient by themselves; they must be supplemented by the signposts already referred to. Transitional words and phrases, like *however, moreover, in conclusion, to be sure,* are often used between sentences to make explicit the relationship intended. Between paragraphs, introductory or summarizing sentences may be used. In a longer piece of writing, short transitional paragraphs may serve as signposts to indicate major divisions of thought.

Transitional devices are especially important when the line of thought takes a sudden turn, or reverses itself.

> Many people think that heavy fishing of a lake will eventually cause serious depletion of the stock of fish. In a lake with a limited food supply, heavy fishing often increases the supply of game fish: by reducing the population, it enables the remaining fish to grow up to legal size.

To the student who wrote this, it seemed clear enough; he knew that the second sentence was a qualification of the first statement — a correction of an erroneous belief. However, the reader, unprepared for this sudden turn of thought, may well be left behind. Without a transitional device as signpost, he will probably assume that the second sentence expands or develops the first, and he will be puzzled and annoyed by the apparent contradiction. Beginning the second sentence with a transitional phrase clears things up:

> *On the contrary* [or *in fact* or *actually*], in a lake with a limited food supply, heavy fishing often increases. . . .

The following transitional words and phrases are useful for indicating a turn of thought or the qualification of an idea: *Yet, still, nevertheless, however, none the less, in spite of this, on the contrary, on the other hand, the fact is, actually, in fact.*

The time to check the coherence of a theme is during the revision of the first draft. Read it over, trying to see it with the eyes of a person who does not already know what you wish to say. Wherever he might have trouble, help him follow the line of thought by inserting a transitional expression.

This can be overdone, of course. Beginning every sentence with a transitional phrase can make a theme sound mechanical, or painfully obvious. Moreover, too many transitional aids may suggest that you distrust the reader's intelligence and are babying him. How far to go is a matter of judgment; it depends on the kind of material and the audience for whom you are writing. In general, however, most college themes would be improved by more, rather than fewer, transitions. It is better to be too clear than not clear enough.

### EXERCISE

Write pairs of sentences illustrating the transitional use of one word or phrase from each of the groups listed below. The second sentence of each pair should begin with the transitional expression.

**Example.** *Therefore.* A survey showed that delivery costs were increasing steadily but that the volume of sales was going down. *Therefore,* it was decided to discontinue free delivery service.

1. Connectives indicating a conclusion or result:
   *Accordingly, Under these circumstances, As a result, This being true.*

2. Connectives indicating a concession:
   *To be sure, Doubtless, It must be admitted that, Actually.*
3. Connectives indicating an illustration or example:
   *For instance, To illustrate, For example, A case in point is.*
4. Connectives indicating an expansion or addition:
   *Moreover, Besides, Furthermore, That is, In other words.*
5. Connectives indicating a summary:
   *In short, On the whole, Briefly, As we have seen.*
6. Connectives marking a change in tone or point of view:
   *At least, To speak frankly, Of course, Seriously, In fact.*

See if the other transitional expressions in each group will fit between the sentences you have written. If not, why? What are the differences in meaning of the transitional expressions that do not fit?

## 3b Beginning a Composition

It is not necessary, in a short paper, to "introduce" a subject. Plunge into your topic at once, without an introductory paragraph of verbal foot-shuffling and throat-clearing. An editor of a popular magazine advised a contributor to write his story, throw away the first page and the last page, and send in the rest. Properly interpreted, this is good advice for any writer. When you have finished a paper, check to see if it would not be improved in directness and force by the omission of the first paragraph. Here is an example.

The Voice of America

Short-wave voice broadcasting has become a well-established and important medium for world-wide communication. It began with the experimentation of amateurs, who talked to each other on home-made equipment. Later it was put to use by government agencies, like the police, and by ships and aircraft. Now it is widely used for international broadcasting. Since it can reach people in isolated areas who have no other means of quick communication, it may be a means of promoting better understanding among the peoples of the world.

The Voice of America aims radio programs at both our friends and our enemies. To our fellow-Americans south of the border, it tries to interpret our way of life; to the captive nations of Europe and Asia, it brings news uncolored by an official party line. . . .

The first paragraph of this student theme does not contribute much to the subject announced in the title. It corresponds to the nervous clearing of the throat with which many speakers begin a talk — a kind of tuning up of the instrument. Such paragraphs often help a writer to get started, and are not out of place in a first draft. But they need not be retained in the final revised version. The theme above really gets down to the business at hand in the second paragraph, and the paper would gain in directness and force if it began there.

Unless you are writing advertising copy, you do not need to sweep the reader off his feet in your first few sentences. Actually, the kind of sensational opening to which popular journalism and the radio have accustomed us is out of place in a paper addressed to an intelligent audience. But there is a happy medium between sensationalism and the dreary colorlessness of many opening paragraphs found in student papers. If your beginning is as dispirited and limp as the following, you had better do something about it.

Religion in Tibet

The nature of religious beliefs and practices in Tibet is widely regarded as being attributable to the geographic situation of the country, as well as to the attitude of the inhabitants. Tibet is located in south central Asia, behind high mountain ranges, which have tended to keep out travelers. Since the people are generally hostile to foreigners, outsiders have seldom gone there, and accordingly the language, government, and customs of Tibet are different from those of the countries which are located nearby.

Asked to revise this feeble beginning, the student produced the following paragraph, which is certainly more compact, vivid, and forceful.

Religion in Tibet

For centuries, Tibet has been veiled in mystery. Isolated from the rest of the world by the highest mountains on earth, the people have cultivated a hostility toward foreigners which has discouraged many of the travelers hardy enough to attempt the Himalayas. Remote and aloof, Tibet has developed a unique culture, which differs from that of her neighbors not only in language, government, and folkways, but most of all in religious beliefs and practices.

The improvement here is partly due to more vivid phrasing, partly to the rearrangement of ideas. The paragraph begins with a short, sharp characterization and leads up to the central idea: the unique religious practices of Tibet.

Other ways of beginning forcefully are illustrated by the following quotations from Wolfgang Langewiesche's *A Flier's World.*

**1. Paradox.**

What makes an airplane fly is not its engine or its propeller. Nor is it, as many people think, some mysterious knack of the pilot or some ingenious gadget inside. What makes an airplane fly is simply its shape.

This sounds absurd. But gliders do fly without engines; model airplanes do fly without pilots. As for the insides of an airplane, they are disappointing, for they are mostly hollow. No, what keeps an airplane up is its shape— the impact of the air upon its shape. Whittle that shape out of wood, or cast it out of iron, or fashion it, for that matter, out of chocolate and throw the thing into the air: It will behave like an airplane. It will *be* an airplane.

**2. Question.**

After the war, the airlines suddenly started flying twice as fast as they had ever flown before. Such sudden jumps in development are not supposed ever to happen, either in business or in engineering. What's the magic?

**3. Incident.**

He did it probably just from exuberance of spirit; a high-speed dive is a wonderful sensation. He was at 30,000 feet in his fighter, doing some 350 m.p.h. So he rolled over and pointed his nose at the ground and let her go. The speed built up: 400, 450, 500 m.p.h. . . . At 25,000 feet, approaching 525 m.p.h., he crossed the frontier from the known to the unknown.

**4. Arresting Statement.**

The birds, who ought to know all about flying, cannot fly blind; but men can.

**5. Contrast.**

Amelia Earhart became a public figure when she flew the Atlantic: as a *passenger!* An Atlantic flight was then the ultimate adventure. Of those who tried, some failed to get off with their overload of fuel, and some burned to death horribly in front of the newsreel cameras. Of those who got off, some turned back in time; some "ditched" near a passing steamer; some disappeared. Of those who got across, many cracked up on hasty landings, out of fuel or out of nervous endurance or both. They wound up in bogs, in cow pastures, in the surf, on subarctic islands. And remember, most of this happened at a time when the airlines were already shuttling all over the United States.

Today, 125 airliners cross the North Atlantic every day, and not a single pay passenger has yet been lost at sea. Some crashes have occurred at the two ends of the run. . . . Even if you count those crashes in, a North Atlantic flight is still safer, mile by mile, than a transcontinental one: it is the safest kind of flying you can buy.

**6. Description and Interpretation.**

A puff of wind comes down the street. An old newspaper stirs in the gutter, jumps up on the sidewalk, spirals up to second-story height and flaps about there for a moment; then, with a new burst of energy, it sweeps upward again, and when you last see it, it is soaring high above the rooftops, turning over and over, blinking in the sunlight.

The wind has picked up a piece of paper and blown it away. What of it? A generation ago, in a philosophical discourse, one might have chosen this as an example of an event completely devoid of significance, completely chance. But not in the air age. The tiny occurrence demonstrates an important fact concerning the air ocean—one that is only now becoming the practical knowledge of practical airfaring men: there are winds which blow neither east nor west, neither north nor south, but in the third dimension: straight up.

**7. Justification.**

In this part, I tell you about a trip I took, a couple of years after the war, over a lot of foreign countries. This is embarrassing. It sounds too much like a young lady writing: "My Trip Abroad." Who cares? What does *she* know anyway? What does a pilot know about a country from merely flying over it?

But that's just it. I print this not because I kid myself that I have something new to say about those countries. I print it simply because I want to show you the peculiar way in which a pilot sees the world.

It's a barbarous way. But it is also magnificent.

It's barbarous because the technicalities of flying keep popping into the foreground of your mind. To tell you how it really went, I would have written in double lines — one line as it stands, the other line full of the job of flying, like this:

Over the wine-colored sea on which Ulysses bore so many
*Manifold pressure 27 inches, r.p.m. 1,700. Where is that*

pains we felt no pain at all. A twin-engined airplane, with
*computer? Air speed reads 157, altitude 7,500, air temperature*

Atlantic ferry tanks in its belly, is just too barbarously able. *15° C. That makes a true air speed of — let's see — 178 m.p.h.*[2]

### 3c Ending a Composition

An ending ought to sound final. It should let the reader know (not necessarily in so many words) that your treatment of the subject has been completed.

It is not necessary, in a short composition, to add a summarizing paragraph as a formal conclusion. Such a recapitulation is often useful at the end of a long essay or term paper, where it serves to remind the reader of the central ideas which unify the material. But the ordinary freshman theme is not improved by a concluding paragraph beginning "Thus I have tried to show . . ."

When you have said what you have to say, stop. Do not tack on a vague generalization, an unimportant detail, or an afterthought. (Careful planning in advance should prevent this, in any case.) A composition should not be left hanging in mid-air; try to give your last sentence a tone of finality. Here are some examples. Ending of a 500-word composition, "Medicine as a Career":

> Above all, the physician has the satisfaction of knowing that his service to mankind is everywhere appreciated and honored.

Ending of a 700-word composition, "Isolationism":

> No modern nation can afford to follow Candide's cynical advice and selfishly cultivate its own garden, ignoring the rest of the world. The garden we must now cultivate is all mankind.

Ending of a 1,000-word composition, "The Modern Cowboy":

> Today the jeeps and station wagons of the new-style cowboy

[2] From *A Flier's World* by Wolfgang Langewiesche. Reprinted by permission of the author and the publisher, McGraw-Hill Book Company, Inc.

> speed across the ranges where the old-timers used to spread their bedrolls beside the chuck wagon.

Ending of a 1,500-word composition, "The Ascent of Mt. Everest":

> The conquest of Everest was a cooperative enterprise. Each expedition made use of the experience of those who had attacked the mountain before them, and the men who waited patiently at the lower camps made possible the advance of their comrades. It is symbolic that the final victory should have been won by two men, working together.

### EXERCISE

1. Consider the suitability of the following subjects for 500-word compositions. If you find the subjects too large, suggest subdivisions that might be treated in 500-word papers.

Modern furniture
Recruiting college football players
World War II
Conformity in American life
Abraham Lincoln
The parking problem in ____
Freedom of the press
The ritual of "Going to a dance"
Double features
Amateur theatrical performances
Democracy
Modern painting and the average citizen
Happy endings in the novel

2. Choose one of the topics above or one of your proposed subdivisions, and make a formal outline showing how material on the subject might be organized.

3. Run through an issue of *Harper's Magazine* or the *Atlantic Monthly* looking particularly at the beginnings and endings of the articles. These magazines are aimed at the kind of audience for whom your themes ought to be written — educated general readers. Notice what devices are used to achieve forceful beginnings, and how an effect of finality is given to the conclusion.

Copy out two effective beginnings, giving also the titles of the two articles. Explain why these beginnings are good.

Copy out two effective conclusions. Before each, give the title and summarize the central theme of the article in a sentence or two. What makes these endings seem conclusive?

4. Criticize the following student themes, considering especially unity, organization, coherence, and the effectiveness of beginnings and endings.

A Living Pump: The Plant

Since the days of the early Greeks, men have been trying to explain various natural phenomena and find the laws governing them. Sir Francis Bacon pointed out a method which promised to give better results than had been obtained by medieval scholars, who tended to accept and pass on whatever "the authorities" had said.

Bacon urged scientists to examine particular instances instead of arguing over theories. This is called the inductive method and has been used by scientists ever since. Of course they weren't called scientists in Bacon's day.

Many mysteries regarding plant life have baffled scientists for centuries. One of these is the way in which a plant gets water to its topmost branches and leaves.

All plants must have water constantly in order to live and grow. Some plants in the desert need relatively little water, since they have developed ways of storing and conserving water. They are usually prickly to discourage foraging animals, and they often have shiny leaves which check evaporation.

Sequoia redwood trees in California have grown to a height of

264 feet. Some eucalyptus trees are said to have been even taller. Obviously some force is required to get water to the tops of these giants.

Air pressure cannot lift water higher than thirty-four feet. It was once thought that trees might have tiny water pumps built into their structures, but the microscope soon disproved this theory. In reality, plants use forces found within the water itself.

Water is made up of tiny particles called molecules. There is a vast number of these particles in water. It has been said that if a person were to take a cup of water to the Pacific Ocean, pour it in, and then stir the ocean thoroughly, he would have eight or ten of the original molecules in the cup if he filled it again with ocean water.

Each of these molecules has a strong force pulling on the other molecules of water near it, much as the gravity of the Earth holds things to its surface. This force in water is known as molecular cohesion. The strength of cohesion has been measured to be about thirty times the pressure of air. Of course this force is effective at only a very short distance.

Through a complicated process, which is not yet clearly understood, a tree uses this force to send water to its top. If such a process did not exist, the upper parts of a tree would die. As water is used by the leaves to make sugars, each cell, of which there are many in each leaf, draws water from another nearby. This drawing of water by its cohesive forces goes on in chain fashion all the way from the leaves, down through the trunk, on to the roots in the moist ground. It sends water to the top of the tallest tree. This same process goes on in all plants, even ordinary flowers. This can be seen by the fact that if a flower is cut under water, it will last much longer than if it is cut out of water. When the stem is cut under water, the attraction chain is not broken, so the flower will keep on "pumping" water.

Seemingly, water would travel very slowly by this method. Actually, water can rise in a plant at a rate of four feet in an hour.

The Two-Party System

Everybody has some special political interest which is not adequately served by either the Republican or the Democratic party. You may be a farmer who wants a very high percentage of parity, or a pacifist who wants the draft and defense spending abolished.

But you never get a chance to vote for someone who represents exactly the program you favor. Why not? The Democrats and the Republicans are the only parties that have a chance of winning an election. Why are there only these two parties?

One of the main functions of a political party is to gain power by criticizing the party holding office. The opposition party makes charges against current policies: the government is mishandling the school situation or foreign affairs. Since there is more effective opposition in united action, the dissatisfied groups get together, try to compromise their disagreements, and agree to carry on a united front. Here is one reason why our two parties have developed.

The United States is divided up into many districts, and each district elects one member by majority vote to the House of Representatives. This means that a party may get quite a few votes in many districts, but not enough to elect a candidate. The party's total vote when added together might be significant, even though it gained no seat in Congress. The people whose votes are thus wasted are not adequately represented in the government.

It is difficult for a new party to get a majority, and without success in the form of representation, new parties die out. In France the situation is different: seats in the legislature are apportioned to different parties according to the percentage of votes they win throughout the entire country. When a new party receives a certain number of votes, it has some representatives in the Chamber of Deputies and has therefore some voting power. From this start it may grow. Poujade had only a few seats after his first election, but the second time he ran he caused a landslide. But since the United States uses the other system of representation, the growth of minor parties is checked. They have no power at all until they can win a majority in some district.

Of course if we had too many parties, it would not be good either. If we used the French system, we might have twenty or thirty small parties, and none of them would represent a majority of the voters in the country. What would our national policy be then? Maybe there is some advantage in having only two parties, even though their platforms do not accurately reflect the wishes of all the people. For example, the Republican party has a right and a left wing, and the Democrats include most Southerners and some big metropolitan political machines.

# The Paragraph

## 4. THE PARAGRAPH AS A UNIT

- **a.** Paragraph division
- **b.** Length of paragraphs
- **c.** Short paragraphs for transition and for emphasis
- **d.** Paragraphing dialogue
- **e.** Paragraph unity
- **f.** Topic sentence

## 5. PARAGRAPH COHERENCE

- **a.** Logical order of ideas
- **b.** Transitional words
- **c.** Linking pronouns
- **d.** Repetition of words
- **e.** Parallel construction
- **f.** Connections between paragraphs

## 6. PARAGRAPH DEVELOPMENT

- **a.** Specific detail
- **b.** Descriptive detail
- **c.** Definition
- **d.** Contrast
- **e.** Illustration and analogy

# 4 THE PARAGRAPH AS A UNIT

A paragraph is both a unit in itself and also part of a larger unit. As subdivisions of a larger whole, paragraphs help to indicate the structure of a composition. The indention marking a new paragraph is a signal to the reader that one point has been completed and that the writer is going on to the next point. The paragraph divisions must therefore be logical divisions of the subject matter of the whole composition and each paragraph should follow naturally from the one preceding and lead smoothly into the following paragraph. But though it is a subdivision of a larger whole, a paragraph must also be complete in itself. A writer therefore needs to ask the following questions about each paragraph: Is the paragraph unified? Does it hang together and read smoothly? Is the idea of the paragraph adequately developed?

## 4a Paragraph Division

The essential principle in dividing material into paragraphs is to make the paragraph breaks come at natural turning points in the thought. Each paragraph will then represent a logical subdivision of the paper as a whole, and will thus help to make the writer's argument or train of thought clear. Each paragraph will be a step in the presentation of the material.

If a writer has prepared a detailed outline, he may have as many as fifteen or twenty subdivisions of what he wishes to say. The number of paragraphs in his paper will not necessarily correspond to the number of subdivisions shown in his outline. Several topics of an outline may be treated in a single paragraph. On the other hand, a single topic of an outline may need to be divided into several steps or paragraphs. The guiding principle is that the paragraphs must represent logical subdivisions of the whole piece of writing. Here is a part of a student outline:

II. Advantages of the two-party system
    A. Channeling opinion
        1. Disadvantages of giving the voter too many choices
            a. No clear-cut definition of issues
            b. No majority decision likely
        2. Value of limiting the alternatives
    B. Making political choices effective in practice
        1. Compromise and unity within the party
        2. Fixing responsibility for political acts

If the writer, planning a short paper, intends to cover this section of the outline in two paragraphs, he should *not* make the division come between 1a and 1b. Such a division would distort the logical structure of his paper, and the two paragraphs would not be unified. A paragraph division between A and B would be natural and would help to indicate the organization of the material.

However, if this section of outline should represent a major part of a long paper, a full discussion of A might require several pages. In that case, several paragraphs would be useful to show the subdivisions of A, and several more for B. The number of paragraph divisions is determined by the length at which subtopics are discussed.

## EXERCISE

The following selection was written as one paragraph. If it were desirable to divide it into three paragraphs, where would the divisions come? Why?

The astronomer seems at first sight to be the most helpless of all scientists. He cannot experiment with the Universe. It is a significant matter of nomenclature that whereas we speak of experimental work in other sciences we speak of *observational* work in astronomy. The astronomer cannot move around the Universe taking an especially detailed look at any object that he finds of interest, as the 'field' worker does in other sciences. He cannot tear objects such as stars to pieces when he wants to find out how they work, which is the method used by physicists — the tough guys of science. Astronomers perforce have to accept a comparatively meek role. They cannot alter the light that comes into the telescope, although they can build larger telescopes to get more light and they can use more efficient devices to analyse the light. Yet the astronomer possesses one well-nigh overwhelming advantage. This lies in the sheer variety of the things that can be observed. The Universe is so vast, and the lengths of time that are of interest in astronomy are so long, that almost every conceivable type of astronomical process is still going on somewhere or other. The astronomer's problem is not a lack of information but an embarrassing excess of it. His is often a problem of disentanglement rather than one of synthesis: among the great wealth of detail he has to decide what is important and what is irrelevant. The light that enters the telescope contains a truly fantastic tangle of information. It is just to assist in the unwinding of the tangle that astronomical theory has been developed, the weapons of astronomical theory being derived directly from physics, chemistry, aerodynamics, and a host of other sciences in lesser degree.

— FRED HOYLE [1]

## EXERCISE

The following selection was originally written as five paragraphs. Indicate where, in your opinion, the divisions should be, and be able to give reasons for your choice.

After Benjamin Franklin invented the lightning rod, the principle was widely accepted but there was much discussion whether sharp

[1] From *Frontiers of Astronomy*. By permission of Harper and Brothers, 1955.

points or round knobs made better conductors. In the absence of conclusive experiments, the discussion became heated. Franklin favored points. King George III, however, belonged to the knob school, and urged the Royal Society to rescind its solution in favor of points and come out for knobs. The argument the King used was guilt by association. He said Franklin was a leader of the insurgent American colonies and that to adopt his type of lightning rod would be to uphold a rebel. The scientists of the Royal Society, unimpressed by the case against the guilty lightning rods, refused to budge. The *Economist* of London, listening in considerable astonishment to the charges coming from investigating committees of Congress in 1952, proceeded to apply their logic to Winston Churchill. As a member of the Church of England, said the *Economist*, Churchill was automatically associated with an admitted fellow traveler, the "Red" Dean of Canterbury. As a member of Parliament, Churchill for fifteen years shared the House of Commons with a card-carrying Communist, William Gallacher. As a member of the Big Three in World War II, Churchill sat at conference tables with Joseph Stalin. Therefore Churchill must be a Communist. Q.E.D. The notion of guilt by association arises in part from the structure of the language we speak, in part from the association process in the memory patterns of the mind. It takes two forms, physical association and verbal. Churchill was physically associated with the Red Dean, though of course he was not contaminated thereby. The case of King George and Franklin, however, was purely a verbal trick. Franklin favored pointed lightning rods; Franklin was a traitor. Therefore anyone who favored pointed lightning rods was a traitor. This spurious identification is one of the major roadblocks in human communication. No animal could be guilty of it, for it is uniquely a phenomenon of language. It has operated so persistently down the ages that elaborate legal defenses have been erected to protect innocent citizens. Spurious identification flourishes when times are out of joint. If citizens feel insecure, frightened, frustrated, they are in the mood to blame somebody for their troubles. Whereupon demagogues and fanatics create scapegoats out of other citizens, condemning them on the principle of guilt by association.

— STUART CHASE [2]

[2] From *The Power of Words*, 1954. By permission of Harcourt, Brace and Company.

## 4b Length of Paragraphs

Ordinarily a paragraph should consist of more than one sentence but of less than a page. Paragraphs vary considerably in length in different kinds of writing. In formal, scientific, or scholarly writing they are often as long as 250 or 300 words. In ordinary magazine articles the average length is about 150 words. In newspapers the average is 50 words or less.

The principle governing paragraph length is the convenience of the reader. If each sentence is a separate paragraph, the reader will not be able to see the groupings of sentences the writer has in mind. If, on the other hand, there are too many sentences in one paragraph, the reader will not be able to see the subdivisions of the material. Paragraphs which run consistently to more than a page are little better than no paragraphing at all.

The student who wrote the following passage did not build it up painfully by adding one paragraph to another; rather, he conceived the passage as a unified and coherent whole. Consequently, it has movement and continuity, the ideas flowing smoothly from beginning to end. Nevertheless, it is too long to appear as a single paragraph, and the division into three, which may well have been made in revision, helps the reader to follow the line of thought.

An American making his first trip abroad will do well to go first to London and then move on to the cities of the continent. In this way, he proceeds gradually from the familiar to the strange and avoids what international travel agencies call cultural shock. England will be enough different from the United States to interest and excite him, but it will not be so totally unfamiliar as to overwhelm and terrify him.

A landing in Genoa or Le Havre may have, on a normally sensitive individual, the effect of a stunning blow. The newly arrived visitor is too dazed by the difficulties of a new language, new money, and new customs, to enjoy or even to see clearly what is around him. By the time he has recovered his self-possession, he has lost some precious days. And then he is confronted with some of the greatest art in the world, and some of the most colorful peoples. His appetite for seeing is soon dulled by an excess of riches. Florence and Rome and Paris are too magnificent to be taken in without some preparation and training. Almost certainly the tourist will suffer from a kind of visual indigestion. It will eventually be cured by his developing a protective immunity: he simply will not see, or even try to see, everything. Overstimulation leads to jaded sensibilities, and by the time he reaches England on his way home, London may well strike him as drab and dingy.

This is unfair to London, which, though not so exotic to Americans as Naples, is still one of the most interesting cities of the world. For an American just arriving abroad, London has the special charm of being new and different but not completely strange. The visitor will be able to understand the language at once, and thus he will have a good start toward understanding the people and their culture. The places and buildings he sees will be memorable because their names and associations are already fixed in his mind. Westminster Abbey, St. Paul's, Buckingham Palace, Downing Street, Bond Street, and Piccadilly — such words represent an existing framework into which he may fit the exciting realities he is now seeing for the first time. And he will be able to really see them, since he will not be dazed by a completely new way of life, nor surfeited with the splendors of St. Peter's and the Pitti Palace and the Champs Élysées.

## 4c Short Paragraphs for Transition and for Emphasis

Two types of very short paragraphs are permissible. To call attention to a very important transition or shift in the line of thought, a single sentence may be written as a single paragraph. Or, a very short paragraph may occasionally be used to indicate rhetorical emphasis.

**Transitional paragraph.**

. . . The amount of specialized training required of a physicist or chemist today is enormous. In high school and college he will need to acquire a thorough grounding in mathematics — the essential tool of engineer and scientist alike. As an undergraduate he will take nearly half of all his work in his special field, and this will consist not of general surveys but of highly technical courses aimed at giving him a thorough knowledge of a few parts of his field and at least an awareness of the areas he has barely touched on. In graduate school he will try to fill in these gaps and at the same time push on in a few areas to the actual frontiers of knowledge. Seven years after graduating from high school, he may have his Ph.D. and the feeling that he is reasonably competent in at least some areas of his field.

*But although this highly specialized study is essential to the making of a competent scientist, something more is needed if we are to produce great scientists.*

The first requirement is . . .

A sentence establishing a transition between paragraphs need not stand alone as a paragraph in itself. It may be included at the beginning of the paragraph which develops a new topic, but it should never be tacked on to the end of the paragraph preceding.

**Short paragraph for emphasis.**

Looking down on those swarming highways I understood more clearly than ever what peace meant. In time of peace the world is self-contained. The villagers come home at dusk from their fields. The grain is stored up in the barns. The folded linen is piled up in the cupboards. In time of peace each thing is in its place, easily found. Each friend is where he belongs, easily reached. All men know where they will sleep when night comes. Ah, but peace dies when the framework is ripped apart. When there is no longer a place that is yours in the world. When you know no longer where your friend is to be found. Peace is present when man can see the face that is composed of things that have meaning and are in their place. Peace is present when things form part of a whole greater than their sum, as the divers minerals in the ground collect to become the tree.

*But this is war.*

I can see from my plane the long swarming highways. . . .

— Antoine de Saint-Exupéry

**EXERCISE**

Make a study of paragraph division in one of the essays in your book of readings or in a magazine article.

*a*) Can you explain the author's paragraph divisions?

*b*) Estimate the number of words in each paragraph.

*c*) Try to account for any unusually long or unusually short paragraphs.

## 4d Paragraphing Dialogue

In narrative, a direct quotation, together with the rest of the sentence of which it is a part, is usually paragraphed separately, in order to make immediately clear the change of speaker. However, a short quoted speech which is closely united with the context is sometimes included in a paragraph of narration.

**Quotation paragraphed separately.**

"You young dog," said the man, licking his lips, "what fat cheeks you ha' got."

I believe they were fat, though I was at that time undersized, for my years, and not strong.

"Darn Me if I couldn' eat 'em," said the man, with a threatening shake of his head, "and if I han't half a mind to't!"

I earnestly expressed my hope that he wouldn't, and held tighter to the tombstone on which he had put me; partly, to keep myself upon it; partly, to keep myself from crying.

"Now lookee here!" said the man. "Where's your mother?"

"There, sir!" said I.

He started, made a short run, and stopped and looked over his shoulder.

"There, sir!" I timidly explained. "Also Georgiana. That's my mother."

"Oh!" said he, coming back. "And is that your father alonger your mother?"

"Yes, sir," said I; "him too; late of this parish."

— CHARLES DICKENS

**Short quotation included with another paragraph.**

The *Tyee* lurched and righted herself slowly, painfully. George gave a gasp of relief. "I thought we were gone that time, Alfie!"

Alfred had thought so, too. They would be gone the next time, or the time after. One more thing they could try, and they would have to try that quickly. "We'll have to run before it," he said. "It's all we can do. . . ."

— ARCHIE BINNS

### EXERCISE

Copy the following extract and make the proper paragraph divisions. Be able to give a reason for each division you make.

I came upon him on a January Sunday in the Botticelli room of the Uffizi Gallery. He was a slight blond young man standing before the vast canvas *Spring*. English, I thought, for he wore a buff camel's-hair coat and carried a copy of George Orwell's *1984*. A pair of middle-aged American tourists entered the room. The husband loitered before *The Birth of Venus;* his wife, busting out of a mink coat, nagged him impatiently on. "The gallery closes in half an hour," she scolded. "How can we see all the paintings if you keep stopping all the time?" The reluctant husband followed his wife into the next room. "She will have to take herself on a bicycle," the young man said in the crisp staccato English of continental Europeans. "There are a thousand more paintings to see." "I'll bet she sees them all," I said. "Americans are very foolish people," the young man said. "They do not look at paintings, they count them." Now I was thinking he was German or Swedish. "I am Italian," he said. I confessed I had been quite certain he wasn't. "I suppose you think I should look like a brother to Anna Magnani," he said. "It is what Americans think, that we are all black-haired peasants who have no dignity or self-control." "Fruit peddlers, gangsters, bootleggers, stone cutters, and opera singers," I said. "And you all eat spaghetti." He looked at me with a pained expression. "Is that what Americans think?" he asked. "That is terrible! That is just terrible." "What do Italians think of as a typical American?" I asked. "A rich man who has no culture and no soul," he said.

"That is terrible," I said. "That is just terrible!" We laughed and moved into a gallery of Del Sartos. I realized I was up against an unusual individual. "Do you like Del Sarto?" he asked. "Not especially," I said. "I like the earlier painters better — like Angelico and Giotto." "For an American your tastes are somewhat superior," he said. "Americans like best the sentimental Raphaels and Del Sartos." "What," I asked, "do you have against Americans?" "Their lack of humility," he said. "Because they know so well how to run machines and make money they think there is nothing else to know." "Is there anything you like about them?" I asked. "Yes," he said. "They are so sure of themselves. They are so hearty and they live passionately." I said that passionate living was a relative thing, that for me it was being in Florence at that moment. "For rich Americans it is easy to live passionately," he said. "For us Italians it is not possible. Our passion is despair, the passion of the poor." The noon bell clanged. On our way out we stopped a moment before a Gozzoli painting of a Medici hunting procession. "I should have liked to live in those times," my companion said wistfully. "Then I should have lived passionately."

— HERBERT KUBLY[3]

## 4e Paragraph Unity

As a unit in itself each paragraph should deal with a single topic. It should have a central idea or purpose, and each sentence in the paragraph should aid in developing this and making it clear. Details that do not contribute to the development of the idea of the paragraph should be struck out in revision. Or, if they are important and you want to include them, put them in another paragraph. Do not change your subject in mid-paragraph, as did the writer of the following.

**Not unified.**

History tells us that in the fifties of the last century thousands of men crossed the plains, the Rocky Mountains, and the desert, in

[3] From *An American in Italy*, 1955. By permission of Simon and Schuster.

search of the magic metal, gold. The California gold rush was a major contribution to the settlement of the Far West. Who of us, however, has ever heard of men stampeding across the country in a rush for iron ore? Iron ore is found in many parts of the United States; in fact, it can be found in some quantity in nearly every state. The greatest deposit of iron ore is in the Lake Superior region. Here the metal lies close to the surface; in most other regions the ore runs in small deep veins.

The first three sentences of this paragraph lead the reader to expect a discussion of the reasons why there was no "rush" for iron as there was for gold. The rest of the paragraph, however, takes up another subject, the location of iron ore deposits. The writer should have either developed each topic in a separate paragraph or cut out one completely and developed the other.

## 4f Topic Sentence

A valuable help in securing paragraph unity, especially in expository writing, is the use of a topic sentence — a sentence which summarizes the central idea or purpose of a paragraph. In revising, the writer can check to see that everything in the paragraph is related to the topic sentence and can cut out any detail which does not contribute to its development. A topic sentence most frequently is found at or near the beginning of a paragraph, where it will prepare the reader for what is to come. But a topic sentence may be placed anywhere in the paragraph — in the middle, after some transitional sentences, or at the end, as a conclusion. Note in the following examples how the topic sentence serves to unify the material of each paragraph.

**Topic sentence first.**

*On the other hand, the plays of Shakespeare stood for everything that Jonson disapproved of in the theatre and everything he had fought against in his long career as a playwright.* Shakespeare had not followed the classical rules except in *The Comedy of Errors*, which came at the very beginning of his career. He had never written a realistic play that mirrored contemporary London and he had not kept to the dramatic types that were so clearly laid down by the rule-makers. He had mingled comedy and tragedy, clowns and kings, in a way that Sir Philip Sidney would have deplored. He had been careless about his sources, brought in farce and dances and melodrama to amuse the lowest elements in his audience, and in general had produced an untidy, sprawling body of work that a true classicist could only regard with something approaching despair. Over and over again, Jonson had deplored the low state of the contemporary theatre and insisted that it could only be raised by following the classic ideal, and long before he mentioned it to Drummond he had made no secret of his conviction that Shakespeare lacked "art."

— MARCHETTE CHUTE [4]

**Topic sentence in the middle.**

Then something unforeseen happened. The waters of the River, shut out from much land, rose higher upon the lands that were left, and so broke over many dikes and again flooded the farms. The white men cursed, thinking that the rains must have been heavier than before; they decided to build levees a little higher, and be safe forever. *In those years that followed, a confusion as of a nightmare fell upon the Valley.* More and more levees were built, and each one made the water rise so that men had to build up the old ones higher still. The white men would not withdraw from the lands, and neither in their peculiar madness would they all work together against the River. Instead, in the dark rainy nights a man might break his neighbor's levee to lower the water-level against his own; so, not with shovels, but with loaded guns, men patrolled the levees, like savages brandishing spears against the river-god.

**Topic sentence last.**

At last, although the white men hated the very sound of the words, they began to talk more and more of "the government" and "regulation." Then finally came engineers who looked shrewdly

[4] From *Ben Jonson of Westminster*, 1953. By permission of E. P. Dutton and Company, Inc.

not at one part of the River, but at the whole. They measured snow and rain, and the depth of streams. They surveyed; they calculated with many figures how high the levees must be and how wide the channels between. Gradually even the fiercest fighters among the white men came to see that the River (which was always the whole River) was too great for any man or any company of men. Only the Whole People could hope to match the Whole River. *So, after many years of disaster, the white men began to live in a truce with the River.*

**Topic sentence first.**

*The terms of the truce are these.* Around the cities and around the best lands shall be the highest levees, and in times of flood men may even pile sand-bags to raise these levees higher. Around other lands shall be lower levees; these lands can be farmed in ordinary years, but in time of high flood they must be overflow-basins and their levees shall not be raised. Finally, broad stretches of land shall have no levees at all; into these great overflow-basins the River can pour, exhausting its fury, and through them as by-passes it can reach the Bay. The land of these by-passes may serve as pasture of sheep and cattle which can be driven behind the levees in time of flood.

**Topic sentence first.**

*It is a truce, but no real peace.* Year by year, the white men work upon their levees; also they build dams in the mountains to cut off the full burst of the River's power. Year by year, too, the River frets openly and in secret against the levees, and sometimes still it pours forth over its ancient flood-plain.

— George R. Stewart [5]

In some cases the topic sentence may be omitted altogether or be merely implied, without violating unity. It should always be possible, however, to summarize the central thought in a sentence. There is, for instance, no definitely expressed topic sentence in the following paragraph; but the central thought may be put thus: Slight differences

[5] From *Storm* by George R. Stewart, copyright 1941 by George R. Stewart. Reprinted by permission of Random House, Inc.

in IQ are not significant because of the statistical error in all intelligence tests.

**Unified: Topic sentence implied.**

Your two children Peter and Linda . . . take intelligence tests. Peter's IQ, you learn, is 98 and Linda's is 101. Aha! Linda is your brighter child. Is she? An intelligence test is, or purports to be, a sampling of intellect. An IQ, like other products of sampling, is a figure with a statistical error, which expresses the precision or reliability of the figure. The size of this probable error can be calculated. For their test the makers of the much-used Revised Stanford-Binet have found it to be about 3 per cent. So Peter's indicated IQ of 98 really means only that there is an even chance that it falls between 95 and 101. There is an equal probability that it falls somewhere else — below 95 or above 101. Similarly, Linda's has no better than a fifty-fifty chance of being within the fairly sizable range of 98 to 104.

— Darrell Huff

EXERCISE

In the following unified paragraphs, do you find a topic sentence? If not, make one. Show how each sentence in a paragraph is related to the topic sentence.

**1.** Hitler decided on the day following his declaration of war to attack American coastal shipping. One month later the U-boats began to strike. Very little had been done to prepare for their visitation. Mine fields had been planted off the Capes of the Chesapeake and certain harbors had been protected by antisubmarine nets; but no new convoys were organized because all available planes and escort vessels were employed in patrol, and none could be spared from transatlantic and transpacific convoys. The antisubmarine air patrol, by April 1942, had been built up to only 170 aircraft, mostly of very short range, based between Bangor and Jacksonville. The result of this lack of defensive measures was devastating. The German Navy, by keeping an average of a dozen U-boats constantly in the Eastern Sea Frontier, relieving them every two weeks and refueling them from tanker submarines stationed 300 miles east of Bermuda, pulled off one of the greatest merchant-ship massacres in history during the first four months of 1942. In round numbers, German submarines sank 82 merchant ships of 491,000 gross tons in the Eastern Sea Frontier, together with 55 ships of 337,000 tons in the Bermuda Area, during January, February, March and April. None of these ships were in convoy and very few, as yet, had been furnished with Naval Armed Guards. During the same four months only 14 U-boats and 5 Italian submarines were sunk (three of the Germans by United States forces); and 80 new ones were added to the underwater fleet.

— Samuel Eliot Morison [6]

**2.** Pepys has, indeed, had full reward for all his pains. Since the appearance of his Diary in the first abbreviated form which printed scarcely half of its contents, much learned and loving labor has been spent on its elucidation. The ingenuity and industry of successive editors have enlarged our knowledge and understanding of the work; the two original volumes, what with inclusion of the parts at first suppressed and a great bulk of comment, have increased to ten. One editor has retranscribed the manuscript, another has compiled a book on Pepys and the world he lived in; the family genealogy has been unearthed and a study made of one of its members as "a later Pepys"; so far has the reflected glory shone. The diarist's early life has been laid bare; his letters published, with his will; his portraits reproduced; a whole book on Pepys as a lover of music has appeared; an essay on the sermons that he heard; even the medical aspects of his married life have been explained by a physician-author. Essayists and bookmakers still find in him an ever-fertile subject for their pens; no biographical dictionary or encyclopedia is without a full account of the great diarist; and rising finally to the full stature of a real biography, few names to-day in English literature are better known, few classics more widely read or more enjoyed.

— W. C. Abbott

**3.** It is easy to idealize Lincoln and to read into him your own views and beliefs until they become his as well. But it is even

[6] From *The Atlantic Battle Won*, 1956. By permission of Little, Brown and Company.

easier to deflate than to idealize, to set him down as just a shoddy horse-trading politician. He was not that. If ever there was a man in our history who had the difficult stuff of heroism, this was the man. He was no absolutist and no program-builder. But neither was there any cant in him, as we know when we read his ironic letter to the delegation of ministers protesting as Christians against the war. He did a hard job well, with dignity, firmness, and — in the midst of desperate measures — with compassion. Always he had the distinguishing mark of greatness, the ability in any problem to get at the jugular. He saw when he came to office that the crux of adequate Presidential power in an emergency lay in the President's role as commander-in-chief. And, although a hard-bitten realist, he could know the meaning and the value of a dream.

— M. LERNER

**4.** There was no corner of the earth in which the Dutch trader was not a familiar figure. In countless early prints of Holland and Japan, his appearance is recorded: a big, hearty man in a millstone ruff, balloon knickerbockers and ten-gallon boots, frequently with a three-foot pipe in his mouth, very often with a monstrous musket in his hand, always wholly at his ease. In every situation, however strange, he preserves his unequalled composure. So he sits like a great cheerful bear in the home of a Japanese samurai, drinking and endeavoring to hold the alarmed daughters of the house on his knee. Anon he is sailing on a high-castled ship along the African coast among canoes full of yelling savages, or trafficking under the trees with American Indians.

— MIRIAM BEARD

**5.** The democratic rule that all men are equal is sometimes confused with the quite opposite idea that all men are the same and that any man can be substituted for any other so that his differences make no difference. The two are not at all the same. The democratic rule that all men are equal means that men's being different cannot be made a basis for special privilege or for the invidious advantage of one man over another; equality, under the democratic rule, is the freedom and opportunity of each individual to be fully and completely his different self.

— H. M. KALLEN

**6.** Out of this system there has come the convenient European fable that "Africa is poor." Europe has found it possible to extract large profits with one hand, and yet gesture sadly at African poverty with the other. Someone has lately calculated, for example, that the revenue of the Government of Northern Rhodesia, a notably "poor" territory, is no larger than the annual sums of money which quit that territory for investors overseas. In 1951 the revenue of the Congo Government was 5322 million francs; the exported profits of the Union Minière — not counting additions to reserve and reinvestment — were 2560 million francs. For the Gold Coast mining industry in 1949, a reliable official source calculates that "of the £6.4 millions earned by the exports of gold, perhaps 3 million pounds can be considered to have been transferred out of the country." In 1954 the Government of South Africa cut down the money it would spend on African education: yet South Africa's big corporations were making record profits. Thus it is obvious that "Africa is poor" not in any inherent sense but only in its social heritage of industrial knowledge and experience, and in accumulated capital — "poor," that is, because the colonial system keeps it so and makes it so.

— BASIL DAVIDSON [7]

[7] From *The African Awakening*, 1955. By permission of The Macmillan Company.

# 5 PARAGRAPH COHERENCE

Within every paragraph the sentences should be arranged and tied together in such a way that the reader can easily follow the train of thought. The relations between sentences must be clear. It is not enough for the reader to know what each sentence means; he must also see how each sentence is related to the one that precedes it, and where all the sentences in the paragraph are going. The means of securing such coherence within a paragraph are, first, the arrangement of sentences in logical order and, second, the use of the special devices illustrated below, in sections **5b–5e.**

## 5a Logical Order of Ideas

The ideas and details which make up a paragraph should be organized into some logical and recognizable order. The method of organization will depend on the kind of material which is to go into the paragraph. If a paragraph deals with different periods of time, putting details in chronological order will make for coherence.

**Incoherent.**

I was by nature a trusting child. [Past] I am still an easy prey to unscrupulous salesmen and young men selling magazine subscriptions to put themselves through college. [Present] When a schoolmate would invite me to look at his new ring, I would always bend down and get squirted. [Past. Detail] I was a born victim for small-boy tricks. [Past. Generalization] I never suspected that the stick of chewing gum so generously offered me concealed a spring that would snap my finger when I pulled the gum out of its package. [Past. Detail] By now I ought to know better than to believe every sales-talk I hear, but I don't. [Present]

The childhood details should come together at the beginning. Also, the illustrative details should be placed together, either before or after the generalization.

**Improved.**

I was by nature a trusting child, and a born victim for small-boy tricks. When a schoolmate invited me to look at his new ring, I would always bend down and get squirted. I never suspected that the stick of chewing gum so generously offered me concealed a spring that would snap my finger when I pulled the gum out of its package. By now I ought to know better than to believe every sales-talk I hear, but I don't. I am still an easy prey to unscrupulous salesmen and young men selling magazine subscriptions to put themselves through college.

A fairly common type of paragraph consists of a general statement with supporting details and necessary concessions and qualifications. Group these details, instead of scattering them throughout the paragraph.

**Incoherent.**

Pelargoniums, sometimes called Martha Washington geraniums, are ideal for an amateur gardener to experiment with. They will grow almost anywhere, and they need very little attention. They are easy to start from cuttings, and the variety of colors and patterns is amazing. Of course, like most plants, pelargoniums need a certain amount of sun. If they are planted in deep shade, they develop long, weak stems and become straggly. It is very difficult to start a successful cutting from such a plant. But a branch from a stocky, short-jointed bush growing in the sun will take root in a few weeks. A row of cuttings set out in the fall will reward the gardener with a blaze of color the following spring. Pelargoniums need relatively little water and will grow in almost any kind of soil. The colors range from pure white through various shades of pink, lavender, orange, and red to a deep maroon. However, if the bushes are not pruned at least once a year, they grow long and spindly, with flowers only at the end of long, snake-like shoots.

**Improved.**

Pelargoniums, sometimes called Martha Washington geraniums, are ideal for an amateur gardener to experiment with. They will grow almost anywhere — in rich or poor soil and in either sun or shade. They require relatively little water, and almost no attention except for an annual pruning. If they are not pruned, the bushes grow long and spindly, with flowers only at the end of long, snake-like roots. The variety of colors and patterns is amazing, ranging from pure white through various shades of pink, lavender, orange, and red to dark maroon. Pelargoniums are very easy to start from cuttings. Cuttings should not be taken from the long weak stems of bushes growing in deep shade, but from the sturdy, short-jointed stems of plants growing in the sun. A row of such cuttings set out in the fall will take root in a few weeks and will reward the gardener with a blaze of color the following spring.

A paragraph which makes comparisons or contrasts should be organized so that the reader does not have to jump back and forth from one subject to another.

**Incoherent.**

Although no flat map is completely accurate, each projection has its characteristic qualities and uses. The Mercator projection, which is commonly seen in maps of the world, was made so that a line drawn between any two points would give the true direction from one point to the other, a great advantage to the seaman. A gnomonic projection has the advantage that any straight line drawn on it represents a great circle on the globe. But it is useless for determining shapes and areas, and distances are very difficult to measure on it. On a Mercator map, distances have to be computed with the aid of a special scale which varies with the latitude. On a conformal conic projection, like that used on most aeronautical charts, distances can be measured directly, and much more easily than on a Mercator map.

Another disadvantage of the Mercator projection is that, especially near the Poles, areas and shapes are badly distorted. A gnomonic chart is even worse in this respect. On a Mercator map of the world, Greenland appears to be almost as large as South America, whereas actually South America is seven times as large as Greenland. The conformal conic projection represents shapes and areas with fair accuracy. It is a kind of compromise map, showing nothing with complete accuracy but approximately correct in all important respects.

**Improved.**

Although no flat map is completely accurate, each projection has its characteristic qualities and uses. The Mercator projection, which is commonly seen in maps of the world, was made so that a line drawn between any two points would give the true direction from one point to the other, a great advantage to the seaman. But it badly distorts areas and shapes, especially near the Poles. On a Mercator map of the world, Greenland appears to be almost as large as South America, whereas actually South America is seven times as large as Greenland. Distances have to be computed on a Mercator map with the aid of a special scale which varies with the latitude. A gnomonic projection has the advantage that any straight line drawn on it represents a great circle on the globe, but it is useless for determining shapes and areas, and it is even worse than the Mercator for measuring distances. The conformal conic projection, which is used on most aeronautical charts, produces a kind of compromise map; it shows nothing with complete accuracy, but is approximately correct in all important respects. Distances can be measured directly, without the variable scale which the Mercator requires, and shapes and areas are represented with fair accuracy.

## 5b Use of Transitional Words

Conjunctive adverbs like *moreover*, *however*, *accordingly*, *therefore* and connecting phrases like *for example*, *in fact*, *to be sure*, *in the first place* help to show the relation between sentences in a paragraph. In the following paragraph, transitional words are in italics.

**Coherent.**

It is hardly necessary to give many instances of these occurrences. It seems desirable, *however*, to illustrate the great strength of these ideas that restrict the freedom of thought of the individual, leading to the most serious mental struggles when traditional social ethics come into conflict with instinctive reactions. *Thus* among a tribe of Siberia we find a belief that every person will live in the future life in the same condition in which he finds himself at the time of death. *As a consequence* an old man who begins to be decrepit wishes to die, in order to avoid life as a cripple in the endless future, and it becomes the duty of his son to kill him. The son believes in the righteousness of this command but *at the same time* feels the filial love for his father, and many are the instances in which the son has to decide between the two conflicting duties — the one imposed by the instinctive filial love, the other imposed by the traditional custom of the tribe.

— FRANZ BOAS

## 5c Use of Linking Pronouns

Sentences in a paragraph may be linked by the use of pronouns which have antecedents in the previous sentence.

**Coherent.**

The great Whig country houses of the eighteenth and early nineteenth centuries are among the most conspicuous monuments of English history. Ornate and massive, with *their* pedimented porticoes, *their* spreading balustraded wings, *they* dominate the landscape round *them* with a magnificent self-assurance. Nor are *their* interiors less imposing. *Their* colonnaded entrance halls, whence the Adam staircase sweeps up beneath a fluted dome; *their* cream and gilt libraries piled with sumptuous editions of the classics; *their* orangeries peopled with casts from the antique; *their* saloons hung with yellow silk, and with ceiling and doorways painted in delicate arabesque by Angelica Kauffmann, all combine to produce an extraordinary impression of culture and elegance and established power.

— LORD DAVID CECIL

## 5d Use of Repetition of Words

The repetition of key words serves to keep the continuity of thought clear to a reader.

**Coherent.**

There is little doubt that *spots on the sun* have an effect upon weather on the earth. They cause great magnetic storms; and, in addition, the amount of energy radiated by the sun appears to be greater at *sun-spot* maxima, less when *sun spots* are few. One of the chief facts of terrestrial climate which seems to be definitely correlated with *sun-spot* number concerns the *track of storms*. If the *tracks followed by heavy storms* are plotted on a map, it will be found that, in North America for instance, there is in any one year *a zone* along which the majority of *storms* travel. Now *this zone shifts* up and down with considerable regularity from year to year, returning to the same position about every eleven years. Such a *shift* in the *storm tracks* will obviously mean a slight *shift* of the margins of all the great climatic *zones*. It will mean that there will be cycles of rainfall, some areas getting more than the average every eleven years, while *other zones* in the same years will be getting less than the average; and this, according to the careful investigations of O. T. Walker, is what actually occurs. Such *changes* are likely to have the most noticeable *effect* upon plants and animals where conditions are difficult for life. For instance, a small *change* in rainfall in a semi-desert region will have much more *effect* than the same *change* in a well-watered country; and quite small temperature *changes* in the Arctic will have disproportionately large *effects* on the animals and plants which live there.

— Julian S. Huxley

## 5e Use of Parallel Construction

Parallel structure in successive sentences helps to indicate the relation of the ideas to each other. Warning: needless or useless parallel structure may make for monotonous sentences.

**Coherent.**

So the American way of war *is bound to be* like the American way of life. It *is bound to be* mechanized like the American farm and kitchen (the farms and kitchens of a lazy people who want washing machines and bulldozers to do the job for them). *It is the army of a nation* of colossal business enterprises, often wastefully run in detail, but winning by their mere scale and by their ability to wait until that scale tells. *It is the army of a country* where less attention is paid to formal dignity, of persons or occupations, than in any other society, where results count, where being a good loser is not thought nearly as important as being a winner, good or bad. *It is the country* where you try anything once, especially if it has not been tried before. *It is a country* which naturally infuriates the Germans with their pedantry and their pathological conception of "honor." *It is a country* that irritates the English with their passion for surface fidelity to tradition and good form. *It is the country* of such gadget-minded originals as Jefferson and Ford. . . .

— D. W. BROGAN

## EXERCISE

In the following paragraphs, point out all the devices for securing coherence:

**1.** That the boom period between 1920 and 1930 was the most spectacular period of our sporting history, the era of the biggest and greatest, the period of the super-champion when the United States not only led the world but admitted it, is beyond question. That it was the boom period of sport in this country is not, however, true. There was more noise and shouting, more exaggeration and hyperbole, more space in the newspapers devoted to sports or what passed at the time for sports; but there were fewer persons actually playing games. The space in the press was devoted to the super-champions, not to the second-raters who play golf and tennis all over the land. No, if we are not yet in the boom period of American sport, we are approaching it. To-day there is a more intelligent appreciation of the values of real sport, there are more persons of average ability competing, there are more participants who are interested in the game for the game's sake, more people playing than ever before in our history. Not merely is this a greater period for athletes than the era of the super-champion, but there is every likelihood of greater times ahead.

— J. R. Tunis

**2.** Perhaps it is true, as Mr. Kilmer said originally very nicely and as countless ladies have reiterated shrilly since, that only God can make a tree. But a man made the Swanee River. The river which Stephen Foster took, misspelling it, from a map where he searched for a better two syllable stream than Peedee, does not run merely to the Gulf from Okefenokee Swamp and its alligators and moccasins and shy, poor white people on occasional prairies and Negroes in the dark shade of its black gum trees. It runs rather from homesickness into memory. Its sources are diverse as its singers. Those English Crimean War soldiers who sang it so long ago had never heard of Florida but they also had childhoods far from the Black Sea shores and beyond the aging of the old folks at home. It is the river behind all of us, with shores simple as sand. . . . It is a river to be sung, not seen.

— Jonathan Daniels

**3.** Let us take some of the rest of the sentence — the mere words "United States." Well, of course, we know what the United States means — we know it so well that we do not even have to think about it. And yet do we? For it took five years of active revolution to make the one word, "States" — twelve years of confederation and argument and, later on, four years of Civil War to make the word "United" an effective word. When you say those particular words — United States — you are not just talking of geography or even of a flag. You are talking of an idea in action — an idea as strong, as deeply rooted as any that has moved the minds of men — an idea that has been served, at one time or another, with singular devotion. I agree that we do not often think of it in that particular way. And yet it is there, in the words. And without the words, and the thought behind the words, it would not be there.

— Stephen Vincent Benét

## 5f Connections between Paragraphs

If a paper is to read smoothly, the reader must be able to see the relation between successive paragraphs. Even though a single paragraph be perfect in itself — its main ideas properly emphasized, the pattern of sentences varied, the ending emphatic and conclusive — it may fail as a functioning part of the entire paper. It is more important that a paragraph should be an effective vehicle carrying the reader along from one point to the next than that it should be a little masterpiece in itself. A striking opening sentence may be less valuable than a sentence linking the paragraph to what has gone before. A final sentence which points ahead is probably more useful than a concluding rhetorical flourish. Paragraphs are not separate jewels making up a necklace; a piece of writing should *move*, and good paragraphs should help it move.

Some of the devices for tying paragraphs together and making them flow are the same as those used to link sentence to sentence within a single paragraph (see **5a–5e**): the repetition of key words, pronouns with antecedents in the preceding paragraph, connecting phrases or sentences. Probably more important is the gradually acquired ability to "aim" a paragraph, to plan the arrangement of material so that a paragraph ends with some reference to the idea that is to be taken up next.

The following paragraphs are part of a discussion of the necessity of tenure for scholars. Notice how the transitions between paragraphs are achieved.

. . . Without tenure the scholar could become the mere hireling of a governing board, bereft of intrinsic dignity and at the mercy of its predilections. Without tenure he would lack any assurance that he can freely express conclusions that may be contrary to the interests, convictions, or prejudices of minority or majority groups. The independence of judgement that is of primary importance both in the search for knowledge and in the interpretation of what is already known would be jeopardized.

The teacher, whether he belongs to the school or to the university, does not possess either the means of defense or the bargaining power that many other groups enjoy. . . . (Examples follow, distinguishing the teacher from members of the professions or of labor unions.) . . . His tenure, offering him a degree of assurance that he can make his scholarly interest his life work, is his necessary mainstay.

It is the more necessary because the powers that rule him often understand so little the nature of the work or of the service, to which the genuine scholar is devoted. . . . They speak as though the duty of the scholar were simply to wait until he had attained demonstrable certainty before he makes a pronouncement on any subject. . . . But for all the testing and examining the scholar can do, there are great areas of the realm of knowledge within which infallible conclusions are not and probably cannot be attained, where all we can hope to reach is a higher degree of probability or predictability. . . . Within this same domain lies the more important part of the work done by the historian, the student of literature, the anthropologist, the economist, the philosopher, the sociologist, and generally all scholars who work in the humanities and in the social sciences. They interpret and they form hypotheses and they draw conclusions. But they are not like mathematicians who can write Q.E.D. at the end of the argument.

When the scholar is occupied in any of these fields, he particularly needs the protection of tenure. It is his right and his duty to throw whatever light he can on the complex and practically important problems that dogma and group interest short-cut by their own convenient ready-made formulas. It is his right and even his duty not to take the safe course of presenting an arid array of fact and figures, expecting some mythical reader to give them form and meaning, but to interpret them and to state, with scholarly discretion and circumspection but also with whatever scholarly imagination he possesses, the conclusions to which they may point.

— Robert M. MacIver[9]

[9] From *Academic Freedom in Our Time*, 1955. Reprinted by permission of Columbia University Press.

### EXERCISE

The following paragraphs are jerky and incoherent. Rewrite them, putting material into logical order, combining sentences, making connections clear, and supplying transitional devices.

Dentistry is a very attractive profession. It offers money and security and respect in the community. Many dentists are active in community affairs, such as local government, service clubs, the Community Chest, etc. Dentistry offers a chance to work hard and to work with one's hands. There is relatively little night work, and the dentist is better off in this respect than a physician. Working with one's hands provides a healthful change from pure brain work. A dentist uses his brain, too, and a liberal education is a necessary foundation to professional training. A dentist is independent. He is his own boss and can set his own hours and pace of work.

The college education of a prospective dentist should be as broad as possible. History may seem to be of no practical value. Literature, art, and music do not help one to earn a living. Economics and government have some practical value, since a dentist is partly a business man. A community leader needs to know something about the community in which he lives. Anyone working with people, like a doctor or teacher or dentist, needs to understand people. Psychology helps to explain why people act as they do, and literature often provides valuable psychological insights. Art and music are community activities which should be supported by all leading citizens.

Of course, science should not be neglected. A knowledge of chemistry is basic for any professional study. Dentists must understand the physical basis of life processes, which depends on a knowledge of chemistry, physiology, and anatomy. The structure of the body, which is studied in anatomy, is especially important. Having a tooth pulled is a surgical operation — minor, perhaps, but possibly serious. The effects of drugs and anaesthetics on the body must be understood. Physiology explains life processes, which depend on chemical reactions. The more science a dentist knows, the better he will be at his job.

# 6 PARAGRAPH DEVELOPMENT

A good paragraph is one in which the central idea is adequately developed. Developing a paragraph does not mean padding out a simple statement nor repeating the same idea in different words. It means filling out the bare statement of an idea with specific details, examples, definitions, comparisons and contrasts, or necessary qualifications. Take time to specify fully what you mean. It is usually better to give adequate development to a few ideas than to make meager comments on a number of topics.

**Underdeveloped paragraph.**

Television is a good example of the never-ending material progress in America. New advancements are being made every day. Television is also an example of social progress, since it increases communication between people. Because of the many people who watch it, television is an aid to advertising, which in turn is an aid to progress.

The student who wrote this wretched parody of a paragraph was not really thinking; he was putting down on paper the first fragmentary ideas that entered his mind when two buttons, marked Television and Progress, were pushed. A little reflection would show that three topics are here hinted at: (1) TV as an example of technical progress, (2) TV and social progress, and (3) TV and advertising. Each of these might be developed into a paragraph.

The following questions suggest the sort of material which might be used to develop the first two topics.

(1) What are other examples of technical and material progress? What are some of the "advancements being

made every day"? Is TV a synthesis of other technical achievements? Does an increase in material goods and technical processes represent progress? What is progress?

(2) How does TV increase communication between people? Are TV addicts more or less likely to have meaningful contacts with their neighbors? Does TV expand one's opportunities for experience? How? Is this good? Why?

Developing a paragraph requires that one think out the implications of his topic sentence, and then take time to express the idea of the paragraph fully, often with specific detail and illustration.

Some methods of paragraph development are illustrated in the following pages. In actual practice a writer is apt to use a combination of methods. The topic sentence of the following paragraph is developed by means of definition, contrast, example, and illustration.

| | |
|---|---|
| **Topic sentence** | London has one great advantage for the American tourist: since he knows the language, he can easily get to know the people and their cul- |
| **Definition** | ture. By culture I do not mean the treasures of the British Museum or the concerts at the Royal Albert Hall. I mean, rather, the underlying assumptions, attitudes, and values which give the specific flavor to British life. In other foreign |
| **Contrast** | countries this sense of the real life of the people is difficult to achieve. An American in Paris may be able to ask simple questions and understand simple directions, but unless he knows French very well, he remains an onlooker, an outsider, and he misses all the subtleties of the French out- |
| **Example** | look on life. In London, every native is a potential acquaintance and a source of knowledge of British life. The porter at your hotel will not only tell you how to get to Buckingham Palace; his incidental remarks may reveal a good deal about the |

**Illustration with Specific Details** English class system. A Cockney street merchant gave me a vivid sense of British feeling toward the Royal Family when he said . . .

The method used to develop an idea will depend on the kind of material and the purpose of the author. In the following paragraphs, notice how the method of development is adapted to the material to be expressed.

## 6a Developed by Specific Detail

When the first loggers, many of whom were State-of-Mainers, saw the fir that grew along the banks of the Columbia, they said there just couldn't be timber that big and tall, and bragged in letters back to Bangor that it took two men and a boy to look to the top of one of these giants. Oregon pine they called it. It was neither pine nor fir, though for more than half a century it has been sold as Douglas fir. Its botanical name is *Pseudotsuga taxifolia*, meaning "false hemlock." It grows to an extreme height of 380 feet. Its average diameter at breast height is from four to six feet. Still standing not far from Astoria is a Douglas fir fifteen feet six inches in diameter, healthy and growing despite the winds and fires and bugs of a thousand years. It is a tree to give a man pause, even a logger.

— STEWART H. HOLBROOK [10]

## 6b Developed by Descriptive Detail

Perhaps the most magnificent exhibition of Indian equestrianship described by white witnesses was at the making of the Medicine Lodge Treaty in Kansas, in October, 1867. . . . In order to make an impression, General Harney formed his whole command into an enormous S and there on the prairie awaited the Indians. Two thousand strong, the mounted warriers, led by Black Kettle, White Antelope, Lone Wolf, Kicking Bird, Satanta and chieftains less notable, appeared over a grass-covered slope about two miles away. They were formed in a great V, the point of it directed towards the middle of the S. They rode slowly, in silence, their horses groomed

[10] From *The Columbia*, 1956. Reprinted by permission of Rinehart and Company, Inc.

and painted, they themselves in war paint and feathers. About a mile away, without a pause or a signal visible to the white spectators, the two thousand riders dashed from V formation into a huge circle. This circle became a revolving wheel, spokeless and hubless, the rim made by five lines of riders. As it rotated, faster and faster, it moved forward until within about a hundred yards of the waiting formation. Then it ceased to revolve, leaving a gap in the forward rim. Now the chiefs gathered to the center of the circle, and a warrior rode through the gap to the flag and ushered the general and commissioners to the chiefs.

— J. Frank Dobie [11]

## 6c Developed by Definition

In spite, or maybe because, of all that has been written on how to acquire friends, exude personality and dazzle dinner parties, America today boasts pathetically few interesting people. By interesting one means, of course, quite the reverse of "interesting"— quite the reverse of travelers who give memorably minute accounts of their trips to the interior of Kenya; or people who have the ear, or hold the hand, or scratch the back, of the great and celebrated. One means people — it seems sad to have to say what one means — who because of their brains, charm, liveliness, responsiveness, wit are a pleasure to be with. And a pleasure whether one chooses to talk sense or nonsense, since the test of interesting people is that subject matter doesn't matter.

— Louis Kronenberger [12]

## 6d Developed by Contrast

Sociologists talk a great deal these days about "adjustment," which has always seemed to me a defeatist sort of word suggesting dismal surrender to the just tolerable. The road runner is not "adjusted" to his environment. He is triumphant in it. The desert is his home and he likes it. Other creatures, including many other birds,

[11] From *The Mustangs*, 1952. Reprinted by permission of Little, Brown and Company.

[12] From *Company Manners* by Louis Kronenberger, copyright 1954. Used by special permission of the publishers, The Bobbs-Merrill Company, Inc.

elude and compromise. They cling to the mountains or to the cottonwood-filled washes, especially in the hot weather, or they go away somewhere else, like the not entirely reconciled human inhabitants of this region. The road runner, on the other hand, stays here all the time and he prefers the areas where he is hottest and driest. . . .

— Joseph Wood Krutch[13]

## 6e Developed by Illustration and Analogy

A basic negotiating technique of Communists is to introduce spurious issues and use them as bargaining points. To illustrate, imagine that two men are discussing the sale of an automobile. Suppose that the seller demands $1,000 for his car; the buyer offers $700. If the seller followed the Communist method, something like the following would occur. The Communist seller would propose that the buyer agree in writing to purchase all his further automobiles from the same Communist salesman. The buyer rejects this, pointing out how unreasonable such an undertaking on his part would be. The Communist seller insists, however, that the buyer should accept the proposal, and continues to so argue over an extended period of time. Naturally, under such circumstances, you or I would terminate the discussion peremptorily and find another source of the automobile we need. This is not possible in international negotiations, however, since matters of life and death are at stake. Accordingly, our analogy must continue. After pressing his proposal to commit the automobile buyer forever to buy from only one source, himself, the Communist seller at last states that he will withdraw his proposal only if the buyer will agree to pay $1,000 for the car in question. When the buyer protests, the Communist seller contends that he has made a great concession in withdrawing his proposal; therefore, the buyer should be willing to make a concession on the price of the car. If this sounds fantastic, read further and observe it in practice.

— Admiral C. Turner Joy[14]

[13] From *The Voice of the Desert*, 1955. By permission of William Morrow and Company.

[14] From *How Communists Negotiate*, 1955. By permission of The Macmillan Company.

### EXERCISE

The following paragraphs are intended for study and analysis. Pick out the topic sentence of each. If there is no topic sentence, make one up. Notice how general statements are illustrated by specific examples, or by metaphors and analogies. Point out other methods by which an idea is developed. Be ready to explain the means used to achieve coherence in each paragraph.

**1.** The American people, more than any other people, is composed of individuals who have lost association with their old landmarks. They have crossed an ocean, they have spread themselves across a new continent. The American who still lives in his grandfather's house feels almost as if he were living in a museum. There are few Americans who have not moved at least once since their childhood, and even if they have stayed where they were born, the old landmarks themselves have been carted away to make room for progress. That, perhaps, is one reason why we have so much more Americanism than love of America. It takes time to learn to love the new gas station which stands where the wild honeysuckle grew. Moreover, the great majority of Americans have risen in the world. They have moved out of their class, lifting the old folks along with them perhaps, so that together they may sit by the steam pipes, and listen to the crooning of the radio. But more and more of them have moved not only out of their class, but out of their culture; and then they leave the old folks behind, and the continuity of life is broken. For faith grows well only as it is passed on from parents to their children amidst surroundings that bear witness, because nothing changes radically, to a deep permanence in the order of the world. It is true, no doubt, that in this great physical and psychic migration some of the old household gods are carefully packed up and put with the rest of the luggage, and then unpacked and set up on new altars in new places. But what can be taken along is at best no more than the tree which is above the ground. The roots remain in the soil where first they grew.

— WALTER LIPPMANN

**2.** Everyone knows the popular conception of Florence Nightingale. The saintly, self-sacrificing woman, the delicate maiden of high degree who threw aside the pleasures of a life of ease to succor the afflicted, the Lady with the Lamp, gliding through the horrors of the hospital at Scutari, and consecrating with the radiance of her goodness the dying soldier's couch — the vision is familiar to all. But the truth was different. The Miss Nightingale of fact was not as facile fancy painted her. She worked in another fashion, and towards another end; she moved under the stress of an impetus which finds no place in the popular imagination. A Demon possessed her. Now demons, whatever else they may be, are full of interest. And it so happens that in the real Miss Nightingale there was more that was interesting than in the legendary one; there was also less that was agreeable.

— LYTTON STRACHEY

**3.** Viewed through a supertelescope by an extramundane astronomer inhabiting, say, one of the outer planets, our earth with its glittering oceans would no doubt be an object of admiration and envy, and would probably be called "the water planet." It certainly forms a striking contrast to its next neighbors in space. Venus, "the cloud planet," coyly hides her charms behind an impenetrable veil of dazzling white clouds. (Spectroscopic analyses indicate these clouds do not contain water, but are largely built up from carbon dioxide.) Her old admirer Mars, "the desert planet," is also deficient in water. Venus is possibly still in a pre-oceanic stage, but Mars is strongly suspected of having consumed his original supply, either drinking it into his crust or perhaps squandering it into interplanetary space. This contrast inevitably suggests that our present oceanic splendor represents a transient stage in the development of the earth, which may be on its way toward the Martian state of complete desiccation. According to some pessimists, in another few thousand million years or so oceanographers will have to learn a new profession.

— HANS PETTERSSON [15]

**4.** Without any doubt, we possess the world's most highly developed technique of combining the efforts of large numbers of scientists and large quantities of money toward the realization of a single project. This should not lead us to any undue complacency concerning our scientific position, for it is equally clear that we are

[15] From *The Ocean Floor*, 1954. By permission of Yale University Press.

bringing up a generation of young men who cannot think of any scientific project except in terms of large numbers of men and large quantities of money. The skill by which the French and English do great amounts of work with apparatus which an American high-school teacher would scorn as a casual stick-and-string job is not to be found among any but a vanishingly small minority of our young men. The present vogue of the big laboratory is a new thing in science. There are those of us who wish to think that it may never last to be an old thing. When the time comes at which the scientific ideas of this generation are exhausted, or at least have come to show vastly diminishing returns on their intellectual investment, I do not see the prospect that the next generation will be able to furnish the colossal ideas on which colossal projects naturally rest.

— NORBERT WIENER [16]

**5.** If the soil is exposed, unprotected from the rains by cover and by roots, the people will be poor and the river will be muddy, heavy with the best soil of the fields. And as a consequence each year the farmers will be forced more and more to use their land in ways that speed up this cycle of ruin, until the cover and then the top soil itself are wholly gone. When that day comes, as in the great reaches of China's sorrowful Yellow River Valley, then rains run off the land almost as rapidly as water runs from the pavements. Even a moderate rainfall forces the river from its banks, and every down-pour brings disastrous flood, destroying crops and homes and bridges and highways, not only where the land is poor, but down the river's length, down in the areas where people are more prosperous, where the soil is still protected and factories have been built at the river's bend. Industries and railroads will be interrupted, farms flooded out, towns and villages destroyed, while heavy silt deposits fill the power reservoirs and stop up the channels of navigation.

— DAVID LILIENTHAL

**6.** It is easier to say what loyalty is not than to say what it is. It is not conformity. It is not passive acquiescence in the status quo. It is not preference for everything American over everything foreign. It is not an ostrich-like ignorance of other countries and other

[16] From *The Human Use of Human Beings*, 1950. By permission of Houghton Mifflin Company.

institutions. It is not the indulgence in ceremony — a flag salute, an oath of allegiance, a fervid verbal declaration. It is not a particular creed, a particular version of history, a particular body of economic practices, a particular philosophy.

— HENRY STEELE COMMAGER

**7.** The trouble with the enormously complex problems of government is that the more you study them, the more complex they seem. This is hard on the human nervous system, which has its limitations. So a large number of American newspapers have hit upon a solution to this. They have developed a very special corps of columnists to explain all in one-syllable words with the least wear and tear on the reader's mind. I mean the ex-sportswriter or Toots Shor school of high-policy writing. Ex-sportswriters are best because in games there are firm rules, only so many plays and possible results and a definite score at the end. The working theory of this group of experts is that if you apply the game approach to the massive, changing affairs of world politics, the box score will be equally clear and final, and we'll know just where we stand.

**8.** Of course, members of this school of commentation have to abide by certain house-rules themselves. They must spring from poor but honest parents, prefer beer to wine, be properly suspicious of foreigners, government officials, college professors, and any American who got past the eleventh grade. One rule is that they must never read government documents or question government authorities, while clinging to the conviction that their favorite barkeep on Third Avenue could run things better than that whole passel of long-haired theorists down in Washington. It is all right for the members to own a country estate — that's an American's privilege, ain't it, bub? — but they must not forget to begin every third column by saying: "I'm just a plain, average grits-and-hominy boy from the farm, Buster, but lemme tell you how it looks to me." They remain faithful to the Horatio Alger tradition; that is, they respect the rich, but they expose as a hollow sham an even older American tradition of respecting deep learning, high art, and specialized knowledge. "That's for the birds, Buster. Dangerous stuff, probably Communist."

— ERIC SEVAREID [17]

[17] From *In One Ear*, 1952. By permission of Alfred A. Knopf, Inc.

**9.** Preparation for fighting a war is like preparation for taking a cruise in a small sailing boat— there is no end to it. It is possible to get so absorbed in the details of preparation as to lose sight of the trip. Anyone who has ever had the experience will know what I mean. If you were to wait until both you and the boat were really ready to put to sea the summer would pass and the autumn would find you still at your home mooring. No boat is ever entirely ready to put to sea, no country is ever fully prepared to go to war; always there remain things which should be attended to, contingencies which should be provided for. But there comes a moment when you have to forget about preparations and think about the stars and the sea and the lengthening nights. You know that if you don't go now you will never go. So you drop off your mooring and shape your course to the wind. From then on things begin to move; you may not be ready in every particular, but you are under way and the ship is alive. And something vital in the ship imparts sudden life and resourcefulness to her crew.

— E. B. WHITE

**10.** Our well-founded distaste for cranks has, however, rather blurred our ability to tell a crank from a mere eccentric, or even an eccentric from an individual. On a very rough-and-ready basis we might define an eccentric as a man who is a law unto himself, and a crank as one who, having determined what the law is, insists on laying it down to others. An eccentric puts ice cream on steak simply because he likes it; should a crank do so, he would endow the act with moral grandeur and straightway denounce as sinners (or reactionaries) all who failed to follow suit. The crank, however, seldom deals in anything so agreeable as steak or ice cream; the crank prefers the glories of health bread or the splendors of soybeans. Cranks, at their most familiar, are a sort of peevish prophets, and it's not enough that they should be in the right; others must also be in the wrong. They are by definition obsessed, and, by connotation, obsessed with something odd. They mistake the part for the whole, the props for the play, the inconvenience for the efficacy; they are spoil-sport humanitarians, full of the sour milk of human kindness.

— LOUIS KRONENBERGER[18]

[18] From *Company Manners* by Louis Kronenberger, copyright 1954. Used by special permission of the publishers, The Bobbs-Merrill Company, Inc.

**11.** What ruled writer and reader alike was the new-found pleasure of talk. The popularity of the coffee-house sprang not from its coffee, but from the new pleasure which men found in their chat over the coffee-cup. And from the coffee-house sprang the Essay. The talk of Addison and Steele is the brightest and easiest talk that was ever put into print; but its literary charm lies in this, that it is strictly talk. The essayist is a gentleman who chats to a world of gentlemen, and whose chat is shaped and colored by a sense of what he owes to his company. He must interest and entertain, he may not bore them; and so his form must be short: essay or sketch, or tale or letter. There was no room for pedantry, for the ostentatious display of learning, for pompousness, for affectation. The essayist had to think, as a talker should think, more of good taste than of imaginative excellence, of propriety of expression than of grandeur of phrase. The deeper themes of the world or man were denied to him; if he touches them it is superficially, with a decorous dulness, or on their more humorous side with a gentle irony that shows how faint their hold is on him.

—J. R. Green

# Analysis of the Sentence

# 7 ELEMENTS OF A SENTENCE

For many years scholars have been trying to make a systematic analysis of the English language which would account logically for every word used in every sentence. It is not an easy task, for English is a highly idiomatic language, often illogical, full of exceptions, and not readily reducible to general grammatical principles. Fortunately, only the specialist needs a complete analysis of the complex details of English grammar. The ordinary person who wishes to use English accurately and with regard to the conventions of his time needs only an understanding of basic grammatical principles. Especially, he needs to know what a sentence is and how its main parts function. This section contains a simplified account of English grammar, omitting minor complications, ignoring exceptions, using a simplified terminology, and stressing an understanding of basic sentence structure.

A useful tool for grammatical analysis is the classification of words into parts of speech: nouns, pronouns, verbs, articles, adjectives, adverbs, prepositions, and conjunctions. (These terms are defined and illustrated in the Glossary of Grammatical Terms, pp. 120–136.) But it is important to notice that a satisfactory classification can be made only of words as they are used in sentences. The word *stone* may be a noun (the name of a certain kind of hard object), or an adjective ("a stone wall"), or a verb, if it is used to mean the act of throwing stones. To tell what part of speech a word is, you must see how it is used in a sentence.

## 7a Subject and Predicate

The essential elements of a declarative sentence are a subject and a predicate. A sentence is a group of words that makes a statement, and to make a statement it is necessary to *say something* about *something*. The word which names what you are talking about is the subject. The assertion you make about it is the predicate.

| Subject | Predicate |
|---|---|
| Washington | crossed the Delaware. |
| I | do not like liver. |
| The temperature | dropped to 30 degrees last night. |

The subject is usually a noun or pronoun, though it may be a phrase or a clause, as will be explained later. The predicate may contain a number of words used in different ways, but the essential part is a verb, a word that asserts something.

Diagraming is a convenient visual device for showing the relation of sentence parts. Subject and verb, the backbone of a sentence, are placed on a horizontal line and separated by a short vertical line:

| Johnson | has been elected |
|---|---|
| **Subject** | **Verb** |

## 7b Modifiers

It is possible to make a complete sentence of two words, a subject and a verb:

Rain fell.

Few sentences, however, are as simple as this. We usually add other words whose function is to describe the subject or the verb.

Cold rain fell steadily.

Here, *cold* describes *rain*, and *steadily* describes the verb *fell*. Such words are called **modifiers,** and they may be attached to almost any part of a sentence. Although modifiers usually describe, they may also indicate how many (*three* books, *few* books), which one (*this* pencil, *the* pencil, *my* pencil), or how much (*very* slowly, *half* sick, *almost too* late).

Modifiers are divided into two main classes: adjectives and adverbs. Any word which modifies a noun or pronoun is an adjective in function; an adverb is any word which modifies a verb, an adjective, or another adverb.

> My very best friend lives quite near.

In this sentence, *my* and *best* are adjectives, since they modify *friend*. *Near* is an adverb modifying the verb *lives*, *quite* is an adverb modifying the adverb *near* (it tells how near), and *very* is an adverb modifying the adjective *best*.

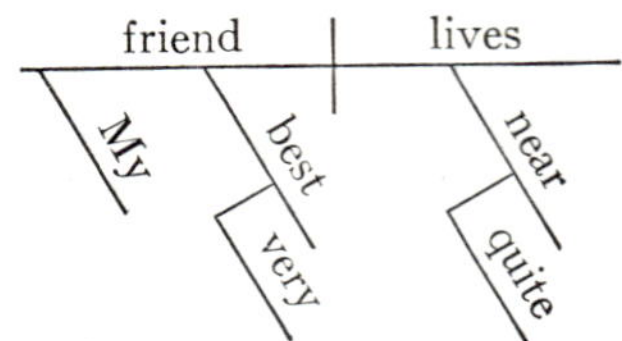


## 7c Identifying Subject and Verb

The analysis of any sentence begins with the identification of the simple subject and the verb. Look first for the verb: a word or group of words that states an action or happening:

> I *cut* my finger.
> Mozart *wrote* three string quintets.
> A tire *blew* out.
> I *had* never *seen* him before. [The two parts of the verb are separated by *never*.]

Some verbs merely assert that something is or was or seems to be:

> I *am* a baseball fan.
> There *were* two reasons for believing his story.
> This book *looks* interesting.
> The class *seems* bored.

When you have found the verb, ask yourself the question, "Who or what ——?" putting the verb in the blank space. The answer to the question is the subject, and if you strip away the modifiers you have the **simple subject.**

> A long, dull speech followed the dinner.

What followed? *A long, dull speech.* But *long* and *dull* are adjectives describing *speech,* and the simple subject is *speech.*

Use of this method is especially helpful when the normal order of the sentence is inverted (that is, when the subject comes *after* the verb) or when the sentence begins with an introductory word like "there."

> Across the Alps lies Italy.

The verb in this sentence is *lies.* What lies across the Alps? The answer is the subject, *Italy.*

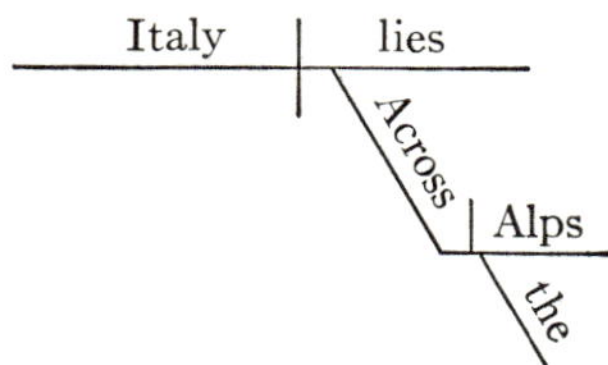


In the sentence "There is a serious error in the first paragraph," the verb is *is,* and the predicate asserts that something "is in the first paragraph." What? Certainly not the word *there.* *There* does not name anything and hence cannot be the subject, it is an idiomatic introductory word.

The answer to the question is "a serious error," and *error* is the simple subject.

Note that in a sentence which asks a question the subject often comes after the verb or after an auxiliary verb.

| Have | you | a match? |
|---|---|---|
| **Verb** | **Subject** | |

| Have | you | returned the books? |
|---|---|---|
| **Auxiliary** | **Subject** | **Verb** |

| What kind of lock | did | you | buy? |
|---|---|---|---|
| | **Auxiliary** | **Subject** | **Verb** |

In an imperative sentence the subject is not expressed. Since a command or request is addressed directly to someone, he need not be named.

| (   ) | Come in. |
|---|---|
| **Subject** | **Verb** |

| Please | (   ) | take | this to the Dean. |
|---|---|---|---|
| | **Subject** | **Verb** | |

| (   ) | Try | it and | (   ) | see. |
|---|---|---|---|---|
| **Subject** | **Verb** | | **Subject** | **Verb** |

A sentence may have several nouns as its subject, since it is possible to make one assertion about several things. Such a construction is called a **compound subject.**

Johnson and Weatherly have been elected.

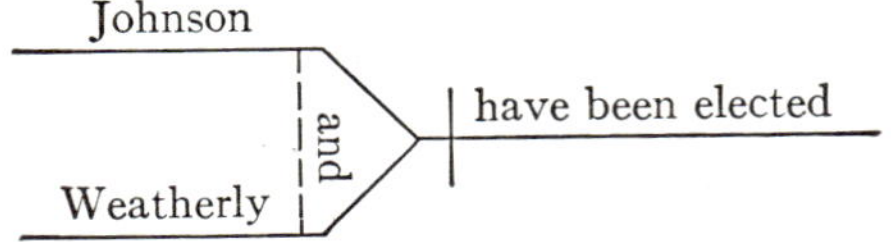


Similarly, it is possible to use a **compound predicate** — that is, to make several assertions about one subject.

The car swerved, skidded, and ran into the ditch.

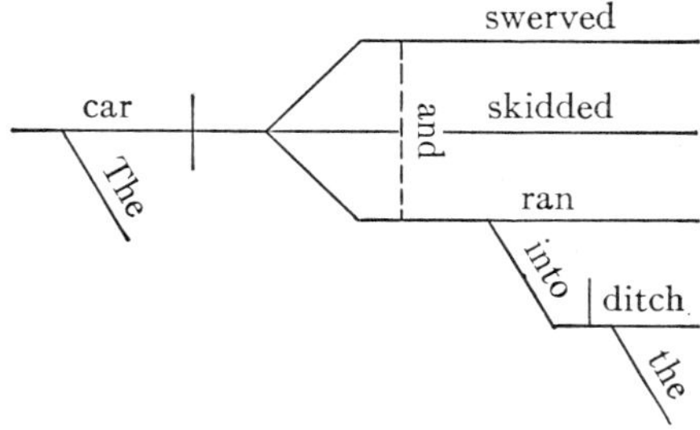


EXERCISE

Pick out the subjects and verbs in the following sentences. Note that either the subject or the verb may be compound.

1. After locking the door, the stewardess sat down at the rear of the plane.
2. Invisible to us, the pilot and copilot were already in their places.
3. Signs warning passengers not to smoke and to fasten their seat belts flashed on.
4. Directly beneath the signs was a door leading to the pilot's compartment.
5. Altogether there were about forty passengers on the plane.
6. In a few minutes the motors turned over, slowly at first, and then roared into life.
7. After taxiing out to the airstrip, the pilot raced each motor to test its performance.
8. Then with a sudden rush of speed the plane roared down the runway and gradually began to climb.
9. Below us, at the edge of the airport, were markers and signal lights.
10. At the edge of town could be seen the furniture factory with cars parked around it.
11. The football field and the quarter-mile track enabled me to identify the high school.

## 7d Direct Object

Some verbs, called *intransitive*, require nothing to complete them; that is, in themselves they make a full assertion about the subject.

> After six months in captivity, the python *died.*
> In a heavy snow a flat roof *may collapse.*

Other verbs, however, are incomplete by themselves; if one says only "I found," the reader is left hanging in mid-air and is apt to ask "What did you find?" Words which answer such a question, and thus complete the assertion, are called **complements** of the verb.

| I | found | a dime. |
|---|---|---|
| **Subject** | **Verb** | **Complement** |

The commonest type of complement is the direct object of a transitive verb, illustrated in the sentence above. The direct object is usually a noun or pronoun, though it may be a phrase or clause, and it usually names the thing acted upon by the subject.

> My cousin built a pigeon trap.

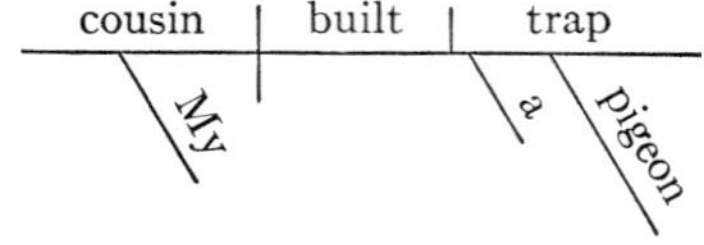


The easiest way to identify a direct object is to say the simple subject and verb and then ask the question "What?" My cousin built what? The answer, *trap*, is the direct object of the verb *built.* Note that the direct object may be compound.

> I bought a pen, a notebook, and an alarm clock.

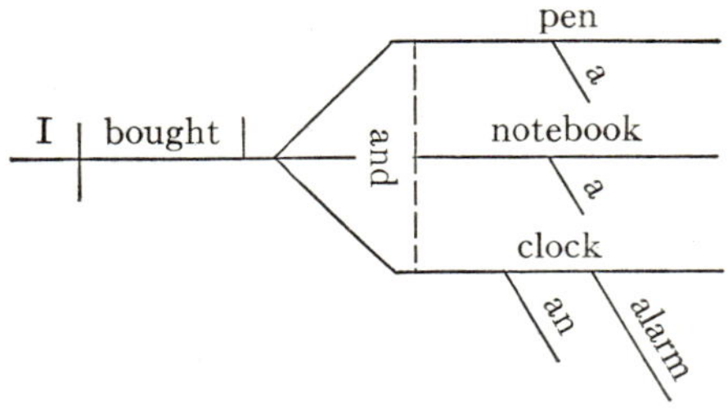


## 7e Indirect Object

In addition to a direct object, certain verbs may take an indirect object, a complement that receives whatever is named by the direct object.

The Constitution grants us certain rights.

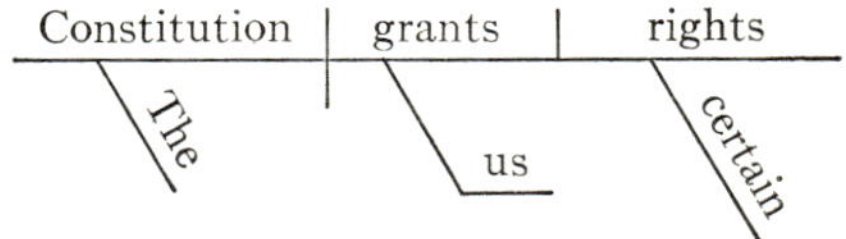


What does the Constitution grant? *Rights* is the direct object. Who receives them? *Us* is the indirect object. Note that the same meaning could be expressed by a phrase.

The Constitution grants certain rights *to us.*

An indirect object is usually the equivalent of a phrase beginning with *to* or *for.*

I told *him* a story = I told a story *to him.*
I wrote *him* a check = I wrote a check *for him.*

## 7f Subjective Complements

Linking verbs, sometimes called copulative verbs, are those which assert, with varying degrees of assurance, that something is or looks or sounds or seems or appears to be.

Linking verbs (all forms of *be*, plus such verbs as *become*, *seem*, *appear*, *look*, *sound*, *feel*, *taste*, etc.) require a **subjective complement,** a word which completes the predicate by giving another name for the subject or describing the subject.

Larson is the president.

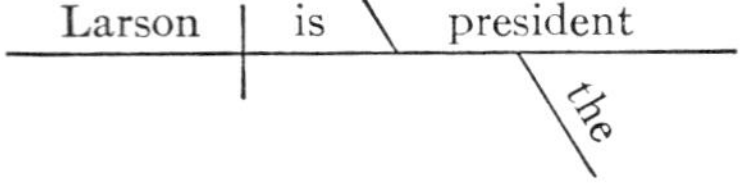


In this sentence, *president* cannot be called the direct object, since it is not acted upon by Larson. It is, rather, another name for Larson, and it can be made the subject of the sentence without changing the meaning.

The president is Larson.

(Contrast "Larson shot the president," in which the direct object, *president*, names another person, who is acted upon by Larson. Making *president* the subject of this sentence changes the meaning entirely.) A noun which serves as complement of a linking verb is usually called a **predicate noun.**

Linking verbs may also be completed by an adjective which describes the subject. Such a complement is called a **predicate adjective.**

His new novel seems imitative and dull.

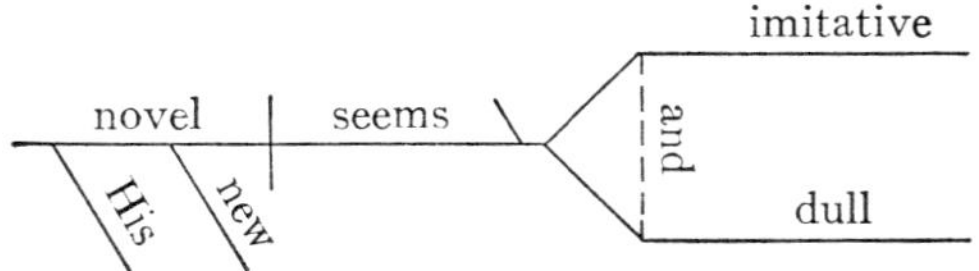


*Imitative* and *dull* describe *novel*, but instead of being directly attached to the noun ("a dull, imitative novel"), they are joined to it by the linking verb *seems* and become predicate adjectives.

### EXERCISE

Pick out the subjects and verbs in the following sentences. Identify direct objects, indirect objects, predicate nouns, and predicate adjectives.

1. As a wedding present, my uncle gave us a picture.
2. It was an original water color by Dufy.
3. The technique was interesting, since Dufy had used only little dabs of color.
4. It seemed an early work, according to a friend to whom I showed it.
5. We hung it in the living room, and it looked good.
6. I wrote my uncle a note and thanked him for the picture.
7. We enjoyed it for several months, until my friend told us its value.
8. Apparently it had been a very expensive present.
9. The idea of having so much money hanging on our wall worried us.
10. On the other hand, storage seemed foolish, since the picture had been painted for people to look at.
11. My uncle settled the matter for us.
12. He was disgusted with us for being so prudent, and he gave us a long lecture on the subject of enjoying works of art.
13. The picture is still hanging on the wall, and everybody is happy.

# 8 PHRASES

A group of words may have the same function in a sentence as a single part of speech. For example, in the sentence

> The train to Portland leaves in ten minutes.

the group of words *in ten minutes* modifies the verb *leaves* in exactly the same way as an adverb like *soon.* Similarly, *to Portland* functions like an adjective: it describes and identifies *train.* Such groups of words, which do not make a complete statement but which function like a single word, are called **phrases.** Phrases may be named for the kind of word around which they are constructed — prepositional, verbal (participial, gerund, infinitive), and noun, or appositive, phrases. But it is often useful to describe them by the way they function in a sentence — as adjective, adverbial, or noun phrases. *To Portland* in the sentence above is a prepositional phrase used as an adjective.

## 8a Prepositional Phrases

A preposition is usually defined as a word showing relationship which combines with a noun or pronoun (its object) to form a modifying phrase: "an agreement *between us,*" "a hotel *in Detroit,*" "slid *under the table,*" "try *with all my strength.*" Some common prepositions are *of, by, with, at, in, on, to, for, between, through, from.* Prepositional phrases usually modify nouns or verbs, and they are described accordingly as adjective or adverbial phrases.

The tree *in the yard* was imported *from Australia.*
**adjective** **adverbial**

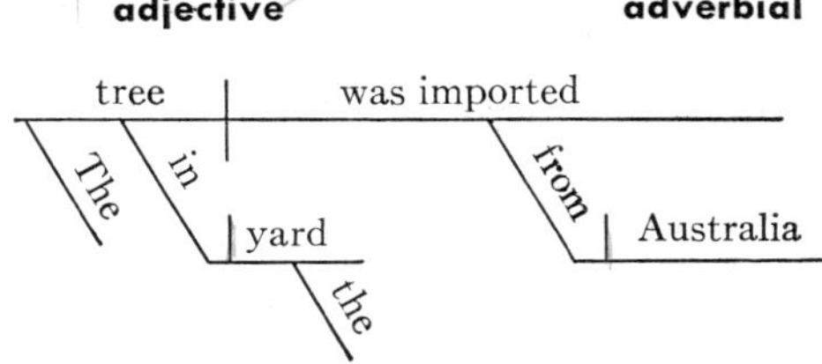


## 8b Verbals and Verbal Phrases

A very common type of phrase is built around a verbal, instead of a preposition. A verbal is a verb form used as some other part of speech. *Flying* is a form of the verb *to fly,* and while it may be used as a part of the verb in a sentence (*was flying, had been flying*), it may also be used as an adjective, to modify a noun: *flying spray.* Such a verbal is called a **participle.** Note that a participle may be in the past tense, as well as in the present — a *used* car, with *worn* upholstery.

When a verb form ending in *ing* is used as a noun, it is called a **gerund.**

*Flying* is his hobby.

In this sentence, *flying* is a gerund since it serves as the subject of the sentence. Gerunds may also be used as objects of verbs or of prepositions.

He loves *flying* and supports himself by *giving* lessons.

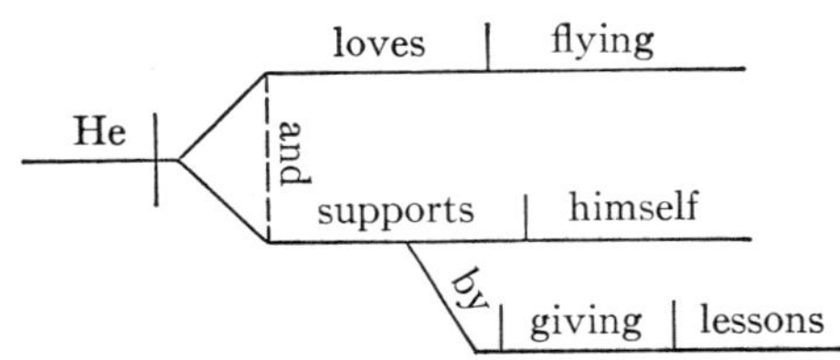

One other type of verbal is common: the **infinitive**. This is the ordinary form of the verb preceded by the particle *to*. Infinitives are frequently used as nouns — as subject or object of a verb.

> *To win* is his chief concern.
> He wants *to win*.

They are sometimes used as adjectives and as adverbs. See page 128.

Since they are verb forms, participles, gerunds, and infinitives may take objects and they may be modified by adverbs or by prepositional phrases. A verbal with its modifiers and its object, or subject, makes up a **verbal phrase** and functions as a single part of speech, but it does not make a complete statement.

**Infinitive phrase.** The sergeant ordered *me to scrub the floor thoroughly.* [The infinitive *to scrub* has a subject, *me*, an object, *floor*, and an adverbial modifier, *thoroughly*. The whole phrase is the object of the verb *ordered*. Note that the subject of an infinitive is in the objective case.]

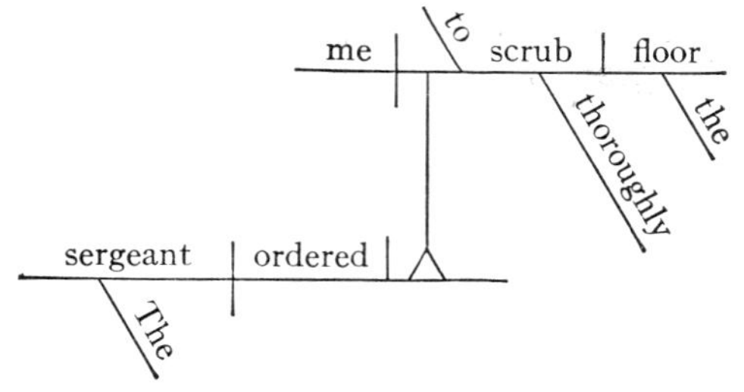


**Participial phrase.** *Flying some strange foreign flag*, a ship was entering the harbor. [Here the participle *flying*, with its object and the modifiers of the object, describes *ship*.]

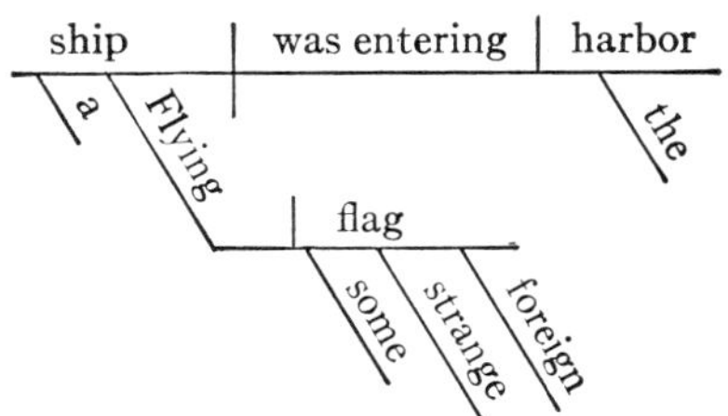


**Gerund phrase.** *Whitewashing a long board fence* is hard work. [Here the phrase — gerund, object, and the modifiers of the object — is the subject of the sentence.]

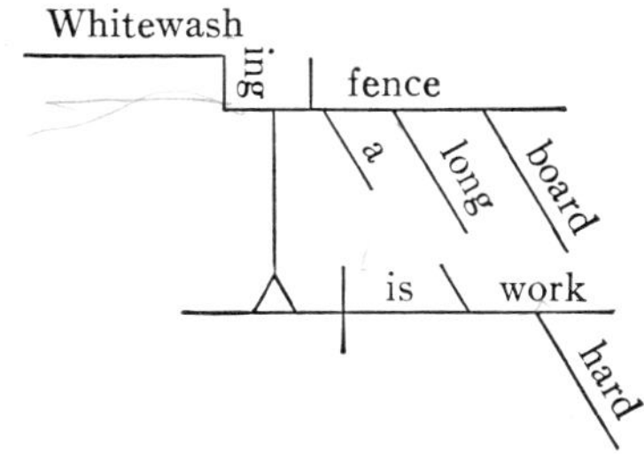


## 8c Appositive Phrases

An **appositive** is another name for something already indicated — a noun added to explain another noun.

Mr. Montgomery, the *cashier,* served as escrow officer.

Appositives with their modifiers may be regarded as phrases, since they function as a unit to give further information about a noun.

**Appositive phrase.** Dinner was served in the patio, *a small open space between the tool shed and the fence.*

For the punctuation of appositives, see Section **32d.**

### EXERCISE

Pick out the phrases in the following sentences. Identify them as prepositional, participial, gerund, infinitive, or appositive, and be ready to describe their function in the sentence.

1. On Tuesday I came home expecting to drive my car, a shiny new Plymouth, into the garage.
2. To my surprise, I found a ditch between the street and the driveway.
3. A crew of men had begun to lay a new water main along the curb.
4. Hoping that I would not get a ticket for overnight parking, I left the car in the street in front of the house.
5. For three days a yawning trench separated me from my garage.
6. Finding a place to park was difficult, since all the neighbors on my side of the street were in the same predicament.
7. By Friday the workmen had filled up the ditch, but my car, stained with dust and dew, looked ten years older.
8. I had to spend the weekend washing and polishing it.
9. My wife, a loyal but impractical ally, suggested sending the city a bill for the job.
10. Unconvinced by my explanations, she sent a bill to the City Manager, and she was much annoyed at not even getting an answer to her letter.
11. When the car next needed to be washed, she wanted me to have it done at a service station, charging it to the City Manager.
12. My refusal convinced her that men are illogical, improvident, and easily imposed upon.

# 9 CLAUSES

Any group of words which makes a statement — that is, which contains a subject and a predicate — is called a **clause.** It follows that every sentence must contain at least one main clause.

## 9a Independent and Dependent Clauses

Not all clauses are sentences; some of them, instead of making an independent statement, serve only as functional parts of the main clause in a sentence. Such clauses are called **dependent clauses,** and they function like single words: adjectives, adverbs, or nouns. **Independent clauses,** on the other hand, are capable of standing alone as complete sentences. They provide the framework to which modifiers, phrases, and dependent clauses are attached in each sentence; and any piece of connected discourse is made up of a series of independent clauses.

"While I was waiting for the bus" is a clause, since it contains a subject, *I*, and a verb, *was waiting*. But it is a dependent clause; in meaning it is incomplete (What happened?) and it would normally be used as a modifier. Its purpose is to tell *when* something happened, and the complete sentence should state *what* happened.

| While I was waiting for the bus, | I found a dollar bill. |
|---|---|
| **Dependent Clause** | **Independent Clause** |

A dependent clause is usually connected to the rest of the sentence by a subordinating conjunction, like *although*, *as*, *because*, *if*, *since*, *when*, *where*, *that*, or by a relative pronoun (*who*, *which*, or *that*). Notice how the addition of a subordinating conjunction to an independent clause makes the clause dependent.

> We went home. It was beginning to rain.

Here are two independent clauses, each a complete sentence. Adding the subordinating conjunction *because* to the second clause makes it dependent; written as a separate sentence, it would now be a fragment. If correctly joined to the preceding clause, however, it modifies the verb *went*, giving the reason for our going.

> We went home because it was beginning to rain.

## 9b Adverbial Clauses

An **adverbial clause** is a dependent clause used to modify a verb or adjective or adverb in the main clause.

> The books were lying *where I had left them.*

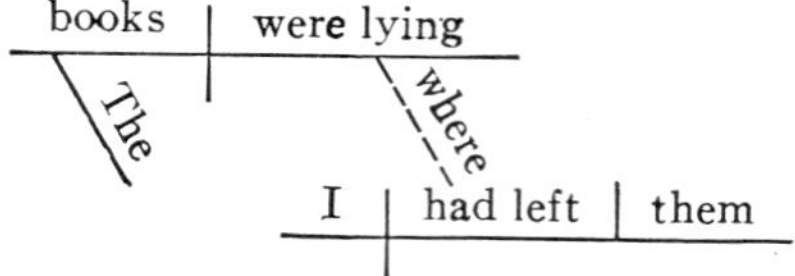


## 9c Noun Clauses

A **noun clause** functions as a subject or a complement in the main clause.

> *That he had made a mistake* was clear. [Noun clause as subject of the sentence.]

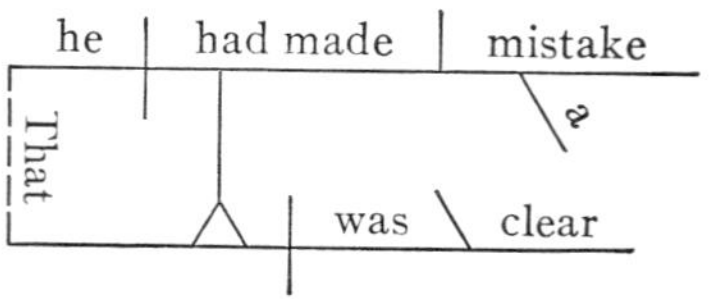

He said *that he had made a mistake.* [Noun clause as direct object of the verb.]

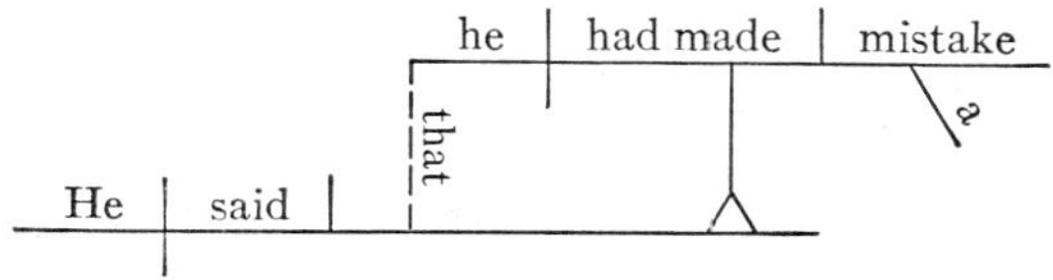


## 9d Adjective Clauses and Relative Pronouns

An **adjective clause** modifies a noun or pronoun.

The man *who rented the room* has a radio *which he turns on early in the morning.*

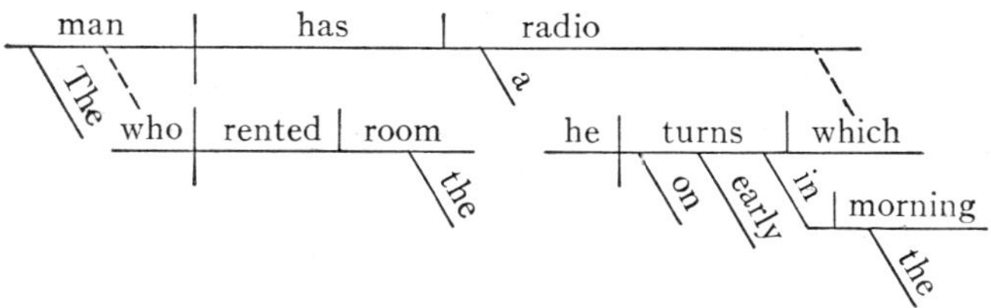


Adjective clauses are usually introduced by a **relative pronoun,** which serves both as a pronoun and as a subordinating conjunction. Its function can best be seen by some examples.

John was a leader; John never failed us.

This sentence consists of two independent clauses, but it would be more idiomatic to substitute a pronoun for the second *John.*

John was a leader; he never failed us.

If, instead of using the personal pronoun *he,* we substitute the relative pronoun *who,* the second clause becomes dependent. "Who never failed us" no longer will stand as an independent sentence; but when it is joined to the first clause, it functions as an adjective, modifying *leader*.

John was a leader who never failed us.

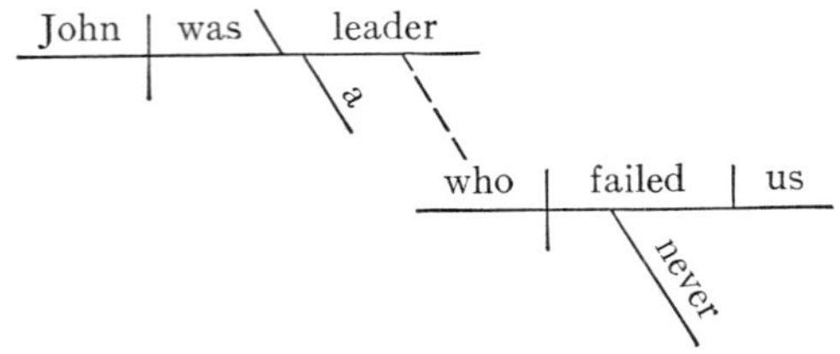


The relative pronouns *who* (and *whom*), *which*, and *that* always have two functions: they serve as subordinating conjunctions, connecting dependent to independent clauses, but they also function like nouns, as subject or complement.

The correct use of *who* and *whom* depends upon your ability to analyze the function of the relative pronoun in a dependent clause. See Section **28b.** For punctuation of dependent clauses, see Section **32d.**

## EXERCISE

Find the simple subject and verb of each clause in the following sentences. Point out the main clauses and the dependent clauses. Be prepared to state the function in the sentence of each dependent clause.

1. The idea that air travel would be pleasanter if each plane carried a woman attendant was first suggested in 1929.
2. Although airline officials were sceptical at first, they agreed to try the plan for three months.
3. Eight nurses who believed in the idea made up the pioneer group of airline stewardesses.
4. As air travel became more popular, other companies adopted the idea, and today the stewardess is an indispensable part of an airline crew.

5. The stewardess who welcomes you when you board a plane has been carefully selected from thousands of applicants for the position.
6. Unless she can meet rigid requirements of size, age, education, and personality, she will not be chosen for training.
7. After being selected, she is sent to a special school where she studies subjects ranging from aeronautics and geography to child care.
8. Some people believe that the chief function of the stewardess is to reassure timid passengers and smile at tired businessmen.
9. Actually, she is the busiest person on the plane, checking tickets, answering questions, inspecting seatbelts, and serving the meals which are now a regular feature of first-class flights.
10. A stewardess works hard when she works, but she has long periods of time off between flights, and she is well paid for filling a responsible position.
11. During her vacations, she receives free air transportation to any place she chooses.
12. Since she has constant opportunity to meet important and eligible men in leisurely and informal circumstances, her chances of remaining single until the time of compulsory retirement are relatively slim.

# 10 SENTENCE FRAGMENTS

It is a basic rule that every sentence must contain at least one independent clause. In writing, it is necessary to mark the end of each sentence by a period. A careless writer, by putting in the period too soon, may cut off a piece of the full sentence. If the piece does not contain an independent clause, the result is a **sentence fragment.** For example:

> The main purpose of the Olympic Games is to create international understanding and friendship. *Thus helping to preserve peace and save millions of people from the destruction of war.*

This was meant to be one complete sentence. If spoken, it would seem to be complete, since there are no periods in speech. As it is written, however, the last part is a fragment, a participial phrase without subject or verb. This phrase should be attached to the previous sentence:

> The main purpose of the Olympic Games is to create international understanding and friendship, thus helping to preserve peace and save millions of people from the destruction of war.

## 10a Common Types of Sentence Fragments

**Fragment (Appositive Phrase).** A major social problem is the number of undesirable people coming into the state. *Professional gamblers and crooks, men who would do anything to make money.*

**Corrected.** A major social problem is the number of undesirable people coming into the state — professional gamblers and crooks, men who would do anything to make money.

**Fragment (Prepositional Phrase).** I had expected to find the laboratory neat and orderly, but actually it was very sloppy. *With instruments strewed all over the workbench and pieces of electronic equipment lying around the floor.*

**Corrected.** . . . Instruments were strewed all over the workbench, and pieces of electronic equipment were lying around the floor. [The fragment might have been simply added to the preceding sentence, but making it into a separate sentence avoids a long trailing construction.]

**Fragment (Dependent Clause).** One lifeguard was trying to hold back the crowd that had gathered to watch the rescue. *While another guard was busy giving the victim artificial respiration.*

**Corrected.** One lifeguard was trying to hold back the crowd that had gathered to watch the rescue, while another guard was busy giving the victim artificial respiration. [Note that the fragment could also have been corrected by omitting the subordinating conjunction *while* and making two complete sentences.]

**Fragment (Participial Phrase).** I was much surprised at the informality of the court. Lawyers, witnesses, and reporters were rushing around all over the place. *Running up to the railing and conferring with the bailiff, the prisoner, and even the judge himself.*

**Corrected.** I was much surprised at the informality of the court. Lawyers, witnesses, and reporters were rushing around all over the place, running up to the railing and conferring with the bailiff, the prisoner, and even the judge himself.

**Fragment (Infinitive Phrase).** The whole expedition was welded into a single highly efficient tool for accomplishing its purpose. *To place at least two men on the highest peak of the mountain and to get them safely down again.*

**Corrected.** The whole expedition was welded into a single highly efficient tool for accomplishing its purpose: to place at least two men on the highest peak of the mountain and to get them safely down again.

Most often the way to correct a sentence fragment is to join it to the sentence of which it is logically a part. Sometimes, however, it is better to change the fragment into a full sentence, by adding a verb or a subject or whatever else is lacking.

**Fragment.** "Fools rush in where angels fear to tread." *A maxim that is often heard but seldom heeded.*

**Corrected.** "Fools rush in where angels fear to tread." This is a maxim that is often heard but seldom heeded.

## 10b Permissible Incomplete Sentences

Certain elliptical expressions are equivalent to sentences because the missing words are clearly understood. Such permissible incomplete sentences are the following:

1. Questions and answers to questions, especially in conversation:

Why not?
Because it is too late.

2. Exclamations and requests:

At last!
This way, please.

3. Transitions:

So much for the first point.
Now to consider the next question.

In addition, fragments are sometimes deliberately used for particular effects, especially in narrative or descriptive writing. In expository writing, however, there is seldom occasion or excuse for writing fragmentary sentences.

**Acceptable.** He watched the needle swing rhythmically from one side of the dial to the other. Back and forth. Over and over.

**Acceptable.** Then to Henderson: "Yes. Let's go back to the station. Sorry to be so much trouble." As they walked he estimated his chances. Not much time left. Have to try it as soon as we get inside.

### EXERCISE

Correct the following fragmentary sentences, in whatever way seems most effective.

1. In 500 B.C. there flourished in the Mediterranean area two civilizations with entirely different types of religion. The Greek civilization, which centered around the Aegean Sea, and the Hebrew civilization along the River Jordan.
2. Many people still believe the ancient superstition that women are the weaker sex. Although it has been proved that women are better able to withstand shock and exposure than men.
3. Not a broken family; just a large, scattered, and disorganized group.
4. Some people just aren't suited for boarding-school life. In which case it is much better for them to go to the public schools.
5. Because there are some animals that will not survive in desert areas, and some seeds that will not grow in desert climates.
6. From the tall, massive buildings of New York, the high, empty deserts of Wyoming, the crowded beaches of

California, to the snow-capped peaks of the Rocky Mountains. I have seen many parts of America thanks to moving pictures.

7. In the East there are many colleges for men only. The reason being that they were founded primarily to train the clergy.
8. Television, a new toy for adults, which is cherished by all tired and unthinking Americans.
9. Another reason for Gallup's erroneous prediction: correct method, incorrect application of it.
10. It now seems to me that my high school was in some ways too conservative and in some ways too progressive. Mostly too progressive, meaning that they didn't teach us to read and write carefully.
11. To Lowell, the canals on Mars appeared as fine, straight lines from 100 to over 1000 miles in length. Not really straight lines, of course, but parts of great circles.
12. Because abolishment of the two-platoon system in college football will mean the development of more versatile players on the teams.
13. I have decided that a good teacher is one with a strong personality. Stern enough to let his students know that what he is teaching them is very important.
14. We remember only the more civilized societies that have existed in the world. The ones that have produced great works of art, science, or technology.
15. The number of the very rich and the very poor having been reduced, leaving the bulk of the population in one large middle class.
16. A vessel under way in a fog should sound a long blast on its whistle at least once a minute. Except when towing other boats or being towed.
17. Long hours of practice after classes, the weekends usually taken up with games, and most evenings spent in study. Athletes have little time for working their way through college.

18. A description of a crash on the desert when the author and his co-pilot have only one orange between them for food.
19. Books are actually a means of communication. A means whereby one person can share his experience with thousands of men, in his own time and in the future.
20. The distance between stars is very great. So great that it is difficult to find a unit of measurement which will enable one to grasp it imaginatively.
21. Every month, the entire research staff spends a day together in informal conference. Mainly to discuss current problems and propose and criticize new ideas.
22. A study by a firm of engineers came up with two proposals for improving traffic conditions. Closing streets inside the campus to automobiles and the installation of traffic lights at two main corners.

# 11 RUN–TOGETHER SENTENCES

Fragments are usually produced by putting in a period too soon, thus cutting off a portion of a preceding sentence. Putting in a period too late — after you have written two complete sentences instead of one — produces a run-together sentence. The term "comma fault," or "comma splice," is used to designate this error. The comma fault is the use of a comma between two independent clauses not joined by a coordinating conjunction — *and, but, or, nor,* etc.

**Run-together sentence.** We will add another story to the house this summer, painting will have to wait until next year.

If there is no punctuation at all between the two independent clauses, a sentence is called a "fused sentence." A fused sentence is even worse than a comma fault, since it suggests that the writer has no sentence sense whatever.

**Fused sentence.** Gambling is like a drug after a while a gambler finds it impossible to stop.

## 11a Correcting Run-together or Fused Sentences

There are three possibilities. You must either (1) use a semicolon between the clauses; or (2) separate the two statements by a period; or (3) join the clauses by a conjunction. There are no hard and fast rules telling which method of correction to use. Judgment is required to decide exactly what the sentence is intended to say.

Correcting a run-together sentence by making two separate sentences gives additional emphasis to each part.

> Gambling is like a drug[. After] ~~after~~ a while a gambler finds it impossible to stop.

But too many short sentences produce a primer style, and it is often desirable to join the two statements into a single statement.

> Gambling is like a drug[;] after a while a gambler finds it impossible to stop.
>
> First I would replace the foundation[;] then I would add another story.

To indicate more specifically the relationship between the two statements a conjunction may be used.

> We will add another story this summer, [but] painting will have to wait until next year.

Finally, it may be desirable to subordinate one statement to the other.

> [Although we] ~~We~~ will add another story this summer, painting will have to wait until next year.

## 11b Punctuation with Conjunctive Adverbs

Many run-together sentences are the result of mistaking a conjunctive adverb for a conjunction. *So*, *therefore*, *hence*, *however*, *nevertheless*, *in fact*, *moreover*, *then*, *also*, *still* are adverbs, not conjunctions. They introduce clauses and indicate relationships, but they do not connect grammatically. A period or a semicolon or a coordinating conjunction must be used along with a conjunctive adverb.

> All powers not given to the Federal Government remain with the states~~,~~[. Therefore] ~~therefore~~ the issue of states' rights is frequently debated in the Supreme Court.

> All powers not given to the Federal Government remain
> ; *and*
> with the states, therefore the issue of states' rights is frequently debated in the Supreme Court.

One way to tell a conjunctive adverb from a pure conjunction is to try to change its position in the sentence. A conjunctive adverb need not stand first in its clause:

> We had been told to stay at home; *moreover*, we knew that we were not allowed to play outside after dark.
>
> We had been told to stay at home; we knew, *moreover*, that we were not . . .

A pure conjunction will fit into the sentence only at the beginning of its clause:

> We had been told to stay at home, *and* we knew . . .

## EXERCISE

Some of the following sentences are run together. Correct them by the method most suitable in each case.

1. There are three movie theaters in town, however, many people prefer the Drive-in on Highway 66.
2. If the discoverer had not been an anthropologist, the bone would probably still be lying in the field, because of its size and shape most people would not have noticed it.
3. Although we saw many interesting decorations cut by the natives out of sheets of tin, we decided to wait until we were farther from the city before buying any.
4. With the new construction, people and money poured into Dawson, until it had changed from a sleepy ghost town to an international crossroads.
5. Then he began to act strangely, he missed most of his meals at the hall and ate crackers and milk in his room.

6. The jet is faster than the propeller airplane of World War II, moreover it can fly at higher altitudes.
7. After two weeks I moved from my hotel to a room with a private family, my idea being to get better acquainted with French life and the French people.
8. But the scientist cannot cut himself off from social responsibilities, the effects of his work are too important.
9. Teaching is definitely not a dying occupation, on the contrary there is a greater demand for teachers today than ever before, and salaries have never been higher.
10. The World Health Organization is trying to popularize a broader principle, the idea that health is not merely an individual problem but a problem of society as a whole.
11. Next the potter rolls the clay between his hands, this gets the air bubbles out of it.
12. It is not enough for a public speaker to be skilled in oratory, to be successful he must have a receptive audience.
13. The new body armor is made of a lighter metal, it has much greater strength, and it is easier to keep clean.
14. The proportion of casualties in the Navy is low, thus the chance of becoming a dead hero instead of a live sailor is relatively small.
15. A prescription seldom costs less than two dollars, however little the ingredients may have cost the druggist.
16. Behind the aquarium was an open-air pool in which a real live whale was swimming, a small one about eleven feet long, which swam around the pool counterclockwise.
17. Helsinki is a young city in comparison with Danzig and other Baltic ports, it was founded in 1550 and reestablished in its present location in the seventeenth century.
18. From the top of Whiteface, one can see miles of rolling mountain country, its valleys studded with lakes and streams.
19. Floating along the surface with his mask under water, he could see urchins and anemones on the bottom, even though the water was twenty feet deep it was very clear.

# 12 TYPES OF SENTENCES

Sentences are traditionally classified, according to their structure, as simple, complex, compound, and compound-complex.

## 12a Simple Sentences

A **simple sentence** consists of one independent clause, with no dependent clauses attached, though it may have modifying phrases:

> Slumped in the bottom of a skiff, I floated peacefully down the river.

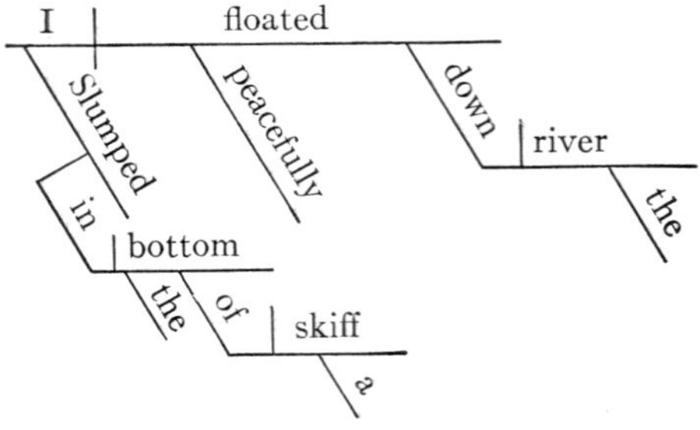


Simple sentences are not necessarily short and jerky, but a habit of overusing them is apt to make one's writing sound both choppy and childish. So-called "primer" style is caused by a succession of short simple sentences. The remedy is to use more complex sentences. See Section **15a.**

## 12b Complex Sentences

The **complex sentence** contains one independent clause and one or more dependent clauses, which express subordinate ideas.

Since the owner of the house refused all proposals which specified immediate possession, we withdrew our offer.

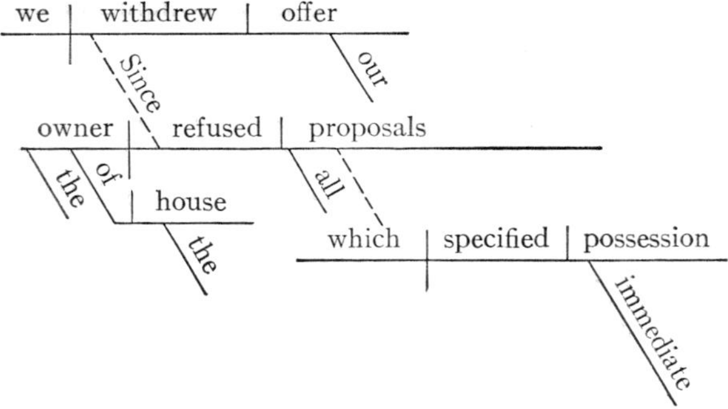


The complex sentence has the advantage of flexibility; it can be variously arranged to produce variety of pattern. It also provides selective emphasis, since the subordination of dependent clauses throws the weight of the sentence on the main clause.

## 12c Compound Sentences

The **compound sentence** consists of two or more independent clauses.

She opened the door, and the dogs rushed into the room.

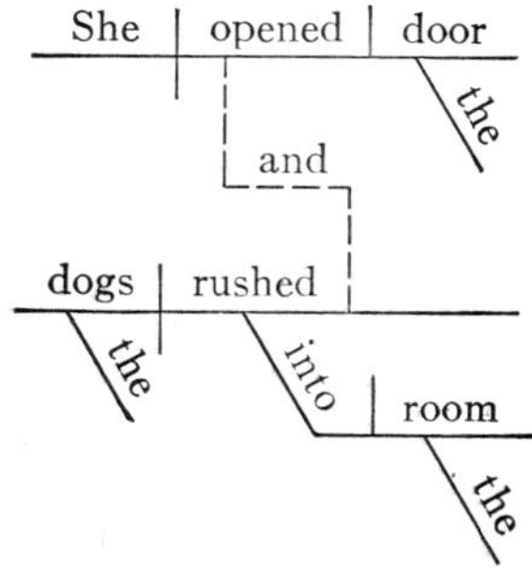

## 12d Compound-Complex Sentences

When a compound sentence contains dependent clauses, the whole is sometimes described as a **compound-complex sentence.**

> Although the critics gave it good reviews, the play never attracted the public, and after two weeks the owners, who had been losing money steadily, reluctantly closed it.

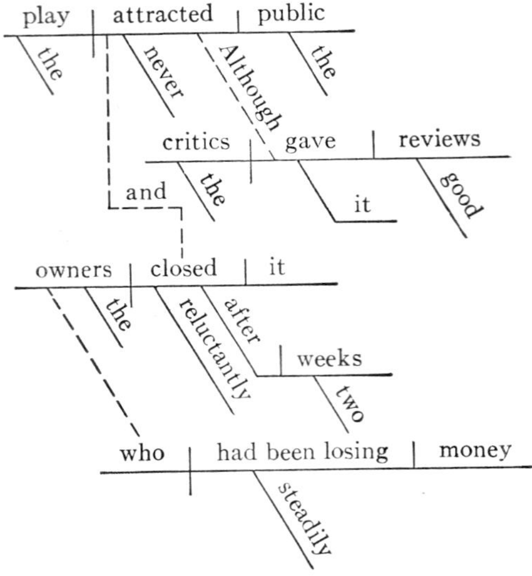


### EXERCISE

Classify the following sentences as simple, compound, complex, or compound-complex. Identify the subject, verb, and complement, if any, of each clause. Describe the function of each dependent clause. Describe phrases both by kind (prepositional, participial, etc.) and by function (adverbial, adjective, etc.)

1. When Renaissance physicians began to study human anatomy by means of actual dissection, they concluded that the human body had changed since the days of antiquity.
2. Galen, an ancient Greek physician, was generally accepted as the authority on anatomy and physiology.
3. His theory of the four humors, blood, phlegm, bile, and black bile, was neat and logical, and authorities had accepted it for centuries.
4. Similarly, his account of the structure of the human body, revised by generations of scholars and now appearing in many printed editions, was generally accepted.
5. If dissection showed a difference from Galen's account, the obvious explanation was that man's structure had changed since Galen's time.
6. One man who refused to accept this explanation was Andreas Vesalius, a young Belgian physician studying in Italy.
7. Asked to edit the anatomical section of Galen's works, Vesalius found many errors in it.
8. Galen said that the lower jaw consisted of two parts, but Vesalius had never found such a structure in his own dissections.
9. Vesalius finally concluded that Galen was describing the anatomy of lower animals — pigs, monkeys, and goats — and that he had never dissected a human body.
10. His realization that Galen could be wrong was a stimulus to Vesalius' own major work, a fully illustrated treatise on the human body based on actual observation.

# 13 GLOSSARY OF GRAMMATICAL TERMS

**Absolute phrase.** See page 251.

**Active voice.** See Voice.

**Adjective.** A part of speech used to describe or limit the meaning of a substantive. There are the following kinds:

**Descriptive:** a *true* friend, a *poor* man.

**Limiting:** *a* boy, *an* apple, *the* man.

**Pronominal:**

*a.* **Possessive:** *my, his, her, its, our, your, their.*

*b.* **Demonstrative:** *this, that, these, those. This* hat, etc.

*c.* **Interrogative:** *whose, which, what. Whose* hat? etc.

*d.* **Relative:** *whose, which.*
The man *whose* house was robbed has just returned.

*e.* **Indefinite:** *any, each, no, some,* etc.
*Each* boy had his own room.

**Numeral:**

*a.* **Cardinal:** *one, two, three,* etc.
*Ten* students were admitted.

*b.* **Ordinal:** *first, second, third,* etc.
He won the *first* game.

**Adverb.** A part of speech used to modify a verb, an adjective, or another adverb. An adverb answers the questions: *Where? When? How? In what manner?* or *To what extent?*

He bowed *politely.* [*Politely* modifies the verb *bowed.*]

A *very* old woman came in. [*Very* modifies the adjective *old.*]

He was *too* much absorbed to listen. [*Too* modifies the adverb *much.*]

Substantives may be used adverbially:

He walked *two miles.* [Modifies the verb *walked.*]
It is worth *ten cents.* [Modifies the adjective *worth.*]
He walked *two miles* farther. [Modifies the adverb *farther.*]

**Antecedent.** A word, phrase, or clause to which a pronoun refers.

I could see the *house* long before I reached it. [*House* is the antecedent of *it.*]

*John* could see the *house* long before he reached it. [*John* is the antecedent of *he; house* is the antecedent of *it.*]

This is a *problem* which cannot be solved without calculus. [*Problem* is the antecedent of *which.*]

*My uncle is paying my tuition,* which is more than I had expected of him. [The clause is the antecedent of *which.*]

**Appositive.** A substantive attached to another substantive and denoting the same person or thing. A substantive is said to be **in apposition** with the substantive to which it is attached.

George, my hostess's *cousin,* was enjoying his favorite sport — *yachting.* [*Cousin* is in apposition with *George; yachting* is in apposition with *sport.*]

**Article.** The word *the* is called the **definite article;** the word *a* or *an* is called the **indefinite article.** Articles are adjectives.

**Auxiliary.** The verbs *be, have, do, shall, will, may, can, must, ought,* with their inflectional forms, when they assist in forming the voices, modes, and tenses of other verbs, are auxiliaries.

I *was* given a message.
He *should have* known better.
He *has been* gone a week.

**Cardinal number.** See Adjective.

**Case.** A characteristic of substantives, indicating the relation existing between a substantive and the other words in the sentence. This relation may be shown by an inflectional form of the word or by its position. In English there are three cases, **nominative, possessive** (or **genitive**), **objective** (or **accusative**).

In nouns the nominative and objective cases are identical, but in personal pronouns they are indicated by different forms (*I*, *me; he*, *him; she*, *her;* etc.). The subject of a verb is in the nominative case. A substantive that shows ownership or origin or a similar relation is in the possessive case. The object of a verb or of a preposition is in the objective case.

My *home* is in Chicago. [*Home* is in the nominative case.]
*John's* hat is lost. [*John's* is in the possessive case.]
We lived within a *stone's* throw. [*Stone's* is in the possessive case.]
He ate the *pear*. [*Pear* is in the objective case, the object of the verb *ate*.]
She sat on the *bench*. [*Bench* is in the objective case, the object of the preposition *on*.]

**Clause.** A group of words containing a subject and a predicate. Clauses that make independent assertions are **independent** (or **principal**) **clauses.** Clauses that are not by themselves complete in meaning are **dependent** (or **subordinate**) **clauses.** Subordinate clauses are used as nouns, adjectives, or adverbs. They are usually introduced by subordinating words.

We heard him when he came in. [*We heard him* is the principal clause; *when he came in* is the subordinate clause.]
*That she will be late* is certain. [Subordinate clause used as a noun.]
The woman *who spoke to us* is our neighbor. [Subordinate clause used as an adjective.]
He will come *when he is ready*. [Subordinate clause used as an adverb.]

Clauses that play the same part in a sentence, whether they are principal or subordinate, are called **coordinate clauses.**

*The bell rang* and *everyone stood up*. [Coordinate principal clauses.]
He left *because he did not like the work* and *because the pay was low*. [Coordinate subordinate clauses.]

**Comparison.** Inflection of an adjective or adverb to indicate an increasing or decreasing degree of quality, quantity, or manner.

**Positive degree:**
Their house is *cold.*

**Comparative degree:**
Their house is *colder* than ours.

**Superlative degree:**
Their house is the *coldest* in town.

When adjectives have one or two syllables, the comparative degree is usually formed by adding *er* to the positive; and the superlative degree is usually formed by adding *est* to the positive. When adjectives have more than two syllables, the comparative degree is usually formed by placing *more* or *less* before the positive; and the superlative degree is usually formed by placing *most* or *least* before the positive. Some adjectives have irregular comparison; e.g., *good, better, best; bad, worse, worst.*

**Complement.** A word or phrase added to a verb to complete the sense of the statement. It may be the direct object of a transitive verb, an indirect object, or a predicate noun or adjective.

**Direct object:** A big wave swamped our *boat.*
**Indirect object:** I told *him* to leave.
**Predicate noun:** Our destination was *Corsica.*
The referee called Sanchez the *winner.*
**Predicate adjective:** The waves were *enormous.*
A limber branch made the tree-house *shaky.*

(*Corsica* and *enormous* are called subjective complements. *Shaky* and *winner* are sometimes called objective complements.)

**Complex sentence.** See page 116.

**Compound sentence.** See page 117.

**Conjugation.** The inflected forms of a verb which show person, number, tense, voice, and mode.

Simplified Conjugation of the Indicative Mode of the Verb *see*.
Principal Parts: see, saw, seen

| Active Voice | | Passive Voice | |
|---|---|---|---|
| SINGULAR | PLURAL | SINGULAR | PLURAL |
| **Present Tense** | | | |
| 1. I see | we see | I am seen | we are seen |
| 2. you see | you see | you are seen | you are seen |
| 3. he (she, it) sees | they see | he is seen | they are seen |
| **Past Tense** | | | |
| 1. I saw | we saw | I was seen | we were seen |
| 2. you saw | you saw | you were seen | you were seen |
| 3. he saw | they saw | he was seen | they were seen |
| **Future Tense** | | | |
| 1. I shall see | we shall see | I shall be seen | we shall be seen |
| 2. you will see | you will see | you will be seen | you will be seen |
| 3. he will see | they will see | he will be seen | they will be seen |
| **Perfect Tense** | | | |
| 1. I have seen | we have seen | I have been seen, etc. | |
| 2. you have seen | you have seen | | |
| 3. he has seen | they have seen | | |
| **Past Perfect Tense** | | | |
| 1. I had seen | we had seen | I had been seen, etc. | |
| 2. you had seen | you had seen | | |
| 3. he had seen | they had seen | | |
| **Future Perfect Tense** | | | |
| 1. I shall have seen, etc. | | I shall have been seen, etc. | |

**Conjunction.** A part of speech used to connect words, phrases, and clauses. There are the following kinds:

1. **Coordinating**
   - *a.* **Pure,** or **simple, conjunctions:** *and*, *or*, *nor*, *but*, *for*, *yet*.
   - *b.* **Correlatives:** *either . . . or*, *neither . . . nor*, *both . . . and*, *not only . . . but* [*also*].
2. **Subordinating**
   - *a.* Conjunctions introducing adjective clauses: *that*, *when*, *where*, *while*, *whence*, etc.
   - *b.* Conjunctions introducing adverbial clauses: *when*, *while*, *where*, *because*, *so that*, *although*, *since*, *as*, *after*, *if*, *until*, etc.

Coordinating conjunctions connect sentence elements that are logically and grammatically equal; i.e., they may connect two subjects or two verbs or two adjective clauses, etc. Subordinating conjunctions connect subordinate (or dependent) clauses with their principal (or independent) clauses. A conjunction may be distinguished from a preposition by the fact that a preposition must always be followed by a substantive, its object.

He fell *into* the cold water. [*Into* is a preposition followed by the noun *water*, its object.]

He remembered the engagement *when* reminded. [*When* is a conjunction followed by the predicate of an elliptical clause.]

**Conjunctive adverb.** An introductory adverb, or sentence modifier, which indicates the relationship between principal clauses: *However*, *moreover*, *therefore*, *nevertheless*, *hence*, *also*, *thus*, *consequently*, *then*, *furthermore*, etc. Between independent clauses it must be reinforced by a semicolon or by a coordinating conjunction.

**Coordinate.** Sentence elements that are equal in grammatical construction and in meaning are coordinate. In the sentence *He and she talked long and earnestly, and at last agreed*, *he* and *she* are coordinate; *talked* and *agreed* are coordinate; *long* and *earnestly* are coordinate; *talked long and earnestly* and *at last agreed* are coordinate.

**Copula,** or **Linking verb.** A verb, like *to be, to seem, to appear, to become,* which acts mainly as a connecting link between the subject and the predicate noun or predicate adjective.

**Correlative conjunctions.** Coordinating conjunctions used in pairs:

*both* my father *and* my mother
*neither* my father *nor* my mother
*not only* cheated us *but also* accused us of cheating.

**Declension.** See Inflection.

**Demonstrative.** See Adjective and Pronoun.

**Direct address.** A grammatical construction in which a speaker or writer addresses a second person directly. Direct address is expressed by the nominative case.

*Mary,* wait for me.
*Friends, Romans, countrymen,* lend me your ears.

**Direct object.** See Object.

**Elliptical expression.** An expression which is grammatically incomplete, but the meaning of which is clear because the omitted words are implied.

Elliptical: If possible, bring your drawings along.
Complete: If it is possible, bring your drawings along.

**Finite verb.** Any verb form that may be used as the predicate of a sentence. Infinitives, gerunds, and participles are not finite verbs.

**Genitive.** See Case.

**Gerund.** A verb form ending in *ing* and used as a noun. It should be distinguished from the present participle, which also ends in *ing* but is used as an adjective. (See Participle.) A gerund may fulfill the principal functions of a noun:

Subject of a verb: Fishing is tiresome.
Object of a verb: I hate fishing.
Object of a preposition: I have an aversion to fishing.
Predicate substantive: The sport I like least is fishing.

Like a noun, the gerund may be modified by an adjective. In the sentence *We were tired of his long-winded preaching*, *his* and *long-winded* modify the gerund *preaching*.

Since a gerund is a verb form, it may take an object and be modified by an adverb.

He disapproved of our taking luggage with us. [*Luggage* is the object of the gerund *taking*.]
Our success depends upon his acting promptly. [*Promptly* is an adverb modifying the gerund *acting*.]

**Idioms.** Expressions characteristic of a particular language which, though they may depart from normal grammatical principles or from logical usage, are accepted as correct.

A friend *of my brother's*.
*The bigger the better*.
We *went swimming*. [An idiomatic verb: *to go swimming*. See also *to take over*, *to get out from under*. Colloquial are *to stick up for* and *stuck-up*.]

**Imperative.** See Mode.

**Indicative.** See Mode.

**Indirect object.** See Object.

**Infinitive.** That form of the verb usually preceded by *to*. *To* is called the **sign of the infinitive.** The sign *to* is often omitted, especially after the auxiliaries *do*, *can*, *shall*, *will*, *may*, *must*, etc., as in the sentence *I can go*.

The infinitive has two tenses, present and perfect, and if the verb is transitive, both active and passive voices.

The infinitive, since it is a verb form, can have a subject, can take an object or a predicate complement, and can be modified by an adverb.

We asked her to come. [*Her* is the subject of *to come.*]
They asked to meet him. [*Him* is the object of *to meet.*]
We hope to hear soon. [*Soon* is the adverbial modifier of *to hear.*]

The infinitive may be used as a noun:

*To meet her* is a pleasure. [Subject.]
His chief delight is *to tease her*. [Predicate complement.]
He wished *to see the dog*. [Object of verb.]

The infinitive may be used as an adjective:

He gave me a book *to read*. [Modifies the noun *book.*]
He is *to be congratulated*. [Predicate adjective.]

The infinitive may be used as an adverb:

We waited *to see you*. [Modifies the verb *waited.*]
We are able *to help*. [Modifies the adjective *able.*]
He is old enough *to travel alone*. [Modifies the adverb *enough.*]

**Inflection.** A change in the form of a word to show a change in meaning or use. Nouns and pronouns may be inflected to show case (*he*, *him*), person (*I*, *you*), number (*man*, *men*), and gender (*his*, *hers*). Verbs are inflected to indicate person (I *go*, he *goes*), number (he *is*, they *are*), tense (he *is*, he *was*), voice (I *received* your message, your message *was received*), and mode (if this *be* treason). Adjectives and adverbs are inflected to show relative degree (*strong*, *stronger*, *strongest*). The inflection of substantives is called **declension**; that of verbs, **conjugation**; that of adjectives and adverbs, **comparison.**

**Intensive pronoun.** The pronouns *myself*, *thyself*, *himself*, *herself*, *itself*, *ourselves*, *yourself*, *yourselves*, *themselves*, *oneself*, when they are used in apposition, are called intensives because they serve to intensify or emphasize the substantives that they are used with; e.g., *I myself will do it. I saw the bishop himself.* When one of these words is used as the object of a verb and designates the same person or thing as the subject of that verb, it is called a **reflexive pronoun;** e.g., *I hurt myself. They benefit themselves.*

**Interjection.** A part of speech that expresses emotion and that has no grammatical relation with the rest of the sentence; e.g., *oh, alas, ha, ah, hello, hurrah.*

**Interrogative pronoun.** See Pronoun.

**Intransitive.** See Verb.

**Irregular verb.** A verb which forms its past tenses by a change of the root vowel: *sing, sang, sung.* Also called a **strong verb.**

**Linking verb.** See Copula.

**Mode (Mood).** Inflection of a verb to indicate whether it is intended to make a statement or command, or to express a hypothetical possibility.

The **indicative mode** is used to state a fact or to ask a question.

The wind is blowing.
Is it raining?

The **imperative mode** is used to express a command or an urgent request.

Do it immediately.
Please answer the telephone.

The **subjunctive mode** is used to express a wish, a supposition, a doubt, an exhortation, a concession, a condition contrary to fact. The subjunctive mode is being largely replaced by the indicative.

Wish: I wish that I *were* able to help you.

Supposition: We can go provided he *consent.* [The indicative would be more commonly used here.]

Exhortation: Heaven *forbid!*

Condition contrary to fact: If she *were* younger, she would understand.

**Modify.** To describe or limit the meaning of a word or group of words. In the sentence *I dislike sour oranges*, the word *sour* describes the word *oranges;* i.e., it modifies it. In the sentence *Call softly*, *softly* describes or modifies *call.* The modifiers of substantives are adjectives (including participles), adjective phrases, adjective clauses, appositives, and substantives in the possessive case. The modifiers of adjectives, verbs, and adverbs are adverbs, adverbial phrases, and adverbial clauses.

**Nominative.** See Case.

**Nonrestrictive modifier.** A dependent clause or phrase which adds information without limiting or identifying the word it modifies. See Section **32d.**

**Noun.** A part of speech, the name of a person, place, thing, or idea. There are the following kinds:

A **common noun** is the name that is applied in common to all the members of a group of persons, places, things, or ideas; e.g., *man*, *village*, *book*, *courage*. Common nouns are not usually capitalized.

A **proper noun** or **proper name** is the name of a particular person, place, or thing; e.g., *Franklin Roosevelt*, *Chicago*, *Domesday Book*, *Revolutionary War*. Proper nouns are capitalized.

A **collective noun** is the name of a group or class considered as a unit; e.g., *flock*, *class*, *group*, *crowd*, *gang*.

A **concrete noun** is the name of something that can be perceived by any one of the senses; e.g., *tree*, *sugar*, *perfume*, *shriek*, *velvet*.

An **abstract noun** is the name of a quality or general idea; e.g., *strength*, *love*, *bravery*.

**Number.** Inflectional changes in verbs, nouns, and pronouns to indicate singular or plural.

**Object.** The **direct object** of a verb names the person or thing that is acted upon by the verb or that completes the assertion made by a transitive verb. It answers the question *what* or *whom*.

Father dried the *dishes* and broke a *plate*.
I believed his *story*, but I had some *doubts*.

The **indirect object** of a verb is the person or thing indirectly affected by the action of the verb. The indirect object can usually be made the object of the preposition *for* or *to*.

I built *my wife* a house. [I built a house *for my wife*.]
I wrote *him* a letter. [I wrote a letter *to him*.]

**Objective (accusative).** See Case.

**Objective complement.** Either a noun or an adjective that completes the predicate by telling something about the direct object.

They called him a *fool*. [Noun.]
I like my coffee *hot*. [Adjective.]

**Ordinal number.** See Adjective.

**Participle.** A verbal adjective. The present participle ends in *ing;* e.g., *eating*, *running*. The past participle ends in *ed*, *d*, *t*, *en*, *n*, or is formed by a vowel change; e.g., *stopped*, *told*, *slept*, *fallen*, *known*, *sung*. If the verb is transitive, there are both active and passive participles.

Since a participle is a verbal adjective, it has the characteristics of both a verb and an adjective. Like an adjective, it modifies a substantive:

The *inquiring* reporter stopped him.
*Encouraged* by his help, we shall continue the work.
*Having* just *returned* from my vacation, I had not heard of the accident.

Like a verb the participle may take a direct or an indirect object and may be modified by an adverb.

Wishing *us success*, he drove away. [*Us* is an indirect object, *success* a direct object, of the participle *wishing*.]
Stumbling *awkwardly*, he came into the room. [*Awkwardly* is an adverb modifying the participle *stumbling*.]

**Parts of speech.** The classification of words according to the special function that they perform in a sentence. In English there are eight parts of speech: nouns, pronouns, verbs, adjectives, adverbs, prepositions, conjunctions, interjections.

**Passive voice.** See Voice.

**Person.** Inflection of verbs and personal pronouns to indicate the speaker (**first person**), the person spoken to (**second person**), and the person spoken of (**third person**).

First person: I am, we are
Second person: You are
Third person: He is, they are

**Phrase.** A phrase is a group of words without a subject and predicate, and used as a single part of speech: as a substantive, verb, adjective, or adverb. See Section **8**.

**Predicate.** A word or group of words that makes a statement about the subject of a sentence. Thus in the sentence *John drove the car*, *drove the car* is the predicate, for it tells what the subject *John* did. The predicate contains a finite verb, either a simple verb or a verb phrase; e.g., *drove*, *was driving*.

The **simple predicate** is the verb alone. The **complete predicate** is the verb and its modifiers and complements.

John drove the car into the garage. [*Drove* is the simple predicate. *Drove the car into the garage* is the complete predicate.]

**Predicate adjective, Predicate noun.** See Complement.

**Preposition.** A part of speech that shows the relation between a substantive and another word in the sentence; e.g., *in*, *on*, *into*, *toward*, *from*, *for*, *against*, *of*, *between*, *with*, *without*, *within*, *before*, *behind*, *under*, *over*, *above*, *among*, *at*, *by*, *around*, *about*, *through*. The word that completes the meaning of a preposition is called the object of the preposition. In English many words may be used as either prepositions or adverbs, their classification depending on their function in the sentence. If they are followed by a substantive which with them forms a phrase, they are prepositions; if by themselves they modify a verb, they are adverbs.

He stood *behind* the chair. [Preposition.]
He walked *behind*. [Adverb.]
He is *in* the bank. [Preposition.]
He came *in* while we were there. [Adverb.]

**Principal clause.** See Clause.

**Principal parts.** In English, the three forms of a verb from which all the other forms are derived. They are (1) the present infinitive, (2) the first person singular of the past tense, and (3) the past participle: e.g., *send, sent, sent; choose, chose, chosen; swim, swam, swum.* All present and future tense forms are derived from the first principal part: I *send*, he *chooses*, we *will swim*. The second principal part is used for the simple past tenses: he *sent*, I *chose*, you *swam*. Compound past tenses and the forms of the passive voice employ the third principal part: he *has chosen*, they *had swum*, the package *was sent*, or *may be sent, is being sent, will be sent*, etc.

In learning a foreign language or in correcting unconventional English, it is important to know the principal parts of the irregular verbs. See Section **30c.**

**Pronoun.** A part of speech, a word used instead of a noun. Pronouns may be classified as follows:

1. **Personal:** *I, thou, you, he, she, it,* and their inflectional forms.
   *I* listened to *her*.
2. **Demonstrative:** *this, that, these, those.*
   *This* is my favorite book.
3. **Interrogative:** *who, which, what.*
   *Who* can answer this question?
4. **Relative:** *who, which, that,* and such compounds as *whoever.*
   The house *that* they bought was built many years ago.
5. **Indefinite:** *any, anyone, some, someone, no one, nobody,* etc.
   *Everyone* is invited.
6. **Reflexive:** *myself, yourself,* etc.
   I hurt *myself.*

7. **Intensive:** *myself, yourself,* etc.
   He *himself* is to blame.

8. **Reciprocal:** *each other, one another.*
   They blamed *each other.*

**Regular verb.** A verb which forms its past tenses by adding *ed* or *t: start, started; dream, dreamed* or *dreamt; buy, bought.* Also called **a weak verb.**

**Relative pronoun.** A pronoun (*who, which,* or *that*) used with a double function: to take the place of a noun and to connect clauses like a subordinating conjunction. See page 103.

**Restrictive modifier.** A dependent clause or phrase intended to define, limit, or identify the word it modifies. See Section **32d.**

**Sentence.** A group of words containing a subject and a predicate and expressing a complete thought. From the point of view of structure, sentences are classified as simple, compound, complex, or compound-complex. See Section **12.**

1. A **declarative sentence** makes a statement.
   The boy closed the door.

2. An **interrogative sentence** asks a question.
   Is the door closed?

3. An **imperative sentence** expresses a command.
   Close the door.

4. An **exclamatory sentence** expresses strong feeling.
   What a glorious view you have!

**Strong verb.** See Irregular verb.

**Subject.** The part of a sentence or clause naming the person or thing about which something is said. The subject of a sentence is usually a noun or pronoun, but it may be a verbal, a phrase, or a noun clause. The subject can most easily be determined by phrasing the predicate as a question, using *who* or *what* as a temporary subject. The answer to such a question is the true subject.

**Noun:** Beyond the ridge lay a high *plateau.* (What lay beyond the ridge?)

**Verbal:** Nowadays *flying* is both cheap and safe.

**Phrase:** *To err* is human.

**Clause:** *That he will be promoted* is certain.

The **simple subject** is a substantive, usually a noun or pronoun. The **complete subject** is the simple subject and its modifiers.

The young trees that we planted last year have grown well.
[*Trees* is the simple subject. *The young trees that we planted last year* is the complete subject.]

**Subjective complement.** See Complement.

**Subjunctive.** See Mode.

**Subordinate clause.** A dependent clause. See page 101.

**Substantive.** Any word or group of words used as a noun. It may be a noun, a pronoun, a clause, an infinitive, or a gerund.

**Superlative.** See Comparison.

**Tense.** A characteristic of verbs shown by different forms that indicate the time of the action. There are six tenses: the present tense, the past tense, the future tense, the perfect (present perfect) tense, the past perfect tense, and the future perfect tense. See **Conjugation** for examples.

**Transitive verb.** See Verb.

**Verb.** A part of speech used to assert an action, a condition, or a state.

He hit the ball. [*Hit* expresses action.]
He is poor. [*Is* expresses condition or state.]

*a.* A **transitive verb** requires a direct object to complete its meaning; i.e., it must be followed by a word that answers the question *whom* or *what.* In the sentence *The girl mailed the letter, mailed* is a transitive verb because it requires a direct object like *letter* to complete its meaning.

*b.* An **intransitive verb** does not require an object to complete its meaning. In the sentence *The girl ran down the hill*, *ran* is intransitive.

**Verbals.** Forms of a verb (*stealing*, *stolen*, *to steal*) used as nouns, adjectives, or adverbs. See **Gerund, Participle, Infinitive.**

**Voice.** Inflection of a verb to indicate the relation of the subject to the action expressed by the verb. A verb is in the **active voice** when its subject is the doer of the act. A verb is in the **passive voice** when its subject is acted upon.

**Active voice:** I rang the bell. [The subject *I* did the act of *ringing*.]

**Passive voice:** The bell was rung by me. [The subject *bell* was acted upon by *me*.]

**Weak verb.** See **Regular verb.**

## Good Sentences

**14.** SENTENCE UNITY

**15.** SUBORDINATION

**16.** PARALLELISM

**17.** FAULTY REFERENCE OF PRONOUNS

**18.** DANGLING MODIFIERS

**19.** MISPLACED SENTENCE ELEMENTS

**20.** UNNECESSARY SHIFTS

**21.** INCOMPLETE CONSTRUCTIONS

**22.** MIXED CONSTRUCTIONS

**23.** WEAK AND UNEMPHATIC SENTENCES

**24.** WORDY SENTENCES

**25.** VAGUE SENTENCES

# 14 SENTENCE UNITY

A sentence is unified if the various ideas it contains all contribute to making one total statement and if the unifying idea, which ties the various parts together, is made clear to the reader. Faults in sentence unity are most often caused either by the inclusion of ideas which are not related to the main purpose of the sentence or by the inclusion of excessive detail — that is, too many ideas, even though the ideas may be relevant.

## 14a Avoiding Irrelevant Ideas

Unrelated ideas creep into a sentence when the writer temporarily forgets what he is talking about and wanders away from his main point:

**Irrelevant idea.** Mac always brings out a person's good qualities, and when a person discovers good qualities in himself, he is apt to develop them into habits and thus become a better person with a stronger character. [What is this sentence supposed to be about: Mac or self-improvement? If it is a part of a character sketch of Mac, then the generalization about self-improvement should be omitted.]

**Irrelevant idea.** The captain of a ship, whether he commands a tugboat or the *Queen Elizabeth*, a giant sister-ship to the *Queen Mary* and one of the fastest liners on the Atlantic, leads a very lonely life. [The *Queen Elizabeth* is mentioned here only to provide a contrast with a tugboat. All other information about the liner is irrelevant to the purpose of this sentence.]

**Improved.** The captain of a ship, whether he commands a tugboat or a giant liner like the *Queen Elizabeth*, leads a very lonely life.

**Irrelevant idea.** Six weeks of coaching by a retired bicycle racer improved my riding remarkably: I developed a faster start in sprints, which are generally 1,000-meter races where the last two hundred meters are covered at top speed, and I did much better in long-distance road races. [The main point of this sentence is improvement in riding, and the definition of "sprint" should be omitted altogether or inserted elsewhere.]

**Improved.** Six weeks of coaching by a retired bicycle racer improved my riding remarkably: I developed a faster start in sprints, and I did much better in long-distance road races.

Even though the relation between two ideas is perfectly clear to the writer, the sentence may baffle a reader if the unifying principle is only implied. Make sure that someone else will readily understand why two ideas are brought together into one sentence.

**Seeming lack of unity.** Radio stars have to practice hard to develop pleasant speaking voices; it is very important that they acquire a sense of timing so programs will begin and end promptly. [These two statements were probably connected in the writer's mind by the idea of the necessity of hard practice. Emphasizing this idea makes the sentence seem unified.]

**Improved.** Radio stars have to practice hard to develop pleasant speaking voices and to improve their sense of timing so that programs will begin and end promptly.

Each sentence break should come between two logically unified thoughts. Careless placing of sentence breaks may bring unrelated ideas into one sentence.

**Faulty sentence break.** Van Gogh did not belong to any one school of painting. He borrowed from all schools, and moreover he developed a brush technique that was uniquely his own.

**Improved.** Van Gogh did not belong to any one school of painting; he borrowed from all schools. Moreover, he developed a brush technique that was uniquely his own.

EXERCISE

Improve the unity of the following sentences.

1. The changed political conditions do not mean that we shall have a socialist government; they do mean that our government will be much more centralized, and in the future we will probably have to import more and more of our raw materials.
2. One of the great advantages of our system of government is that American citizens may work wherever they want to, and at present jobs are plentiful in America.
3. According to the contractor, a native of the town and superintendent of the local Sunday School, the granite ledge would have to be blasted out before excavation could begin.
4. For supper that evening we cooked the trout, two mature specimens of the cutthroat variety, *Salmo clarkii*, which I had caught in the late afternoon.
5. Borrowing a pen from the salesman, who seemed to prefer the ball-point type which seldom runs out of ink though it never writes very well, I signed the contract.

## 14b Avoiding Excessive Detail

If a sentence contains too many ideas, none of them will stand out; the sentence will seem overcrowded and pointless.

**Overcrowded sentence.** When the cry for woman's suffrage was first heard there was immediate opposition to it, which continued for a long time until people finally began to realize that women were entitled to the same rights as men, and in 1920 the Nineteenth Amendment was ratified. [This sentence includes too many ideas: the beginning of the woman's suffrage movement, opposition to it, continued opposition, gradual change of public opinion, and ratification of the Nineteenth Amendment. It should be broken into at least two sentences.]

**Improved.** When the cry for woman's suffrage was first heard there was immediate opposition to it, and this opposition continued for a long time. Gradually, however, people realized that women were entitled to the same rights as men, and in 1920 the Nineteenth Amendment was ratified.

Even though two ideas clearly belong together in the sense that one ought to follow the other, they do not necessarily belong in the same sentence. Putting them into one sentence may suggest a closer relationship than actually exists.

**Lack of sentence unity.** After locking the house, I left the key with the real estate agent, and I hope you will soon find another tenant.

**Improved.** After locking the house, I left the key with the real estate agent. I hope you will soon find another tenant.

## EXERCISE

Revise the following sentences to make them more unified.

1. When Roderick was on his way back to England, he was shipwrecked, but was saved and secured a place as servant to a poetess in England.

2. The Basques are marked by an exceptional pride of race and great physical sturdiness and endurance, as well as great conservatism and self-respect, and their language is different from any known tongue.
3. King Bladud reigned at Bath, according to the legend, in honor and splendor for years, until despair over his increasing senility prompted him to jump from the pinnacle of a temple dedicated to Minerva, and thus he ended his life.
4. The fact that each member of the cast felt himself part of a team was chiefly responsible for the success of the play, which was Shaw's comedy *Androcles and the Lion*, our first production of the year.
5. After his attacks on slave owners in Kansas had earned him a reputation as a violent enemy of slavery, John Brown moved his men to Virginia, took the town of Harpers Ferry, was defeated and captured by a small detachment of marines under Colonel Robert E. Lee, and soon after was tried and hanged for treason, becoming a martyr in the eyes of Northern abolitionists.
6. On the forward end of the boat I built a little deck of plywood, which extended about one third of the way aft and into which I cut a hole for the mast, made of two pieces of plywood glued together, and the boom was made the same way.
7. Fra Junipero Serra, known as the Father of the Missions, traveled north to Monterey Bay and at the mouth of the Carmel River founded the Mission San Carlos, in which he was finally buried and which has become a great tourist attraction because of its architectural beauty and excellent state of preservation.

# 15 SUBORDINATION

To make main points stand out clearly, less important points must be made less conspicuous. That is, main ideas should be expressed in independent clauses, which are the backbone of any sentence. Minor descriptive details, qualifications, and incidental remarks should be put into subordinate constructions — dependent clauses, appositives, or modifying phrases.

## 15a Avoiding Primer Sentences

A series of short independent sentences may produce the jerky primer style of second-grade readers. A more serious disadvantage of such writing is that no one statement seems to be more important than any other. Primer sentences should be combined into longer, unified sentences with the less important ideas subordinated.

**Primer sentences.** Last semester I wrote a book report. It was on *A Sailor's Life*. This is a book by Jan de Hartog. It discusses every aspect of life at sea. It was a very interesting book.

**Unified and improved.** Last semester I wrote a book report on *A Sailor's Life*, by Jan de Hartog, a very interesting book which discusses every aspect of life at sea.

**Primer sentences.** The train was three hours late. There had been a freight wreck ahead somewhere. We finally reached Riverbank. The station was dark and deserted.

**Improved.** The train was three hours late because of a freight wreck ahead, and the station was dark and deserted when we finally reached Riverbank.

**Primer sentences.** Mr. Dean usually teaches our section of History 1. Yesterday he left a note on the blackboard. It asked us to join another section. He could not meet the class.

**Improved.** Yesterday Mr. Dean, who usually teaches our section of History 1, left a note on the blackboard asking us to join another section, since he could not meet the class.

EXERCISE

Revise the following groups of primer sentences to make them more compact and forceful.

1. Some people think that guarding a swimming pool is easy. These people are wrong. A lifeguard has a big responsibility. Everyone in the pool is dependent on him.
2. The Russians came to the last Olympic Games. Their athletes were surprisingly good. Their best event was gymnastics. They took almost all the gold medals in gymnastics.
3. In ancient Greece there were two cities of great importance. They were Athens and Sparta. The distance between them was not great. Their governments differed greatly.
4. These planes carried small cannon. A few bombs were placed under the wings. Sometimes a torpedo was added. They were also equipped with self-sealing gas tanks.
5. Television also attracts the youngsters. Children comprise a considerable proportion of television viewers. It consumes much of their leisure time.

### 15b Illogical Coordination

When sentence elements are joined by *and* or another coordinating conjunction, the implication is that the elements are of equal weight and importance. If they are not really coordinate in importance, one of them should be subordinated.

**Illogical coordination.** A large refinery was built to provide fuel for construction equipment and is now used to supply passenger cars and planes.

**Improved.** A large refinery, built to provide fuel for construction equipment, is now used to supply passenger cars and planes. [The change of tense in the original sentence is an indication that the two predicates are not of equal weight and that one of them should be reduced to a modifier.]

**Illogical coordination.** The potter must roll the clay out on a flat surface, and a surface that the clay will not stick to.

**Improved.** The potter must roll the clay out on a flat surface which is smooth enough so that the clay will not stick to it. [The *and* in the original sentence is misleading. The writer is not talking about two surfaces, but is describing two necessary qualities of the surface.]

**Illogical coordination.** I got the note from Mr. Lewis, and I gave it to my boss, but he just scowled at me, and finally he said I could take the afternoon off.

**Improved.** When I gave the note from Mr. Lewis to my boss, he just scowled at me, but finally he said I could take the afternoon off.

### EXERCISE

Improve the effectiveness of the following sentences by suitable subordination.

1. In English we had to learn many rules of grammar, and very few of these rules are used today.
2. I am a law-abiding citizen, but I will discuss my reasons for disliking policemen.

3. The Tamalpais School for Boys was formerly known as the Hitchcock Military Academy, but has recently been sold.
4. Five hundred men were too many to meet at one time, and instead the Council was divided into ten smaller groups.
5. Our new property was about a quarter of a mile from the highway, and our first problem was to clear a road through the trees and shrubs.
6. The team came onto the field, and the crowd cheered, and the band played.
7. Smollett's next novel was *Peregrine Pickle*, and it shows considerable improvement in characterization, but the plot is even looser than that of *Roderick Random*.

## 15c Faulty Subordination

When the main idea of a sentence is placed in a subordinate construction — a dependent clause or a modifying phrase — the resulting upside-down subordination makes the sentence weak. The context, of course, determines which ideas are relatively more, and which are relatively less important. In a personal narrative the following sentence would be satisfactory:

> I used to work for the Ace Manufacturing Company, which went bankrupt yesterday.

In a report on the Ace Manufacturing Company, the first idea would be subordinate:

> The Ace Manufacturing Company, where I used to work, went bankrupt yesterday.

**Faulty subordination.** I was living in Sacramento when my father was made district manager, which resulted in our moving to San Francisco.

**Improved.** While I was living in Sacramento, my father was made district manager, and as a result we moved to San Francisco.

**Faulty subordination.** The novel has a beginning which some readers find dull and wordy.

**Improved.** Some readers find the beginning of the novel dull and wordy.

**Improved.** The beginning of the novel, according to some readers, is dull and wordy.

### EXERCISE

Improve the distribution of weight in the following sentences by revising the faulty subordination.

1. The horse came up to the first jump, when he stumbled and threw Jean off.
2. This is called the cryptozoite stage, after which the plasmodia break out of the liver cells and float about in the blood stream.
3. An especially big wave rolled in, when I finally managed to get my line unsnagged.
4. The night watchman walked past the building, noticing that the door was unlocked.
5. Saint-Exupéry's past books have consisted of fragments of his philosophy, which are brought together in this one book, *La Citadelle.*

### EXERCISE

Improve the unity and subordination in the following sentences.

1. A good cook is very conscious of food, but often the people who eat the food discourage the cook, for many people are very particular and they may dislike certain things, and a cook likes to please all the people he serves.
2. The shabbiest of the three buildings was the auditorium, which was dark brown in color, and plaster was missing

from its ceiling, and the stage was badly in need of repair.

3. He was trying to kill a bee inside the car, driving off the road as a result.
4. There were about ten boys out for wrestling, and we only had ten weeks before our first match, so we worked very hard to get in condition, but three of our best men caught the flu and we didn't do well against our rival.
5. The train to Albany was two hours late, causing me to miss my appointment in that city.
6. The picture which won first prize, though it was criticized bitterly by most of the visitors to the gallery, was an abstraction in water color.
7. The first book I consulted lacked an index, and next I tried an encyclopedia.
8. A last desperate pass had just been knocked down when the gun went off, thus ending the game.
9. The dinner was over at nine, but we couldn't get a taxi, and we had to wait almost an hour and consequently were late in arriving at the dance.
10. The swimming pool was intended for college students only, but is now open to townspeople as well.
11. I picked up my tool box and went to work, first jacking the automobile up off the ground and then taking out all the bolts around the oil pan, but still unable to get the pan off.
12. The Greek word *papyros* originally meant thin sheets made from a certain Egyptian reed, from which we have borrowed our modern word *paper* and which now means any kind of writing material.

# 16 PARALLELISM

Parallel thoughts should be expressed in parallel grammatical form. For example, an infinitive should be paralleled by another infinitive, not by a participle; a subordinate clause by another subordinate clause, not by a phrase. Parallel structure is one method of showing the reader the relation between your ideas.

## 16a Coordinate Constructions

The coordinating conjunctions (*and*, *or*, *nor*, *but*) are sure signs of a compound construction. Any sentence elements which can logically be joined by a coordinating conjunction should be parallel in grammatical construction.

**Not parallel.** Among the primitive uses of fire were protection from wild animals and for preparing food. [In this sentence, *and* joins the two complements of the verb *were*, but one of these is a noun and the other a prepositional phrase.]

**Improved.** Among the primitive uses of fire were protection from wild animals and the preparation of food. [Two nouns are joined by *and*.]

**Not parallel.** The range of airplanes has improved greatly, partly because the motors have been made more efficient and partly the new technique of refueling in mid-air. [In this sentence, *and* joins a dependent clause with a noun, *technique*.]

**Improved.** The range of airplanes has improved greatly, partly because the motors have been made more efficient and partly because it is now possible to refuel in mid-air.

**Improved.** The range of airplanes has been improved greatly, partly because of more efficient motors and partly because of the new technique of refueling in mid-air.

**Not parallel.** Every player is taught to work with the team and that good sportsmanship must be shown.

**Improved.** Every player is taught to work with the team and to show good sportsmanship.

EXERCISE

Correct the faulty parallelism in the following sentences.

1. When I was a small child, my parents spent a lot of time preparing me for school, and then letting me use my own judgement when I got to high school.
2. In an effort to foster good relations with other people of the world as well as preserving the economic health of friendly countries, the United States has spent billions on foreign aid.
3. Adding chocolate flavoring and vitamins makes milk not only enjoyable but a healthy drink as well.
4. The inefficiency of our cadet officers causes us to look very ragged and frequently getting mixed up in drill exercises.
5. I think sports stars should be well paid because of their relatively short period of greatness and they must make some provision for later life.

## 16b Elements in Series

Sentence elements in a series (*a*, *b*, and *c*) should express parallel ideas and be parallel in grammatical form.

**Faulty parallelism.** She is young (a), well educated (b), and has an aggressive manner (c). [**a** and **b** are adjectives, and **c** is a verb.]

**Improved.** She is young, well educated, and aggressive.

**Faulty parallelism.** He was tall, slim, and wore a black coat. [*Tall* and *slim* are adjectives, but *wore* is a verb and has an object, *coat.*]

**Improved.** He was tall and slim and wore a black coat. [One *and* joins two adjectives; the other joins the two verbs *was* and *wore.* It would be correct but awkward to say . . . "*tall*, *slim*, and *black-coated.*"]

**Faulty parallelism.** By this time the guests were showing signs of boredom, hunger, and some of them were beginning to leave.

**Improved.** By this time the guests were showing signs of boredom and hunger, and some of them were beginning to leave.

## EXERCISE

The following sentences contain elements in series. Revise the sentences to make the elements parallel in grammatical form.

1. Before coming to college a student has had someone to look after him, urge him to get his work done, and has led a rather sheltered life.
2. Now all the boys started running the way Stan ran, walking the way Stan walked, and they even started using his facial expressions.
3. Voltaire was a true European: French by birth, a great admirer of England, and was very friendly with Frederick the Great of Prussia.
4. Applicants for this position must be United States citizens, willing to work abroad, and qualify under security regulations.

5. Most homes contain such modern conveniences as the electric iron, the electric refrigerator, the washing machine, and the radio and television could also be included in this group.

## 16c Repetition of Prepositions and Other Introductory Words

In order to make a parallel construction clear it is often necessary to repeat a preposition, an article, a relative pronoun, a subordinating conjunction, an auxiliary verb, or the sign of the infinitive.

**Obscure parallelism.** The captain must be quick to see just what movement will get his company out of close quarters and give the order clearly.

**Clear parallelism.** The captain *must* be quick to see just what movement will get his company out of close quarters and *must* give the order clearly.

**Obscure parallelism.** The registrar told him that he could not have credit for his half year of German and he must be put on probation because of his poor grades in English.

**Clear parallelism.** The registrar told him *that* he could not have credit for his half year of German and *that* he must be put on probation because of his poor grades in English.

**Obscure parallelism.** The place is often visited by tourists who are fond of rugged scenery, and especially amateur photographers.

**Clear parallelism.** The place is often visited *by* tourists who are fond of rugged scenery, and especially *by* amateur photographers.

When the parallel elements are short and stand close together, repetition of the connective word is usually unnecessary.

**Clear.** The sheep may stray and be lost.

**Clear.** He has lived in Cuba, Panama, and Haiti.

**Clear.** Has she learned to dance, play bridge, and make herself agreeable?

EXERCISE

In the following sentences insert the words necessary for satisfactory parallelism.

1. The critics say that he has no sense of timing nor ear for dialogue, and he ought to give up trying to write plays.
2. Ruskin is referring to those people who are not strong enough to be consistently evil but when an opportunity arises, will take advantage of others.
3. In industry women can make electrical equipment, instruments, light metal goods, and excel in airplane building.
4. A teacher should note what points the students have trouble with and explain them carefully.
5. In the course of the summer I planned to read a dozen books, earn some money, and to have as good a time as possible.

## 16d Correlatives

Correlative conjunctions (like *either . . . or*, *neither . . . nor*, *not only . . . but also*) should be followed by parallel sentence elements.

**Undesirable.** He is not only discourteous to the students but also to the teacher. [*Not only* is followed by an adjective with a prepositional phrase modifying it; *but also* is followed by a prepositional phrase.]

**Improved.** He is discourteous not only to the students but also to the teacher. [The correlatives are each followed by a prepositional phrase.]

**Undesirable.** He either was a magnificent liar or a remarkably naive young man. [*Either* is followed by a verb and its noun complement; *or* is followed by a noun and its modifying adjectives.]

**Improved.** He was either a magnificent liar or a remarkably naive young man. [Each correlative is followed by a noun complement of the verb.]

### EXERCISE

Revise the following sentences so that the correlatives are followed by elements that are parallel in grammatical form.

1. Everyone should know something of zoology, not only so that he will understand his own body but also to understand man's relation to the other animals.
2. Rossetti was not only famous as a poet, but also for his painting.
3. The bumper crop of rice neither helped the farmers nor the consumers.
4. He won the approval of not only his school friends but also of his teachers and counselors.
5. John Brown was either regarded as a patriotic martyr or a crazed fanatic.

## 16e *And which* Clauses

Avoid joining a relative clause to its principal clause by *and* or *but.* These conjunctions are coordinating conjunctions and therefore should connect elements which are grammatically coordinate. An undesirable *and which* construction can be corrected by (*a*) omitting the coordinating conjunction, (*b*) changing the relative clause to a principal clause, or (*c*) inserting a relative clause before the conjunction.

**Undesirable.** On the way we met a Mr. Osborn from the neighborhood of Denver and who had the typical Western breeziness.

**Improved.** On the way we met a Mr. Osborn from the neighborhood of Denver, who had the typical Western breeziness.

**Improved.** On the way we met a Mr. Osborn, who came from the neighborhood of Denver and who had the typical Western breeziness.

**Undesirable.** The witness appeared at the committee meeting with a long written statement, but which he was not allowed to read.

**Improved.** The witness appeared at the committee meeting with a long written statement, but he was not allowed to read it.

## EXERCISE

Revise the following sentences to make the elements grammatically parallel.

1. A dictionary is one of the most useful books a student can own, and which he will continue to use when he leaves college.
2. A truck driver sometimes has twelve different gears at his disposal and which he must adapt to the steepness of the grade and the weight of his load.
3. Around the edge of the sun dial a motto had been engraved, but which was almost obliterated by rust and grime.
4. Keep on the top shelf all drugs containing poison or which might be harmful to children.
5. In the middle of the square was a statue dating from 1870 and which showed General Lee on horseback.

# 17 FAULTY REFERENCE OF PRONOUNS

The antecedent of every pronoun should be immediately clear to the reader. A pronoun usually refers to a definite person or thing. The relative pronoun *which* may in some instances refer to a clause or phrase (see **17e**), but even then the antecedent should be readily identifiable. Faulty reference of pronouns is particularly hard to detect in a first draft. Check each pronoun carefully when you are revising.

## 17a Ambiguous Reference

Do not use a pronoun in such a way that it might refer to either of two antecedents. If there is any possibility of doubt, revise the sentence to remove the ambiguity.

**Ambiguous.** With only six miles completed, the company stopped work on the canal because of lack of support by the legislature; it was more interested in economy than in progress. [The company or the legislature?]

**Clear.** With only six miles completed, the company stopped work on the canal because of lack of support by the legislature, which was more interested in economy than in progress.

**Ambiguous.** People often blame ski accidents on poor ski bindings, but a little common sense would eliminate most of them.

**Clear.** People often blame ski accidents on poor ski bindings, but most accidents could be prevented by using a little common sense.

**Ambiguous.** Queen Victoria determined for the rest of her life to follow Albert's example, and she told her uncle that all his plans and wishes were to be her law.

**Clear.** Queen Victoria determined for the rest of her life to follow her husband's example, and she told her uncle that all Albert's plans and wishes were to be her law.

Avoid the device of explaining an ambiguous pronoun by repeating its antecedent in parentheses.

**Awkward.** King Henry is talking to Hal about his (Hal's) past life.

**Improved.** King Henry is reproving Hal for his past life.

## 17b Reference to Remote Antecedent

A pronoun need not be in the same sentence as its antecedent, but the antecedent should not be so remote as to cause possible misreading. If a considerable amount of material stands between the antecedent and the pronoun, repeat the antecedent.

**Undesirable.** The author draws a panoramic picture of an army air base and describes the encounters and cross-purposes of the people working on it, from generals to buck privates. Dozens of characters appear during the three days in which the action takes place, but he seems to be most interested in the thoughts and actions of an aging colonel.

**Improved.** . . . but the author seems to be most interested in the thoughts and actions of an aging colonel.

**Undesirable.** Holton organized a six-piece band which played exclusively the kind of traditional Dixieland jazz which originated in New Orleans. It was not well received by the students, but he would make no concessions to popular taste.

**Improved.** . . . but Holton would make no concessions to popular taste.

## 17c Reference to Implied Antecedent

Do not use a pronoun to refer to a noun which is not expressed but has to be inferred from another noun.

**Antecedent implied.** In the curriculum feminine interests are regarded as relatively unimportant compared with masculine interests, and consequently they are given the same kind of education as the men.

**Improved.** . . . and consequently the women are given the same kind of education as the men.

**Antecedent implied.** I once knew an old violinist who repaired them very expertly.

**Improved.** I once knew an old violinist who repaired violins very expertly.

## 17d Reference to Inconspicuous Antecedent

Do not use a pronoun to refer to a noun in a subordinate construction where it may be overlooked by the reader. A noun which is used as an adjective, especially the possessive form of the noun, is likely to be too inconspicuous to serve as an antecedent.

**Inconspicuous antecedent.** Adobe brick was used in the wall, which is a Spanish word for sun-dried clay.

**Improved.** The bricks in the wall were made of adobe, which is a Spanish word for sun-dried clay.

**Inconspicuous antecedent.** The professor told us the plants' names which were all around us.

**Improved.** The professor told us the names of the plants which were all around us.

**Allowable.** Henderson's room was unlocked, and he had left a note on the dresser. [There is sufficient emphasis on the antecedent to prevent misreading.]

## 17e Broad Reference

Using a relative or demonstrative pronoun (*which*, *that*, *this*) to refer to the whole idea of a preceding clause, phrase, or sentence is acceptable if the sense is clear and if a change would be awkward or wordy.

**Acceptable broad reference.** At first glance, the desert seems completely barren of animal life, but this is a delusion.

**Acceptable broad reference.** The game ended a little before ten, which gave us plenty of time to catch our train home.

Frequently, however, broad reference makes a sentence sound awkward. It may also be ambiguous if the preceding clause contains a noun which might be mistaken for the antecedent. Hard and fast rules will not serve here; you must use your judgement. If you are in doubt, revise the sentence.

**Undesirable.** In 1591, Sir Richard was sent out with a small squadron to intercept a Spanish treasure fleet, the result of which is told in Tennyson's poem.

**Improved.** In 1591, Sir Richard was sent out with a small squadron to intercept a Spanish treasure fleet, and the result of this expedition is told in Tennyson's poem.

**Ambiguous.** The beginning of the book is more interesting than the conclusion, which is very unfortunate.

**Improved.** Unfortunately, the beginning of the book is more interesting than the conclusion.

**Awkward.** In the eighteenth century more and more land was converted into pasture, which had been going on to some extent for several centuries.

**Improved.** In the eighteenth century, more and more land was converted into pasture, a process which had been going on to some extent for several centuries.

### 17f Personal Pronouns Used Indefinitely

Although the indefinite *you* is suitable in informal writing, it is generally out of place in formal compositions. Instead, use the impersonal pronoun *one*, or put the verb in the passive voice.

**Informal.** You should not take sulfa drugs without a doctor's prescription.

**Formal.** One should not take sulfa drugs without a doctor's prescription.

**Formal or informal.** Sulfa drugs should not be taken without a doctor's prescription.

The indefinite use of *they* is always vague and usually sounds childish or naive.

**Undesirable.** Thirty years ago there was no such thing as an atomic bomb; in fact, they did not even know how to split the atom.

**Improved.** . . . in fact, scientists did not even know how to split the atom.

**Undesirable.** They have good roads in Minnesota.

**Improved.** The roads in Minnesota are good.

The indefinite *it* is correctly used in impersonal expressions, such as *it is raining*, *it is hot*, or in such sentences as *It seems best to go at once*, in which *it* anticipates the real subject, *to go at once*. Avoid, however, the unexplained *it*, the *it* that needs an antecedent and has none. The expression "it says here that . . ." is an example of such colloquial usage, which should not be used in writing.

**Undesirable.** There would be enough room if the building were extended in width, but it would involve removing the front wall.

**Improved.** There would be enough room if the building were extended in width, but such a change would involve removing the front wall.

**Undesirable.** It says in the paper that they are having severe storms in the West.

**Improved.** The paper says there are severe storms in the West.

**Undesirable.** Does it say *For Sale* on that sign?

**Improved.** Does that sign say *For Sale?*

## 17g Demonstrative Pronouns and Adjectives

The pronouns *this*, *that*, *these*, *those* are frequently used as adjectives, to modify nouns. Using one of these words as a modifier, without an expressed or clearly implied antecedent, is a colloquialism which should be avoided in serious writing.

**Acceptable.** After struggling through the poetry assignment, I decided that I would never read one of those poems again.

**Colloquial.** It was just one of those things.

**Colloquial.** The building was one of those rambling old mansions.

**Improved.** The building was one of those rambling old mansions that are found in every New England town.

### EXERCISE

Correct any faults in reference in the following sentences.

1. Machines are constantly being invented to do work previously done by men, and this tends to increase unemployment.
2. It won't hurt people to read about criminals; they live in a different kind of world, and they don't have to follow their example.

3. When she first saw Albert, her attitude toward men changed completely, which resulted in their marriage.
4. All jobs at the office proved to be tedious at times, but on the whole it was fun.
5. The government is trying to stop swindlers from taking advantage of the loopholes in our tax laws, but this is not easy.
6. In Nevada they have less trouble with crime than they do in California.
7. Ted was dressed in his best clothes, but he was driving one of those old cut-down cars.
8. The men went trout fishing early the next morning, but they didn't catch any.
9. To qualify for a career in the State Department, you must study foreign languages in college.
10. From the castle's elaborate gardens, it looked like an illustration from a book of fairy tales.
11. Johnson's father was governor of the state, which gave him considerable social prestige.
12. Lobbyists can provide helpful information to the legislators, but when they resort to bribery and other disreputable methods, it becomes a felony under the law.
13. Legalized gambling would bring many tourists to the state, which would be a help to the economy as a whole, although it might also attract an undesirable criminal element.
14. Engineering is the profession that harnesses natural forces to do man's work, and it is my ambition to become one of them.
15. Axel Heyst's chief difficulty is that he is trying to escape the outside world, which is impossible.
16. In England they serve tea every afternoon at four or five o'clock.
17. American men wear bright ties and loud socks which usually do not match.

18. If intercollegiate sports were banned, they would each have to develop an elaborate intramural program.
19. Under Roosevelt's leadership, the Democratic party became united for a time, which had not happened for many years previously.
20. I don't think that a radio star has to work as hard as a movie star, but it is still a hard job.
21. A few people are very wealthy but show almost no outward signs of it.
22. Since the sun's rays are striking the side of the greenhouse as well as the roof, its maximum surface area is being warmed, which means that the maximum amount of sun heat is being received.
23. The Navajos believe that if they make images of their gods, they will come to their ceremonies.
24. When there is no harmony in the home, the child is the first to feel it.
25. I deduced the year in which the story was supposed to take place from a statement that one of the characters was born in 1904 and was at that time nineteen years old.

## 18 DANGLING MODIFIERS

A modifier is a "dangling modifier" when there is no word in the sentence for it to modify. In the sentence "Swimming out into the lake, the water felt cold," the writer took it for granted that the reader would assume that someone was swimming. Actually the only noun in the main clause is *water*, and the participial phrase cannot logically modify *water* — the water was not swimming. Hence this participial phrase is a dangling modifier. Dangling modifiers can be corrected in either of two ways:

(1) By supplying the noun or pronoun which the phrase logically describes:

> Swimming out into the lake, I felt the water grow colder.

(2) Or by changing the dangling construction to a complete clause:

> As I swam out into the lake, the water felt colder.

Introductory modifiers are apt to be connected, in the reader's mind, with the subject immediately following:

> Having come of age, I took my son into partnership with me.

Even though such modifiers are not strictly dangling (in this case, the participial phrase modifies *son*), they often produce ludicrous misreadings. They may usually be corrected by rearranging the sentence or by changing the participial phrase to a clause:

Having come of age, my son entered into partnership with me. [*Or*, When my son came of age, I took him into partnership.]

## 18a Dangling Participles, Gerunds, and Infinitives

**Dangling participial phrase.** Walking carefully across the trestle, a train suddenly appeared around the curve. [Who was walking across the trestle?]

**Improved.** Walking carefully across the trestle, I saw a train suddenly appear around the curve.

**Improved.** As I was walking carefully across the trestle, a train suddenly appeared around the curve.

**Dangling participial phrase.** Having followed directions carefully, my cake was a great success.

**Improved.** Since I had followed directions carefully, my cake was a great success.

**Dangling gerund phrase.** After explaining my errand to the guard, an automatic gate swung open to let me in. [Who explained the errand?]

**Improved.** After I had explained my errand to the guard, an automatic gate swung open to let me in.

**Dangling infinitive phrase.** In order to become a top entertainer, all types of audiences must be pleased.

**Improved.** In order to become a top entertainer, an actor must please all types of audiences.

## 18b Dangling Elliptical Clauses

Subject and main verb are sometimes omitted from a dependent clause (*while going* instead of *while I was going*, or *when a boy* instead of *when he was a boy*). If the subject of such an elliptical clause is not stated in the rest of the sentence, the construction may dangle.

**Dangling.** When six years old, my grandfather died.

**Improved.** When I was six years old, my grandfather died.

**Dangling.** Do not apply paint until thoroughly stirred.

**Improved.** Do not apply the paint until it has been thoroughly stirred.

## 18c Permissible Introductory Expressions

Some verbal phrases, like *generally speaking*, *taking all things into consideration*, *judging from past experience*, have become stock introductory expressions and need not be attached to any particular noun. Similarly, verbals expressing a generalized process, like *in swimming*, *in cooking*, are often used without being attached to a particular noun.

**Acceptable.** Generally speaking, women are more sensitive to color, and men are more sensitive to sound.

**Acceptable.** Taking all things into consideration, the decision was a fair one.

**Acceptable.** Judging from past experience, he is not to be trusted.

**Acceptable.** In swimming, the head should not be held too high.

**Acceptable.** In cooking, only the best ingredients should be used.

### EXERCISE

Correct any dangling constructions in the following sentences.

1. The next day the boys began to put on the roof, and except for occasionally inspecting and supervising the job, they finished with very little assistance from me.
2. In order to maintain a productive farm, it must have an adequate water supply.

3. After correcting all my original mistakes, the problem was finally solved.
4. Considering the condition of the roads, it is a wonder that we reached home that night.
5. The directions were clearly explained, and if followed correctly, my trouble could have been prevented.
6. Football games are very popular with the general public, resulting in a large profit for the college.
7. Upon opening the motor housing, I found that a loose wire was causing a short circuit.
8. A trip abroad requires a good deal of money on hand before starting.
9. In determining social standing in this country, education and occupation are two very important factors.
10. The ozonosphere is our chief protection against ultraviolet rays from the sun, which would seriously injure plants and animals if exposed to the sun's rays directly.
11. Having read Thackeray's *Henry Esmond*, my attitude toward the historical novel has changed completely.
12. Generally speaking, a beginner spoils fifteen or twenty sheets of metal the first day on the job.
13. While living with one parent, expensive gifts might encourage antagonism toward the child's other parent.
14. Although large, a jet engine is long, round, and narrow, making it ideal for use in an airplane.
15. Upon arriving in San Francisco, the steep streets running straight up the hills are the first thing to be noticed.
16. Not counting auditors, there are over a hundred students in the class.
17. Swift wishes the reader to become disgusted with man's vices by showing the resemblance between the vile Yahoos and the people of Europe.
18. When waiting for the dentist, even a favorite paper or magazine seems dull and trivial.

# 19 MISPLACED SENTENCE ELEMENTS

Normal sentence order in English is subject, verb, and complement, with modifiers either before or after the word modified. This permits considerable flexibility in the placing of subordinate sentence elements, but two cautions should be observed:

(*a*) place modifiers as close as possible to the words they modify, and

(*b*) do not needlessly split a grammatical construction by the insertion of another sentence element.

## 19a Misplaced Clauses and Phrases

Some dependent clauses and modifying phrases can be moved around to various positions in a sentence without affecting the meaning. For example, an introductory adverbial clause can sometimes be shifted from the beginning to the middle or the end of a sentence.

> *Whatever the natives may say*, I am convinced that the best fishing is at low tide.
>
> I am convinced, *whatever the natives may say*, that the best fishing is at low tide.
>
> I am convinced that the best fishing is at low tide, *whatever the natives may say*.

This freedom, however, has its dangers. Movable modifiers may be placed so as to produce ridiculous misreadings or real ambiguities. In revision, make sure that no movable modifier is placed so that it might mislead the reader.

**Misplaced modifier.** Like many artists of the period, Hogarth lost the opportunity to make large profits on his paintings through the work of imitators and plagiarists.

**Corrected.** Like many artists of the period, Hogarth lost, through the work of imitators and plagiarists, the opportunity to make large profits on his paintings.

**Misplaced modifier.** She wore a ribbon in her hair which was of a peculiar shade of green.

**Corrected.** In her hair she wore a ribbon of a peculiar shade of green.

Such difficulties are particularly likely to arise when two movable modifiers describe the same word. It may be desirable to revise a sentence completely.

**Misplaced modifier.** The cowboy returns to a warm meal around the campfire, which usually consists of meat from a fat calf and sourdough biscuits.

**Corrected.** The cowboy returns to the campfire and a warm meal, which usually consists of meat from a fat calf and sourdough biscuits.

**Corrected.** The cowboy returns to a warm meal around the campfire — usually meat from a fat calf and sourdough biscuits.

**Misplaced modifier.** His oldest hat was pulled low on his forehead, dingy and battered by years of exposure to the weather.

**Corrected.** His oldest hat, dingy and battered by years of exposure to the weather, was pulled low on his forehead.

## 19b Misplaced Adverbs

Theoretically, limiting adverbs like *only*, *almost*, *never*, *seldom*, *even*, *hardly*, *nearly* should be placed immediately before the words they modify.

**Correct.** We caught only two flounders, though we got dozens of mudcats.

**Correct.** We only caught the flounders; we didn't eat them.

By strict logic, "We only caught two flounders" would mean that we did nothing except catch those two fish. But general usage avoids such logic-chopping, and the construction with the adverb before the verb is found in all but very formal writing. "We only caught two flounders" sounds more natural than "We caught only two flounders," and either construction is acceptable unless it is awkward or genuinely ambiguous.

**Formal.** He introduced the subject only to start an argument.

**Informal.** He only introduced the subject to start an argument.

**Acceptable.** He seldom seems to be at home.

**Acceptable.** The gull hardly appeared to be alive.

**Awkward.** What would a foreigner think of us if he only got his impression of America from gangster movies?

**Improved.** What would a foreigner think of us if he got his impression of America only from gangster movies?

**Ambiguous.** I nearly ate the whole dozen.

**Improved.** I ate nearly the whole dozen.

## 19c Squinting Modifiers

Avoid placing a modifier in such a position that it may refer to either a preceding or a following word.

**Ambiguous.** The person who steals in nine cases out of ten is driven to do so by want.

**Improved.** In nine cases out of ten, the person who steals is driven to do so by want.

**Ambiguous.** Since a canoe cannot stand hard knocks when not in use it should be kept out of the water. [A comma after *knocks* would help to make the meaning clear, but it is better to revise the sentence.]

**Improved.** Since a canoe cannot stand hard knocks, it should be kept out of the water when not in use.

## 19d Awkward Split Constructions; Split Infinitives

Any needless splitting of a grammatical construction by the insertion of a modifier may give the reader an unpleasant jolt.

**Awkward.** Swift made the horses, animals that we consider of no use for anything but brute labor, portray an ideal society.

**Improved.** Swift portrays an ideal society by means of horses, animals that we consider good only for brute labor.

**Awkward.** I, more than the rest of my family, have been losing sleep since we got a television set.

**Improved.** More than the rest of my family, I have been losing sleep since we got a television set.

Split infinitives, that is, infinitives with a modifier between the *to* and the verb form (*to personally supervise*), may be awkward, especially if the modifier is long.

**Awkward.** I should like to, if I ever get the chance, take a trip to Mexico.

**Improved.** I should like to take a trip to Mexico, if I ever get the chance.

Frequently, however, an adverb fits most naturally between the two parts of an infinitive:

> Some young people regard children as an unpleasant responsibility, but as they grow older they begin to actually look forward to having a family.

This is acceptable. "Actually begin to look forward" would change the emphasis slightly. "Begin actually to look forward" is possible.

**Acceptable.** Advertisers urge us to always brush our teeth after meals.

**Acceptable.** We expect in the coming year to more than double our assets.

### EXERCISE

Revise the following sentences to correct the misplaced modifiers.

1. As well as being poorly dressed, like his brother, he was badly undernourished.
2. I put the book on the mantel which I had brought home from school.
3. Standing there placidly switching his tail and chewing grass, Henry still did not trust the bull.
4. Under the influence of narcotics I believe that his judgement was unreliable.
5. Miss Spencer only wanted us to read good books.
6. He wrote his book on gambling in England.
7. I had nothing but books to base my opinions on of Italy.
8. I have followed the advice given by this book faithfully.
9. At the end of the period we were told to immediately hand in our bluebooks.
10. It is important that we maintain friendly relations with such nations as our former mother country and present close ally, England.
11. We camped in a small cabin on the edge of a cliff which had been uninhabited for years.
12. The term *reactionary* is generally applied to political, social, economic (or a combination of the three) beliefs.

### REVIEW EXERCISE

In the following sentences correct the dangling constructions and misplaced modifiers.

1. After completing this last process, your plastic jewelry is ready for use.
2. When attending high school in the city, a hot dog and a bottle of pop often served in place of lunch.
3. Having carefully wiped my feet, the door was opened by a uniformed butler, and I entered a long hall.
4. After several hours of work, the shingles were in place and the roof completed.
5. The one perhaps flaw in our social system is that it is so materialistic.
6. Even though it costs a little more, it is advisable to choose colors for painting a house which will last.
7. After having controlled his desire for action for several months, it began to get the best of Ricardo.
8. I found a lump of fresh putty on the windowsill which had been left by the carpenters.
9. Flashing and fluttering in the wind, each lamp post was covered with tinsel.
10. Placing the tone arm carefully on the record, a loud squawk was all I heard.
11. Invaluable experience can be gained at school which will always be a source of satisfaction to the individual.
12. Having had an ulcer myself, the treatment just described is known to be effective.

# 20 UNNECESSARY SHIFTS

Structural consistency makes sentences easier to read. If the first clause of a sentence is in the active voice, do not shift to the passive voice in the second clause unless there is some reason for the change. Similarly, avoid needless shifts in tense, mode, or person within a sentence.

## 20a Shifts of Voice or Subject

Shifting from the active to the passive voice almost always involves a change in subject; thus an unnecessary shift of voice may make a sentence doubly awkward.

**Shift in subject and voice.** When I finally found the trouble in an unsoldered wire, the dismantling of the motor was begun at once.

**Improved.** When I finally found the trouble in an unsoldered wire, I began at once to dismantle the motor. [The sentence would be logically consistent if both verbs were in the passive voice: "When the trouble was found, the dismantling was begun." But the passive voice is needless and awkward here. See Section **41b.**]

**Shift in voice.** The pocket edition costs so little that it can be afforded by anyone who wants it.

**Improved.** The pocket edition costs so little that anyone who wants it can afford it.

**Shift of subject.** Radio amateurs stay on duty during emergencies, and messages to and from disaster areas are their particular job.

**Improved.** Radio amateurs stay on duty during emergencies and send messages to and from disaster areas.

## 20b Shifts of Tense

Do not change the tense unless there is reason to do so. (See Sequence of Tenses, Section **30b.**)

**Shift of tense.** The family was usually quarreling over money matters, and when this new problem arises, the family is broken up.

**Improved.** The family was usually quarreling over money matters, and when this new problem arose, the family was broken up.

**Shift of tense.** The tourist now decides to invest a few dollars in a poker game. He was sure four aces would show up in his hand, but they never did. In a short time he is poorer, but wiser.

**Improved.** The tourist now decides to invest a few dollars in a poker game. He is sure four aces will show up in his hand, but they never do. In a short time he is poorer, but wiser.

## 20c Shifts of Mode

If you begin a sentence with an order or command (imperative mode), do not shift without reason to a statement (indicative mode).

**Shift of mode.** First stir in the flour; then you should add the butter and salt. [The first clause is an order; the second is a statement giving advice.]

**Improved.** First stir in the flour; then add the butter and salt.

**Improved.** After you have stirred in the flour, you should add the butter and salt.

**Shift of mode.** On my ideal ranch, the chief crops would be corn, oats, alfalfa, and wheat, but I will have about ten acres bearing nothing but vegetables.

**Improved.** On my ideal ranch, the chief crops would be . . ., but I would have . . .

## 20d Shifts of Person

The commonest shift in student writing is from the third person (*he*, *she*, *they*, *one*) to the second person (*you*). This error usually occurs when the writer is thinking not of a particular individual but of anyone or everybody and is stating a general truth applicable to all.

**Needless shift.** A person should spend the morning hours on work requiring mental effort, for your mind is freshest in the morning.

**Correct.** *You* should spend the morning . . ., for *your* mind is . . .

**Correct.** *A student* should spend the morning . . ., for *his* mind is . . .

**Needless shift.** I could find only one fault with my new gun. When you fired it, gas would leak through the action.

**Correct.** I could find only one fault with my new gun. When I fired it, gas would leak through the action.

### EXERCISE

Correct shifts in voice, mode, tense, or person in the following sentences.

1. In the following months I would design the cabin, order materials, and rent a truck to bring the materials up to the lot. Now I am ready to begin the construction of the cabin.

2. Because the powder was packed so tightly that it will not explode, I felt safe in carrying it to the laboratory.
3. The chance for a foreman to be promoted used to have been good.
4. After I finished planting my garden, the seeds were watered daily.
5. In some of these contests a person may answer a simple question and expect to win a prize, but in order to get the prize you must sell subscriptions to the newspaper.
6. If you plan to build a new house, some thought should first be given to the typical activities and interests of your family.
7. My brother entered the contest and was lucky enough to win. You were judged on the performance of the model plane and on your skill in handling it.
8. The individual builds up an unconscious dislike, which is shown by him in his everyday actions.
9. For example, suppose a man was going about five miles over the speed limit and got a ticket from a policeman. From then on you will probably dislike policemen.
10. Don't ride the clutch; you should keep your left foot off the pedal.
11. My uncle always maintained that one could do anything if you tried hard enough.
12. I hate to think what would happen if the owner comes along.
13. The club members tried to keep girls out of the cave, but they always manage to get in somehow.
14. If one has little social standing in the community, you are not expected to live like the upper class.
15. Given a few decades of peace, economists would have time to experiment as best they can with a stable economy.

# 21 INCOMPLETE CONSTRUCTIONS

Sentence constructions are incomplete if words and expressions necessary for clarity are omitted.

## 21a Auxiliary Verbs

Do not omit auxiliary verbs that are necessary to complete a grammatical construction. When the two parts of a compound construction are in different tenses, it is usually necessary to write the auxiliary verbs in full.

**Incomplete.** Fishing has and always will be a very profitable industry in Alaska.

**Correct.** Fishing has been and always will be a very profitable industry in Alaska.

When there is no change in tense, it is permissible to omit part of a compound verb, instead of repeating the compound construction in full.

**Correct.** Tickets will be sent to all students who have signed up for the trip and [who have] paid the fee.

## 21b Idiomatic Prepositions

English idiom requires that certain prepositions be used with certain adjectives: we say, for example, "interested *in*," "aware *of*," "devoted *to*." Be sure to include in compound constructions all necessary idiomatic prepositions.

**Incomplete.** No one could have been more interested or devoted to her students than Mrs. Allen.

**Correct.** No one could have been more interested in or devoted to her students than Mrs. Allen.

## 21c Comparisons: *As* and *Than; One of the . . . if not the . . .*

In comparisons do not omit words necessary to make a complete idiomatic statement. We say "as tall *as*," but "taller *than*," and if these constructions are combined, both words must be included.

**Incomplete.** He is as tall, if not taller than his brother. [As it stands, this sentence says that he is "as tall . . . than his brother."]

**Complete, but awkward.** He is as tall as, if not taller than, his brother.

**Improved.** He is as tall as his brother, if not taller.

**Incomplete.** Leonardo had one of the greatest, if not the greatest, minds of all time. [Two idioms: "one of the greatest *minds*" and "the greatest *mind*."]

**Correct.** Leonardo had one of the greatest minds, if not the greatest mind, of all time.

## 21d Incomplete Comparisons

Comparisons should be logical and unambiguous.

**Illogical.** Her salary was lower than a typist. [Is a typist low?]

**Improved.** Her salary was lower than that of a typist. [*Or* . . . than a typist's.]

**Illogical.** The life of a peasant was sometimes happier than a prince.

**Improved.** The life of a peasant was sometimes happier than that of a prince.

**Illogical.** The John Hancock Building is taller than any building in Boston. ["Any building in Boston" includes the John Hancock Building.]

**Improved.** The John Hancock Building is taller than any other building in Boston.

**Illogical.** She is as good a singer as any girl in the Glee Club.

**Improved.** She is as good a singer as any other girl in the Glee Club.

Avoid comparisons which are ambiguous or vague because they are incomplete. A comparison is ambiguous if it is hard to tell what is being compared with what. It is vague if the standard of comparison is not indicated.

**Ambiguous comparison.** Lawrenceville is farther from Albany than Gibbstown.

**Clear.** Lawrenceville is farther from Albany than Gibbstown is.

**Clear.** Lawrenceville is farther from Albany than from Gibbstown.

**Vague comparison.** Manufacturers have come to see that electric power is more economical. [Than what?]

**More definite.** Manufacturers have come to see that electric power is more economical than steam power.

If it is clearly indicated by the context, the standard of comparison need not be specified.

**Acceptable.** Boulder Dam is big, but Grand Coulee Dam is bigger.

Note that the words *so*, *such*, and *too* when used as comparatives are completed by a clause or phrase indicating the standard of comparison.

**Correct.** I'm so tired that I could drop. I had such a small breakfast that I was starving by ten o'clock, and when we stopped for lunch, I was too tired to eat.

### EXERCISE

Fill out any incomplete constructions in the following sentences.

1. Swift shows that man is capable of, and probably has, altered the traditional aims of the Christian religion.
2. I derived much knowledge and had much respect for my high school history teacher.
3. I thought *My Fair Lady* was as good, if not better than *South Pacific*.
4. Trying to analyze my good points and weaknesses made me a happier and secure person.
5. The distributor has been cleaned, and the points adjusted.
6. This bank never has and never will contribute money to any political party.
7. The curriculum of a coeducational college is usually more attractive to men than women.
8. Paris is one of the most beautiful, if not the most beautiful city in the world.
9. The Parkers invited me to go swimming, but I was too tired.
10. Already in college I have had access and understanding of a great deal of new information.
11. Van Gogh's style has been ranked with the greatest painters.
12. The flowers grown in Hawaii can be matched by no other area in the world.
13. Foreigners have a more contemptuous attitude toward American women than American men.
14. I believe the Japanese people are basically as inventive as the United States or any other nation.

15. The houses, clothes, and furniture of aristocrats a hundred years ago were almost as comfortable as the middle class of today.
16. Our class president had a more successful term of office than any president in the history of the school.
17. The new detergents cost less and wash clothes cleaner.
18. My pride in the boat I made myself is greater than those who sail manufactured boats.
19. The father and mother work so hard, and the children are so irresponsible.
20. Every day more prospective buyers came to look at the house, but none of them were too interested in our proposal.

## 22 MIXED CONSTRUCTIONS

Do not begin a sentence with one construction and shift to another to conclude the sentence. English is full of alternate constructions, and it is fairly easy to confuse them in a first draft and produce a monster with the head of one sentence and the tail of another. For example, here are two ways of saying the same thing — two different constructions, not just different words.

1. Fishing in Alaska is superior to that of any other region in North America.
2. Alaska is superior to any other region in North America for lake and stream fishing.

The first sentence compares fishing in two regions; the second compares two regions in regard to fishing. Either sentence is correct, but the combination of the first half of one with the second half of the other produces confusion:

**Mixed construction.** Fishing in Alaska is superior to that of any other region in North America for lake and stream fishing.

The following example is more complicated:

**Mixed construction.** Often it wouldn't be until late in the evening before my father got home.

**Correct.** Often it would be late in the evening before my father got home.

**Correct.** Often my father wouldn't get home until late in the evening.

Many mixed constructions involve comparisons. For example:

**Mixed construction.** The backyard mechanic will find plastic much easier to work with than with metal.

Either of the two constructions here mixed is correct:

**Correct.** The backyard mechanic will find plastic easier to work with than metal.

**Correct.** The backyard mechanic will find it much easier to work with plastic than with metal.

Using a modifying phrase or clause as subject or complement of a verb often produces a badly mixed construction:

**Mixed.** Without a top gave the Model A Ford a very odd look.

**Correct.** Without a top, the Model A Ford looked very odd.

**Mixed construction.** One thing I know will keep me from enlisting, and that is when I think of kitchen police.

What is the thing that will keep the writer from enlisting? Not "when I think of kitchen police." That clause is a modifier, not a thing. What is needed to round out the sentence is some kind of substantive.

**Correct.** One thing I know will keep me from enlisting — the thought of kitchen police.

**Mixed construction.** The good performance of American teams at the Olympic games is because the Americans have such a large number of athletes to choose from.

**Corrected.** American teams perform well at the Olympic games because the Americans have such a large number of athletes to choose from.

**Acceptable informal English.** The reason American teams perform so well at the Olympics is because the Americans have such a large number of athletes to choose from.

Technically, this last sentence is wrong, since it uses an adverbial clause, "because . . . from," as the complement of *is*. A similar construction, "An accident is when the causes of an event are not known," would be felt to be awkward by most readers.

**Improved.** An accident is defined as an event of which the causes are not known.

But usage has established the "reason . . . is because . . ." construction as acceptable in all but formal English.

### EXERCISE

Eliminate the mixed constructions in the following sentences.

1. With large numbers in a class it also makes it impossible for the teacher and student to discuss problems.
2. To children, the thrill of being shipwrecked on an unknown island like Lilliput appeals to their love of adventure.
3. I was really getting beaten up; every hold I tried, my opponent would counter it.
4. As long as man is a sinner, that is how long a government with authority and power will be needed.
5. Even though these ancient customs have been preserved through the years does not mean that Hawaii is backward in her outlook.
6. It was only when he compared the English nobility to the societies on the continent did he realize how good the English system was.
7. Emerson points out that just because a person reads books or is a librarian is no sign that he is wiser than the rest of mankind.
8. For college students, I feel that the teaching assistants who read papers for the professors are really advantageous to the students.

9. Sanding was a long job, but when this was finished, which took me three hours, made me very proud of myself.
10. In the container is where the experiment takes place.
11. For the more we spend our leisure time looking at television, we have little opportunity to read books.
12. It was only when I heard the whistle give three sharp toots, I remembered the lifeguard's warning.
13. As the volume of sound increases in the earphones, the nearer the submarine is approaching.
14. It would be hard to say what the outlook on life a person with this disease would have.
15. What safer way can one learn about these vices than by reading books on the subject?
16. Nicotine is habit-forming, and like most other drugs, when taken continuously, they affect the human body.
17. From the shelves of the market to the ultimate appearance of the dish on the restaurant table requires much skill on the part of the chef.
18. In my former high school, which is considered one of the best in the state, it seems to me that it was much too easy.
19. Of course, once he chooses a special trade to specialize in during his Army career doesn't mean that it is too late to change his specialty.
20. In order to qualify for relief, it requires a birth certificate.

## REVIEW EXERCISE

Some of the following sentences contain dangling constructions, misplaced modifiers, unnecessary shifts, incomplete constructions, and illogical comparisons. Revise those that need revision.

1. Readers of the sport page only know the names of the colleges which are famous for athletics.
2. In this small community there are so many people who have done such interesting things.

3. As more of the students learn to set up their own experiments, the less time is required of the teacher.
4. Unlike the rest of the United States, Hollywood is a city of extremes; you are either rich or poor, beautiful or ugly, famous or unknown.
5. Eight enormous pillars, said to be copied from a Roman temple, form the portico of Arlington House, the former home of General Robert E. Lee.
6. Just because our diplomacy is stalemated is no reason to risk a world war.
7. I find that removing the engine is a relatively simple job providing you have a chain hoist and a little patience.
8. The new dress uniform of the Army is darker than the Marines.
9. The best moccasins are handmade, and if possible have an Indian make them for you.
10. Generally speaking, colors used for painting houses have become brighter and more varied compared with those in common use thirty years ago.
11. Inspectors were checking brand marks, to see if any cattle had been stolen that were going to be slaughtered.
12. I like my British skirt better than any of my clothes.
13. A good player always uses the best clubs he can afford, because the importance of good equipment is well known to him.
14. The friendliness of the Spanish people and the low cost of living in Spain are factors to consider when planning a long vacation abroad.
15. Beethoven often demonstrated his fondness and skill in improvising variations on a theme.
16. The Lilliputians are much more like the human race than the giants.
17. Mr. Strachey has pointed out that Victoria's greatness was due to contact and reflection of the great minds of her time.

# 23 WEAK AND UNEMPHATIC SENTENCES

Even though a sentence is technically correct, with its elements properly subordinated to throw the stress on the most important ideas, it may still lack force and impact. Weak sentences are usually caused either by shaky structure — as when the end of a sentence dwindles away in a feeble string of unimportant details or subordinate constructions — or by dilution with needless words and repetitions.

## 23a Trailing Constructions

A sentence should not trail away in a tangle of dependent clauses and subordinate elements. The end of a sentence is an emphatic position. Put some important idea there. It is not necessary that all your sentences should be "periodic" — that is, arranged so that the meaning is suspended until the very end of the sentence. Periodic sentences may sound contrived and formal:

> It was Swift's intention that mankind, despite its ability to deceive itself, should be forced to look steadily and without self-excuse at the inherent evil of human nature.

Although such sentences are compact and forceful, too many of them make one's writing sound "literary" and stilted.

On the other hand, there is no excuse for the weak, flabby structure of the following sentence:

> A trip abroad would give me a knowledge of foreign lands, thus making me a better citizen than when I left, because I could better understand our foreign policy.

The participial construction "thus making me a better citizen" is particularly weak. Not only is it technically "dangling" (see Section **18**), but it sounds tacked on, as though it were an afterthought. Actually, it contains one of the most important ideas of the sentence. The structure of this sentence can be strengthened by trimming and rearrangement:

> The knowledge gained on a trip abroad would help me to understand our foreign policy and thus make me a better citizen.

**Trailing construction.** Harper lacked the qualities of decisiveness and assurance which are essential to any man who hopes to be a success in a position of authority, with the result that he was a failure as an executive.

**Improved.** Since he lacked the qualities of decisiveness and assurance which are essential for success in a position of authority, Harper was a failure as an executive.

**Trailing construction.** It is in this scene that Lear finally realizes that he has been deceived by the promises that his elder daughters have made.

**Improved.** In this scene Lear finally realizes that he has been deceived by the promises of his elder daughters.

**Trailing construction.** In a totalitarian society, conformity is enforced on the individual by keeping him in constant fear that he might do something illegal for which he would be punished by the state.

**Improved.** In a totalitarian society, constant fear of punishment for illegal acts is used to enforce conformity on the individual.

## 23b Avoiding Anticlimax

When a sentence ends in a series of words varying in strength, they should be placed in climactic order, the strongest last, unless the writer intends to make an anticlimax for humorous effect.

**Anticlimactic.** The new sales manager proved himself to be mercilessly cruel in discharging incompetents, stubborn, and impolite.

**Improved.** The new sales manager proved himself to be impolite, stubborn, and mercilessly cruel in discharging incompetents.

Catchall expressions like *and others, etc., and the like* suggest that the writer has run out of examples, or is too lazy to specify them. Do not use such phrases unless there is good reason for them.

**Weak.** Many towns in the state have names borrowed from Spanish, Italian, etc., and a few in the mountains have Indian names, such as Siskiyou, Klamath, and others.

**Improved.** Many towns in the state have names borrowed from Spanish or Italian, and a few in the mountains have Indian names, such as Siskiyou and Klamath.

Sentences ending with prepositions are by no means incorrect. A sentence with a preposition at the end is often more emphatic, and more natural, than the stilted sentence with the preposition buried within it.

**Stilted.** This is a picture of the girl with whom I am in love.

**Improved.** This is a picture of the girl I am in love with.

### EXERCISE

Revise the following sentences to make them more forceful.

1. The Industrial Revolution has progressed during the last two centuries, changing the life of everyone in the Western world.
2. The meadow was surrounded by tall blossoming trees which gave off a sweet fragrance which lent an atmosphere to the grove which seemed to make it an ideal place to hold a concert.
3. The customs of different civilizations throughout the world are not alike, varying considerably in religious observances and marriage practices, especially.
4. There have been increasing evidences of student vandalism, such as the near-flood last Sunday morning in the East Wing of the Auditorium caused by the water of a fire hose which someone had unrolled, turned on, and then left.
5. In grade school hardly a week passed without my being beaten up by the big boys, scolded by the teacher, teased by the girls, etc.
6. Although Dr. Wells was supposed to be a good teacher, little encouragement was given to aspiring scientists by him, I found.
7. There are two holidays which I specially dislike, which are Labor Day and Christmas.
8. A scientific fact is one in which the conditions by which the fact was discovered can be duplicated by someone else, achieving the same result.
9. A capable wife does more to improve the human race by being such than she could in almost any other way.
10. A student will not get high grades in college unless he has a reasonable proficiency in writing, which is necessary if he is to express his ideas clearly and forcefully.

# 24 WORDY SENTENCES

Unnecessary words and repetitions dilute the strength of a piece of writing and make sentences as flat and watery as weak coffee. Be as concise as clarity and fullness of statement permit. Note that conciseness is not the same as brevity. A brief statement does not give detail; for example, "I failed." A concise statement may give a good deal of detail so long as it does not waste words: "Last month I sold only 60 per cent of the quota set by the company." Being brief is not always a virtue; there are times when a fairly detailed statement is required. But it is always good to be concise. In revision, check your sentences for unnecessary words. Look with suspicion on such circumlocutions as "along the lines of," "of the nature of," "it was during . . . that." Avoid redundant expressions: "repeat that again," "in this modern world of today," "pink in color," "this country of ours," "nine A.M. in the morning," "large in size."

**Wordy and repetitious.** If I should be required to serve a term with the armed forces, I would prefer to enter the Air Force, because I think I would like it better than any other branch of the service, as I have always had a strong interest in and liking for airplanes.

**Improved.** If I have to enter the armed forces, I would prefer the Air Force, as I have always liked airplanes.

**Wordy.** An announcement was made by the manager to the effect that beginning on the first of July breakfast at the Lodge would be available for guests of the hotel only between the hours of seven and ten in the morning.

**Improved.** The manager announced that after June 30 breakfast at the Lodge would be served only between 7 and 10 A.M.

**Wordy.** I am happy to state that I shall be glad to accede to your request.

**Improved.** Yes.

### EXERCISE

Revise the following sentences to make them more concise.

1. It is my opinion that it is most desirable that a candidate for President should have had the opportunity of becoming acquainted at first hand with the problems that an administrator must deal with.
2. Recently I read an excellent book, *Madame Curie*, which was interesting and highly enjoyable throughout the entire book.
3. Perhaps what I have previously said might give a reader the impression that I do not place a very high value on the acquiring of a college education, but this is not true; I consider that in this modern world of today a college education is an absolutely indispensable attribute of a successful career.
4. One of the most important things that intercollegiate sports offer is that they bring fame and national recognition to a college.
5. If my father had been so unfortunate as to lack the gift of understanding the importance of being able to see the comedy in the minor mishaps of life, he would not be the wonderful personal counselor that I have always found him to be.
6. As to the overall effect on people who have television sets, I don't think the effect is good because people will sit and watch television and forget everything that ought to be done along the lines of schoolwork and housework.

## REVIEW EXERCISE

Make the following sentences more forceful by proper subordination and the elimination of trailing constructions, awkward constructions, and unnecessary words.

1. The science of government attempts to regard political events with an unbiased attitude, attempting also to find and apply valid general principles.
2. In any society there are always some people who cannot seem to progress in the way others, including most of the population, do.
3. Parts of Asia and Europe have already become communistic, but the people do not know what communism is.
4. A rough wooden cross marks the place at which the Mission was originally located.
5. Even though nothing prevents student activities from being equally shared by the men and women, they usually are not, the men running most of the campus activities.
6. The style of painting Van Gogh has was borrowed from Cézanne.
7. In assessing the local political trends, the fact that Roberts won over Mrs. Elwood cannot be left out of account.
8. The use of airplanes was vital in the construction of the road, making it possible to choose the best route.
9. A long period of time to the average person is usually just about the length of time that he has lived; but to a historian, his own lifetime would seem rather insignificant.
10. She is certainly not worried about financial matters, for she puts on an act at the Flamingo Club, bringing her in $500 a week.
11. The common cold is a communicable disease which can be transferred from one person to another.
12. Many times I would come home and ask for help on my schoolwork, when the reply would be, "I'm sorry but I'm memorizing a speech for my luncheon group."

# 25 VAGUE SENTENCES

If your sentences are to be clear, you must express your meaning fully, in exact and definite language. In the heat of composition it is easy to omit essential steps in your line of thought, and it is almost certain that a first draft will contain inexact words and vague phrases. Revision of a first draft is essential to fill up gaps in thought, to sharpen the phrasing, and to make your statements definite and specific.

## 25a Gaps in Thought

Try to put yourself in the place of the reader and try to see your first draft through his eyes. Would it be clear to someone who has no previous knowledge of what you are trying to say? Lack of clarity is often caused by "short circuits": the writer, who knows what he is trying to say, jumps ahead and omits necessary steps in his train of thought.

**Not clear.** Maturing faster because of parents' divorcing does not hold true in all cases. The child may be rendered timid and insecure.

**Gaps filled in.** When his parents are divorced, the shock may hasten the maturation of the child. But this does not always happen; divorce may also retard maturation and make the child timid and insecure.

**Not clear.** Senator Robinson could buy only ten hours of TV time, which illustrates the importance of publicity in political campaigns.

**Gaps filled in.** Senator Robinson was not able to buy as much TV time as his opponent, and Robinson's consequent defeat illustrates the importance of TV publicity in political campaigns.

**Not clear.** Because I wanted to play in the orchestra, I stopped practicing the clarinet. On that day my career as an oboe player began.

**Gaps filled in.** I wanted to play in the orchestra, but there were already too many clarinetists. Accordingly, I gave up the clarinet and began practicing the oboe.

### EXERCISE

Rewrite the following sentences, filling in the gaps in thought.

1. The head nurse is supposed to answer most of the questions asked by parents; if not, there are many books on child care in the office of the nursery.
2. A man may think that when he gets married both members of the marriage will never be employed at the same time, which case may become very necessary.
3. Such legislation as legalized gambling would have to be passed upon and approved by many organizations.
4. The most common difference in social standing is a person's wealth.
5. Another situation that might arise is the hate of the opposite sex by one of the parents being instilled in the child.

## 25b Inexact Statement

In speech you can repeat a statement in different ways if you doubt that you have been understood. In writing you have just one chance to make yourself clear. A reader will expect that you have phrased your sentences carefully and that you mean what you have written. If what you have written, literally interpreted, is nonsense, the reader may assume that what you are saying is nonsense.

**Inexact phrasing.** Luxurious living results in expensive bills at the end of the month. [The bills are not expensive; the bills are high. It is luxurious living that is expensive.]

**Improved.** Luxurious living brings high bills at the end of the month. [*Or*, Luxurious living is expensive.]

But, the author of this sentence might protest, "Anyone would know what I meant." Possibly, but this is not good enough. A writer should *say* what he means, not blunder round and round a meaning, relying on the reader's intelligence and good will to make sense of his muddy phrasing. Not all readers have intelligence; not all have good will. Protect yourself by choosing your words with care.

**Inexact statement.** From my home are five high schools which can be reached in a five-minute driving radius. [You can reach a high school in an automobile or a bus, but not in a radius.]

**More exact.** Five high schools lie within a five-minute driving radius of my home.

Some sentences are inexact because the writer has failed to limit a general statement.

**Inexact statement.** Since man is able to think and reason, many questions arise in his mind. In order to be at peace with himself, he must find answers to them. These answers are the basis of religion.

What are some of the many questions that arise in the mind of man? A fairly common one is "What are we having for dinner?" The answer may be steak or corned beef and cabbage, but neither has anything to do with religion. What the writer meant can be made clear by limiting the first sentence:

**Improved.** Since man is able to think and reason, many questions regarding man's destiny and place in the universe arise in his mind. . . .

**Exaggerated statement.** Prince Albert's untiring labors over the details of government won him the respect of even his former opponents, and gradually, almost without notice, he became King of England. [This sentence is simply not true; Prince Albert, though he had great influence on his wife, Queen Victoria, never became King.]

**Improved.** . . . became the virtual ruler of England. *Or* . . . became, for all practical purposes if not in fact, the King of England.]

The time to make such improvements in phrasing is in revision. In a first draft, stopping to find the right word may make you lose the thread of what you are saying, and it is usually better to go ahead and get your ideas down even in approximate form. But before you make a final copy, check to see that you have said exactly what you intend to say.

### EXERCISE

Rewrite the following sentences to make them clear and exact.

1. He promised to revise taxes so that the poor man would fare better, and not the rich man, as his opponent's bill had done.
2. Television also presents an alarming cultural threat in the communication of ideas; too often, content is not emphasized.
3. This course, which concerns itself with the literature written in Latin America until the end of the nineteenth century, is translated into English.
4. The most important step in knitting the sweater is strong eyesight.

5. Plenty of evidence is available in connection with the potential self-sufficiency of Israel.
6. The interests of the average college girl are not concerned with preparing herself to defend her country after graduation.
7. I think the two most important things of foreign aid are food and education.
8. The basement was flooded with water and ruined the books stored there.
9. Danny Kaye has perfected this comic device so that no one can touch him.
10. Of these twelve names, three were chosen to appear before the City Council and present our plan.
11. It is incredible what may be accomplished in the way of military aircraft during the next fifty years.
12. I feel that the classics deserve more of a position of importance than they are presently receiving in education.
13. There are few women who are capable of learning the very strict training demanded by a good medical school.
14. Except for amateur sports, large numbers of people would spend their leisure time becoming fat and lazy.
15. Almost everything that a Zuñi does is governed by ritual, and no Zuñi ever thinks of breaking the ritualistic process of everyday life just to better his own end.

# Grammatical Usage

**26.** AGREEMENT OF SUBJECT AND VERB

**27.** AGREEMENT OF PRONOUN AND ANTECEDENT

**28.** CASE

**29.** ADJECTIVES AND ADVERBS

**30.** TENSE AND MODE OF VERBS

# 26 AGREEMENT OF SUBJECT AND VERB

The general rule is that a singular subject requires the singular form of the verb, and a plural subject requires the plural form of the verb. Violations of this rule occur when the writer does not know which word is the subject, or when the writer is not sure whether the subject is singular or plural.

## 26a Obscured Subject

When there are modifying phrases between the simple subject and the verb, or when the sentence is inverted so that the subject comes after the verb instead of before it, mistakes in agreement are particularly easy to make. Be sure you have correctly identified the simple subject, and make the verb agree with it.

**Wrong.** The assistance of three lawyers, one economic expert, and two advertising men were necessary. [The simple subject is *assistance*, and the verb must be singular to agree with it.]

**Correct.** The *assistance* of three lawyers, one economic expert, and two advertising men *was* necessary.

**Wrong.** A list of the semester's reading assignments have been posted on the bulletin board.

**Correct.** A *list* of the semester's reading assignments *has* been posted on the bulletin board.

**Wrong.** Around us in every direction was miles of empty desert.

[Even though the sentence has been inverted, the simple subject is *miles*.]

**Correct.** Around us in every direction *were miles* of empty desert.

**Correct.** Above a cluster of low buildings *rises* the *dome* of St. Paul's. [*Dome* is the simple subject; it *rises*.]

Modifying phrases which suggest a plural idea do not change the number of the simple subject.

**Wrong.** The chancellor, as well as the provost and the deans, were in full academic regalia.

**Correct.** The *chancellor*, as well as the provost and the deans, *was* in full academic regalia.

**Wrong.** Five members of the class, including John, was going to camp for the summer.

**Correct.** Five *members* of the class, including John, *were* going to camp for the summer.

Distinguish carefully between the subject and a predicate noun, which completes the verb *to be*. The verb agrees with the subject.

**Wrong.** Randall's chief interest in life were airplanes.

**Correct.** Randall's chief *interest* in life *was* airplanes.

**Correct.** *Airplanes were* Randall's chief interest in life.

The word *there* is often used to introduce an idiomatic construction: "There is no reason to worry." In such a sentence, the subject follows the verb.

**Correct.** There *were* two *newspapers* in town, but there *was* only one editorial *policy*.

**Correct.** In this office there *are* four *secretaries*.

**Wrong.** In the office there is a desk, a chair, and a filing cabinet.

**Correct.** In the office there *are* a *desk*, a *chair*, and a filing *cabinet*.

## 26b Compound Subjects

Two or more subjects of the same verb are usually considered plural if they are joined by *and*.

**Correct.** Mathematics and science are my best subjects.

**Correct.** To plan, to direct, and to execute company policy are the functions of the president.

Note, however, that a compound subject which really designates only one person or thing takes a singular verb, and that a compound subject designating closely related ideas may take a singular verb.

**Correct.** Here lies a lawyer and an honest man. [One person is designated in this epitaph.]

**Correct.** Bread and butter is commonly served with tea in England.

**Correct.** His drive and energy were contagious.

**Acceptable.** His drive and energy was contagious.

Compound subjects joined by *or* or *nor* usually take a singular verb. In informal English, a plural verb is sometimes used when a *neither . . . nor . . .* construction expresses a plural idea.

**Correct.** Either the *Times* or the *Herald Tribune* is a reliable source of news.

**Correct.** Neither the plaintiff nor the defendant was satisfied with the decision.

**Acceptable.** Neither the union nor the company seem to be seriously interested in settling the strike.

When one subject is singular and one is plural, the verb agrees with the subject nearest it.

**Correct.** Neither John nor his brothers like golf.

Compound subjects modified by *each* or *every* are regarded as singular.

**Correct.** Every (each) soldier and sailor *was* given a complete examination.

## 26c Indefinite Pronouns

The indefinite pronouns *each*, *either*, *someone*, *somebody*, *anyone*, *anybody*, *everyone*, *everybody* are regularly followed by a singular verb. *None* and *neither* may be either singular or plural, depending on the context and the meaning intended.

**Correct.** *Each* of the suspects *was* questioned by the police.

**Correct.** *Either* of the men *is* qualified for the position.

**Correct.** *Anyone is* welcome to try.

**Correct.** *Everybody* in the room *was* given a present.

**Correct.** *None* of this money *is* to be spent for clothes.

**Correct.** *None are* so deaf as those who will not hear.

**Correct.** *Neither* of the men *has* indicated his preference.

**Correct.** *Neither* of the girls *were* ready when we arrived.

## 26d Collective Nouns

Nouns which refer to a group of people — *class*, *committee*, *team*, *board of trustees*, etc. — take a singular verb when the group is thought of as a unit, and a plural verb when the individuals are thought of separately. The same rule applies to nouns indicating number or a portion.

**Correct.** The *committee was* unanimous in its recommendation.

**Correct.** The *class were* unable to agree on a day for the party. [Many writers would feel this sentence to be awkward, even though correct, and would rephrase it: The members of the class were unable . . .]

**Correct.** A *number* of pages in his notebook *are* illegible.

**Correct.** A large *number* of signatures *is* assured.

**Correct.** Nearly half the *class was* determined to put off the examination, but a *majority* of the students *were* ready to take it at once.

## 26e Relative Pronouns

The relative pronouns — *who, which,* and *that* — take singular or plural verbs depending on whether their antecedents are singular or plural. Be sure you have identified the antecedent correctly.

**Correct.** Bryan is the kind of man who always thinks before he acts. [The antecedent of *who* is *man.*]

**Correct.** Bryan is one of those men who always think before they act. [The antecedent of *who* is *men.*]

**Correct.** Jim Weed is one of the brightest *students who have* graduated from this college.

**Correct.** This is the only *one* of the typewriters *that is* working. [The antecedent of *that* is *one.*]

**Correct.** This is the best of the *typewriters that are* in working order. [The antecedent of *that* is *typewriters.*]

## 26f Singular Nouns with Plural Forms

Some abstract nouns which are plural in form are grammatically singular — e.g., *news, mathematics, physics, acoustics,* etc. But note that certain concrete nouns ending in *s* have no singular form and are always plural: *trousers, scissors, measles, forceps.* Some nouns ending in *ics* (*athletics, politics, statistics*) may be either singular or plural, sometimes with a distinction in meaning.

**Correct.** Intercollegiate athletics are taken seriously in the South.

**Correct.** Athletics is one way of improving muscular coordination.

**Correct.** Politics makes strange bedfellows.

**Correct.** Politics are his chief interest.

**Correct.** Statistics is my most difficult course.

**Correct.** Statistics show that . . .

Words like *data* and *strata* are Latin plurals, but there is a strong tendency in current English to treat them as collective nouns, which may be either singular or plural.

**Correct.** We next classify all the data that have been collected.

**Acceptable.** This data has been assembled by the secretary.

### EXERCISE

Give reasons for using the singular or the plural verb form in the following sentences.

1. There are seven men on a team, and every one of the seven (is *or* are) important.
2. The close relationship with deans, professors, and fellow students (makes *or* make) the small college the choice of many people.
3. He is one of the few who (is *or* are) free from false aspirations and sentimentality.
4. Either rainfall or irrigation (supplies *or* supply) most of the water used for farming.
5. Here is a message of importance to every man and woman who (votes *or* vote).
6. The flour and ground rice (is *or* are) thoroughly mixed to form the dough.
7. The experience of sports stars and movie and TV stars (is *or* are) similar when they are handling publicity.
8. She is one of those fussy housekeepers who (makes *or* make) everyone uncomfortable.
9. There (has *or* have) never been hard feeling between the families living on this block.

10. Next in the waiting line (was *or* were) an old lady and her son.
11. There is always a possibility that the infection will return, but so far there (has *or* have) been no signs of trouble.
12. The letters I receive from my friends and relatives in America (makes *or* make) me think that it is a wonderful place to live.
13. The symptoms of lead poisoning (varies *or* vary) with each individual case.
14. The Rose Festival is an event which every resident as well as the tourists thoroughly (enjoys *or* enjoy).
15. The main building and the gymnasium of Lowell High School (is *or* are) located in one city block.
16. In some countries such penal measures as beating, whipping, and solitary confinement (is *or* are) still prevalent.
17. Evidences of a distrust of nonconformity (is *or* are) no longer so obvious in the rural areas.
18. Such governmental services as public health, public housing, and social security (has *or* have) increased many times in recent years.

# 27 AGREEMENT OF PRONOUN AND ANTECEDENT

Pronouns should agree in number with their antecedents — that is, the nouns they refer to. In general, the rules are the same as for agreement of subject and verb: *a boy* is referred to as *he* or *him; two boys* is referred to as *they* or *them.*

## 27a Collective Nouns as Antecedents

Collective nouns may be considered either singular or plural, depending on the meaning intended. But if the verb shows the antecedent to be singular, consistency requires that the pronoun referring to it also be singular.

**Correct.** The *crowd* showed *its* approval by clapping.

**Correct.** The *family* could never agree about *their* shares of the property.

**Inconsistent.** The jury is about to return and give their verdict.

**Correct.** The *jury is* about to return and give *its* verdict.

When a demonstrative pronoun (*this, that*) is used as an adjective, it should agree in number with the noun it modifies.

**Wrong.** These kind of flowers should be planted in the shade.

**Correct.** This kind of flower should be planted in the shade.

**Correct.** These kinds of flowers should be planted in the shade.

## 27b Compound Antecedents

When two or more antecedents are connected by *and*, the pronoun referring to them is plural.

**Correct.** The *boy* and his *father* started on *their* vacation last Monday.

When two or more singular antecedents are connected by *or* or *nor*, the pronoun referring to them is singular.

**Correct.** Neither *Charles II* nor *James II* succeeded in having *his* own way in religious affairs.

When one of the antecedents connected by *or* or *nor* is singular and the other plural, the pronoun agrees with the nearer.

**Correct.** Either the *members* of the legislature or the *governor* will have to give up some of *his* demands.

**Correct.** Neither *Mary* nor the *boys* had finished *their* jobs.

The masculine pronoun *he* may be used to refer to both men and women in place of the awkward *his or her*.

**Awkward.** Every man or woman must make his or her own decision.

**Correct.** Every man or woman must make his own decision.

**Correct.** Each boy or girl is asked to bring his own bedding.

**Correct.** Boys and girls should bring their own bedding.

## 27c Indefinite Pronoun as Antecedent

A singular pronoun is preferred with the following antecedents: *each*, *either*, *neither*, *someone*, *somebody*, *anyone*, *anybody*, *everyone*, *everybody*, *no one*, *nobody*.

**Correct.** Everyone was on his best behavior.

**Correct.** Each of us is willing to do his share.

**Correct.** Neither of the candidates wanted to state his views on the tax bill.

In speech and in informal writing the plural pronoun *they* is often used when there is a distinct plural implication or when the singular pronoun produces an awkward or stilted effect.

**Correct but stilted.** Everybody there agreed and declared he thought it an excellent plan.

**Acceptable.** Everybody there agreed and declared they thought it an excellent plan.

The word *person*, although singular, is often used to mean "anybody" or "everybody." Be sure that any pronoun used with this antecedent is singular.

**Wrong.** I have always maintained that a person should mind their own business.

**Correct.** I have always maintained that a person should mind his own business.

### EXERCISE

Give reasons for using the singular or plural form of the pronoun in the following sentences.

1. Maybe some day each person will have (his *or* their) own helicopter for commuting to the city.
2. After basic training almost everyone is sent to different training schools, according to (his *or* their) ability.
3. The committee was unable to agree on a policy, and so (it *or* they) decided to meet again next week.
4. The average student likes to dream of the time when (he *or* they) can go to Paris or Rome.
5. Either the janitor or the plumber must have eaten (his *or* their) lunch here.

6. One of the main parts of a military aircraft is (its *or* their) armament.
7. He is suspicious of any new enterprise because he doubts that (it *or* they) will be of any help to our economy.
8. Mary's graduation was a sad day for the school because (it was *or* they were) losing one of the best students (it *or* they) had ever had.
9. There is no need for household servants, for no one has more housework than (he *or* they) can manage.
10. Upon release, the prisoner's attitude toward society is determined by (his *or* their) treatment in prison.
11. The United States has to look out for the rights of (its *or* their) citizens.
12. As the Egyptian priesthood became more profitable, it became a profession and (its *or* their) power increased.
13. A trip to Europe seems to be desired by anyone who is in (his *or* their) right mind.
14. Any parent hopes to obtain the best education possible for (his *or* their) children.
15. The school was preparing to put on (its *or* their) annual Parents' Day.

# 28 CASE

Case means the changes in the form of a substantive to show its use in a sentence. English nouns used to have many case forms; now they have different endings only to indicate the possessives. But most pronouns have three case forms: nominative (to indicate the subject of a verb), possessive, and objective (to indicate a direct or indirect object).

| | | | | | | |
|---|---|---|---|---|---|---|
| NOMINATIVE: | I | we | he | she | they | who |
| POSSESSIVE: | my | our | his | her | their | whose |
| OBJECTIVE: | me | us | him | her | them | whom |

Most people use the correct case forms without deliberation or conscious choice. But there are a few constructions which sometimes cause trouble.

## 28a Case in Compound Constructions and Appositives

A noun and a pronoun used in a compound construction should be in the same case. The same principle applies to constructions like *we boys* and to appositives.

**Correct.** My father and I often go fishing together.

**Wrong.** Professor Henderson invited my brother and I to come to his house on Wednesday evening. [Because a construction like "my brother and I," with the pronoun politely placed second, is so commonly used as the subject of a sentence, it is easy to slip into using the same form even when the objective case is needed.]

**Correct.** Professor Henderson invited my brother and me to come to his house on Wednesday evening.

**Wrong.** Between you and I, Wesley is not to be trusted.

**Correct.** Between you and me, Wesley is not to be trusted.

**Wrong.** My father always told we boys not to stay out late. [Since *boys* is in the objective case, the pronoun must also be objective: "he told *us*."]

**Correct.** My father always told us boys not to stay out late.

**Correct.** We boys were not allowed to stay out late.

**Wrong.** Most of the work was done by two members of the family, my brother and I. [Since the object of *by* is in the objective case, the appositives must be in the same case.]

**Correct.** Most of the work was done by two members of the family, my brother and me.

**Correct.** We all went — my cousin and my sister and I.

## 28b Case of Relative Pronouns

The proper case form, *who* or *whom*, is determined by the use of the relative pronoun as subject or object in the dependent clause. When in doubt, substitute a personal pronoun for the relative. If *he* or *they* fits the context, use *who;* if *him* or *them* fits the context, use *whom*.

**Correct.** Here is a man who can tell you all about it. [*He* can tell you all about it.]

**Correct.** Here is the man whom I told you about. [I told you about *him*.]

A parenthetic expression, like *I think* or *he says*, intervening between a relative pronoun and its verb does not change the case of the pronoun.

**Wrong.** The man whom I thought would be elected came in

third. [The relative pronoun is the subject of *would be elected* and should be in the nominative case.]

**Correct.** The man who I thought would be elected came in third. [I thought *he* would be elected.]

The pronoun *whoever* is sometimes incorrectly put into the objective case because it appears to be the object of a preceding preposition.

**Wrong.** Free theater tickets will be sent to whomever phones us first.

**Correct.** Free theater tickets will be sent to whoever phones us first. [*Whoever* is the subject of *phones*, not the object of *to*. The object of *to* is the whole clause, *whoever phones us first.*]

In formal writing, the interrogative pronouns *who* and *whom* are used exactly like the relative pronouns.

**Correct.** Who is coming for dinner?

**Correct.** Whom are you expecting for dinner? [*Whom* is the object of *are expecting.* Are you expecting *him?*]

In speech and in much informal writing, there is an increasing tendency to use *who* as the interrogative form whenever it begins a sentence, no matter what its construction in the sentence. *Whom* is used when it directly follows a preposition. Since the use of *who* and *whom* is still often considered a crucial test of literacy, it is safer in writing to use the formal case form. But be sure you use it correctly.

**Acceptable.** Who are you expecting for dinner?

**Acceptable.** Who are you staying with?

**Correct.** With whom are you staying?

## 28c Case Forms with *to be*

In formal writing, the complement of all forms of the linking verb *to be* except the infinitive should be in the nominative case.

**Correct.** The members of the committee are you, your brother, and I.

**Correct.** When we heard someone coming up on the porch, we hardly dared hope it would be Captain Little, but it was he.

**Correct.** May I speak to Professor Holmes? This is he.

**Correct.** Even if Jensen is supposed to be the richest man in town, I still wouldn't want to be him. [*Him* is the complement of the infinitive *to be.*]

In speech and in informal writing, the form "It is me" is now generally accepted.

**Acceptable.** Everyone wondered who had taken the money, but no one suspected that it was me.

## 28d Case Forms Following *than, as, but*

The case of a pronoun after *than* or *as* is determined by its use in the elliptical clause which follows. Most commonly the pronoun is the subject, but occasionally it may be the object.

**Correct.** My brother is taller than I. [*Than I* is a shortened form of *than I am.*]

**Correct.** I can do it as well as he. [*As he* is a shortened form of *as he can do it.*]

**Correct.** He likes you better than me. [*Than me* is a shortened form of *than he likes me.*]

*But* is sometimes used as a preposition meaning "except." When so used, *but* is followed by the objective case.

**Correct.** No one but her knew the answer.

**Correct.** By morning everyone had left the house but me.

## 28e Possessive Case

Ordinarily, the possessive case is used only with nouns referring to persons and living things. To show possession by inanimate objects, a phrase beginning with *of* is preferred.

**Correct.** The cat's home was under my uncle's garage.

**Awkward.** At a cold's first sign, go to bed and keep warm.

**Improved.** At the first sign of a cold, go to bed and keep warm.

Good usage approves many exceptions to these rules. Even with persons an *of*-phrase rather than the possessive in *'s* should be used when the modifying noun is separated from the word it modifies by a phrase or clause.

**Wrong.** The boy who came in the door's appearance was shocking.

**Improved.** The appearance of the boy who came in the door was shocking.

Expressions designating time or measure and expressions implying personification normally make use of the form in *'s* rather than an *of*-phrase.

**Correct.** A day's journey, a stone's throw, five minutes' walk, a month's wages, two dollars' worth.

**Correct.** For pity's sake, the law's delay, love's old sweet song.

The double genitive, which uses both an *of*-phrase and *'s*, is permissible in informal writing.

**Correct.** A friend of my brother's, a friend of my brother, one of my brother's friends.

## 28f Possessive Case with Gerunds

A noun or pronoun modifying a gerund is in the possessive case.

**Correct.** Henry's coughing during the lecture annoyed the professor.

**Correct.** I can't understand your failing the examination.

**Correct.** Everyone approved of his applying for the job.

The possessive is not used before the gerund when the substantive has no possessive form or when it is separated from the gerund.

**Correct.** Some students may have cheated, but I do not know of any having done so. [*Any* has no possessive case.]

**Correct.** Who ever heard of anyone in his right mind making such a request?

Note that a pronoun used as the subject of a gerund should be in the objective case.

**Correct.** I tried to imagine him dancing a samba. [The object of *imagine* is the gerund phrase *him dancing a samba.*]

### EXERCISE

In each sentence, choose the proper case form, and give reasons for your choice.

1. My brother is a better skier than (I *or* me).
2. If Joe had not been reliable, my parents would never have permitted Betty and (he *or* him) to get married.
3. There was no comment from the two members (who *or* whom) I thought were sure to protest.
4. All the students (who *or* whom) I talked to seemed to like the new coach.
5. My father told (we *or* us) children never to play in the street, but we didn't obey him.

6. All the family but (I *or* me) went to the party.
7. The new president won't know for several months just (who *or* whom) he can trust.
8. The camp director wanted Bob, Jim, and (I *or* me) to take charge of the younger boys.
9. My father objects to (me *or* my) watching television every evening.
10. As for my sister and (I *or* me), we always prefer to go to the mountains.
11. The Wentworths have not lived here as long as (we *or* us).
12. This year we have a new teacher who wins the respect of all students (who *or* whom) she has in class.
13. I do not want to find myself in a position where the job has me, instead of (me *or* my) having the job.
14. Only two members of the family have red hair, my uncle and (I *or* me).
15. We agreed that anyone but (she *or* her) would have been preferable.
16. Another good reason for (me *or* my) joining the Coast Guard is the chance for special training.
17. The policeman told my brother and (I *or* me) to come with him.
18. The girl (who *or* whom) we thought would be chosen was disqualified.
19. Robert insisted that credit for winning the game should go to two players — his brother and (he *or* him).
20. The ten remaining tickets will be given to (whoever *or* whomever) applies first.

# 29 ADJECTIVES AND ADVERBS

Distinguish between adjectives and adverbs, and use the form required by the construction of a sentence. A word modifying a noun or pronoun should be an adjective; a word modifying a verb, adjective, or adverb should be an adverb. Most adverbs are formed by adding *ly* to the adjective: *clear*, *clearly; easy*, *easily; immediate*, *immediately*. But note that some adjectives end in *ly; friendly*, *manly*, etc. A few adverbs have the same form as the adjective: *far*, *much*, *little*, *right*, *fast*. The dictionary will tell you whether a word is an adjective or an adverb, or both.

**Wrong.** The car stopped quite sudden.

**Correct.** The car stopped quite suddenly.

**Correct.** The car came to a sudden stop.

**Wrong.** She played the sonata as perfect as her teacher.

**Correct.** She played the sonata as perfectly as her teacher.

**Correct.** Her playing of the sonata was perfect. [*Perfect* modifies the gerund *playing*.]

## 29a Adjectives with Linking Verbs

Verbs like *become*, *seem*, *appear*, as well as the verbs indicating the use of the five senses (*look*, *feel*, *sound*, *taste*, *smell*), are often used to link an adjective to the subject of the sentence.

**Correct.** The sailor {looked / seemed / became / felt / sounded} cold.

Do not use an adverb as the complement of a linking verb.

**Wrong.** I felt badly about my mistake.

**Correct.** I felt bad about my mistake.

**Wrong.** The flowers smelled sweetly.

**Correct.** The flowers smelled sweet.

Note the distinction in use between the adjectives and the adverbs in the following sentences:

> The blind man felt the wall cautiously.
> Watching him, I felt miserable.
> Since the soup was hot, I tasted it carefully.
> To my surprise, it tasted sour.
> She looked regretfully at the departing guests.
> She looked regretful after the guests had departed.

## 29b Adverbs without *ly*

Some adverbs have two forms, one the same as that of the adjective and another with *ly* added. *Slow, slowly; loud, loudly; soft, softly; cheap, cheaply; sharp, sharply; quick, quickly* are all adverbial forms. In informal writing and in speech, especially in short imperative sentences, the form without *ly* is often used when the adverb follows the verb. In formal writing the form in *ly* is preferred, and wherever the adverb precedes the verb, the form in *ly* is required.

**Acceptable.** Drive slow. You may have to stop quick. The box was buried deep in the sand.

**Correct.** You should drive slowly on wet pavements. By good luck I was able to stop quickly. I shifted quickly into second. The box was deeply buried in the sand. He dug deeply into the wet soil.

The following adjectives are often used in popular speech to modify a verb or adjective. In writing, use the corresponding adverb or an intensive like *very*.

| *Adjectives* | *Adverbs* |
|---|---|
| sure | surely |
| some | somewhat, some (before a numeral) |
| real | really |
| good | well |
| most | almost |

**Colloquial.** I'm sure glad you came.

**Correct but stilted.** I am surely glad that you came.

**Improved.** I am very glad that you came.

**Colloquial.** She is some better today.

**Correct.** She is somewhat better today.

**Correct.** There are some twenty people in the room.

**Colloquial.** I am real sorry that you are leaving.

**Correct.** I am really sorry (*or* very sorry) that you are leaving.

**Colloquial.** Most all the students finished by noon.

**Correct.** Almost all the students finished by noon.

**Correct.** Most of the students finished by noon.

## 29c Comparative and Superlative

In formal writing the comparative degree of an adjective

or adverb is used in speaking of two persons and the superlative degree in speaking of three or more persons. In speaking and in informal writing this distinction is not always observed, and the superlative degree is often used in comparing two persons.

**Correct.** She was the more beautiful of the two sisters.

**Correct.** She was the most beautiful of all the sisters.

**Acceptable.** Of the two versions proposed, the first was the most popular.

According to logic, adjectives like *perfect*, *round*, *unique* should not have comparative or superlative forms: a thing is either perfect or not perfect, round or not round. Formal writing tends to avoid expressions like *more perfect*, *rounder than*, *most unique*, preferring *more nearly perfect*, *more nearly round*, *unique*. But comparative, superlative, and intensive forms of such adjectives are very commonly used in both speech and writing.

**Acceptable.** We, the people of the United States, in order to form a more perfect union . . .

**Acceptable.** Wilson lived in a very unique house.

### EXERCISE

Correct the use of adjectives and adverbs as may be necessary to bring the following sentences up to the level of standard *written* English.

1. If you listen close, you should be able to hear it quite distinct.
2. The colors in the kitchen contrasted harshly and looked badly.
3. People today live more secure because of new drugs and antibiotics.

4. I know now that I didn't do too good on the final examination.
5. The sun shone brightly and the pine needles smelled sweetly.
6. At the laboratory we were introduced to some of the wonders and seemingly impossibilities of modern technology.
7. An adventure story affects me quite different from the other kinds of stories I read.
8. We were real pleased that the experiment turned out so good.
9. That disastrous Thursday evening started out quite natural.
10. I slept well, but the sky next morning looked threateningly.
11. During the whole time that Norton was chairman, business went along very smooth.
12. The auditorium floors should be built in tiers so that people in the back rows can see more easy.
13. I intend to build the cabin as cheap as I possibly can.
14. If your tooth hurts real bad, take an aspirin or two.
15. Although he doesn't look different, he acts different.

# 30 TENSE AND MODE OF VERBS

Tense means the indication of the time of an action by changes in the form of a verb. There are six principal tenses in English:

**Present.** We *hold* these truths to be self-evident.

**Past.** I *played* the piano, and my brother *sang*.

**Future.** She *will feel* better tomorrow.

**Perfect.** I *have tried* to be friendly, but he *has* never *spoken* to me.

**Past perfect.** Although he *had finished* his dinner an hour before, he still sat at the table.

**Future perfect.** He *will have gone* by the time we arrive.

## 30a Confusion of Past and Perfect Tenses

Note that the past is not one single time, but that a particular event divides the past into two parts, each having its appropriate tense. The past tense is used for a particular event, over and done with; the past perfect tense is used for the time preceding the particular event; the perfect tense is used for time continuing up to the present. Be sure your tenses logically indicate the time intended.

**Illogical.** When he died, his fellow citizens realized how much he contributed to the community, and since then they collected funds for a memorial.

**Correct.** When he *died*, his fellow citizens *realized* how much he *had done* for the community, and they *have been* collecting funds for a memorial.

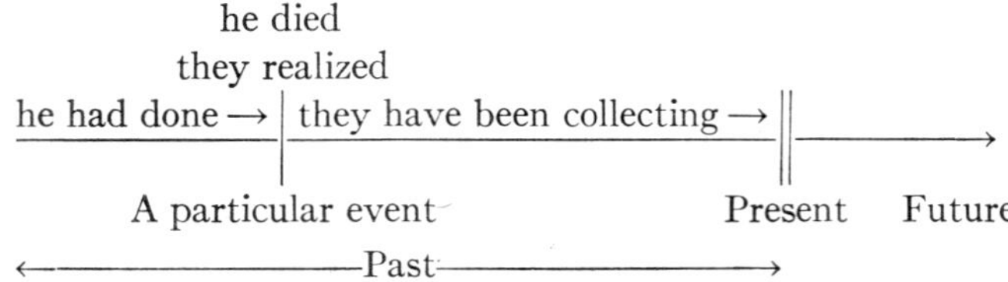


**Illogical.** These fossils represent animals that have lived and died before the dawn of history.

**Correct.** These fossils represent animals that lived and died before the dawn of history.

**Illogical.** Until now the winter was mild.

**Correct.** Until now the winter has been mild.

**Correct.** Until the end of January the winter had been mild, but in February the temperature dropped to zero.

## 30b Sequence of Tenses

The tense of the verb in the main clause governs the tense of the verb in a subordinate clause. The following sentences illustrate consistent sequence of tenses.

**Correct.** When the button *is pressed*, the motor *begins* to run.
When he *pressed* the button, the motor *began* to run.
If you *will press* the button, the motor *will begin* to run.
Now that he *has pressed* the button, he *can begin* to test the motor.
When he *had pressed* the button, he *began* to test the motor.

An infinitive should be in the present tense unless it represents action earlier than that of the governing verb.

**Illogical.** It was not wise to have written such a letter.

**Correct.** It was not wise to write such a letter.

**Illogical.** I should have asked him to have stayed for dinner.

**Correct.** I should have asked him to stay for dinner.

**Correct.** We ought to have gone home hours ago.

Ordinarily, the past participle should be used to represent action earlier than that of the governing verb. The present participle indicates action at the time expressed by the verb.

**Illogical.** Entering the course two weeks late, he soon found it too difficult.

**Correct.** Having entered the course two weeks late, he soon found it too difficult.

**Correct.** Entering the course two weeks late, he expected to find it difficult.

Statements that are permanently true should be put in the present tense, even though the main verb is in the past.

**Illogical.** He insisted that Pikes Peak was higher than Mt. McKinley.

**Correct.** He insisted that Pikes Peak is higher than Mt. McKinley.

**Illogical.** Magellan proved that the earth was round.

**Correct.** Magellan proved that the earth is round.

The present tense is often used in book reviews and criticism for statements of permanent truth regarding a work of art. In statements relating the events of an author's life, the past tense would normally be used.

**Correct.** The setting of Jane Austen's novels *is* the English village that she *knew* so well. [The settings of the novels are still the same; Jane Austen knew them in the past.]

**Correct.** In "Old China" Charles Lamb *describes* charmingly his home life with his sister Mary, to whom he *was* devoted.

## 30c Principal Parts of Irregular Verbs

Irregular verbs are a small group which, instead of forming their past tenses in the usual way by adding *ed* (*start, started*), change the vowel to indicate the past tense and the past participle (*begin, began, begun*). The principal parts consist of (1) the present infinitive (*begin*); (2) the past tense, first person singular (*began*); (3) the past participle (*begun*). All tense forms can be derived from the three principal parts. The first principal part is the basis for all present and future tenses; the second principal part is used for the simple past tense: "I began the job yesterday." The third principal part is used in all the compound past tenses: "I have begun," "he had begun," "the job was begun," etc.

In the speech of uneducated people and children, errors in the use of principal parts of the irregular verbs are common: "I throwed the ball," "We brung it home," "He taken it along with him." The following list gives the principal parts of some irregular verbs which are apt to be confused. Be sure you know these, and add to the list any others which you are likely to confuse.

| | | |
|---|---|---|
| begin | began | begun |
| bid (*offer*) | bid | bid |
| bid (*command*) | bade | bidden |
| bite | bit | bitten |
| blow | blew | blown |
| break | broke | broken |
| bring | brought | brought |
| burst | burst | burst |
| catch | caught | caught |
| choose | chose | chosen |
| come | came | come |
| dive | dived (dove) | dived |
| do | did | done |
| draw | drew | drawn |

| | | |
|---|---|---|
| drink | drank | drunk |
| eat | ate | eaten |
| fall | fell | fallen |
| fly | flew | flown |
| forget | forgot | forgotten (forgot) |
| freeze | froze | frozen |
| get | got | got (gotten) |
| go | went | gone |
| grow | grew | grown |
| know | knew | known |
| lie | lay | lain |
| ride | rode | ridden |
| ring | rang (rung) | rung |
| rise | rose | risen |
| run | ran | run |
| see | saw | seen |
| shrink | shrank (shrunk) | shrunk |
| sing | sang (sung) | sung |
| speak | spoke | spoken |
| spring | sprang (sprung) | sprung |
| steal | stole | stolen |
| swim | swam | swum |
| swing | swung | swung |
| take | took | taken |
| throw | threw | thrown |
| wear | wore | worn |
| write | wrote | written |

## 30d Use of *Shall* and *Will*

In informal writing American practice is to use *will* to express the simple future: "I will go, we will go, you will go, he (she, it, they) will go." To express determination, promise, or prophecy, *shall* is normally used, though *will* is fairly common in the first person.

**Correct.** They shall not pass.

**Correct.** Upon default in payment, the entire amount shall become due at once.

**Correct.** My father expects me to get tired and give up, but I won't. [*Won't* = will not. As stressed in this sentence, it implies determination.]

In questions as to what is proper or expected, *shall* is used with the first person.

**Correct.** Shall I wear a long dress?

**Correct.** Shall we come at the same time tomorrow?

In formal writing, *shall* is used to express the simple future in the first person; *will* is used to express the simple future in the second and third persons.

**Correct but formal.** I shall be glad to see you.

**Correct.** We shall arrive in Boston on Friday, but they will have gone by then.

*Should* is used with all persons to express a condition in an *if*-clause, or to express obligation or duty.

**Correct.** If you should go to Norwich, be sure to see the cathedral. If I (he, she, they) should leave, no one would notice.

**Correct.** I should stay in and study this evening.

**Correct.** A Boy Scout should be courteous and truthful.

*Would* is used with all persons in polite requests and to express a habitual action or tendency.

**Correct.** Would you come to my office at ten?
Contrast the more emphatic "Will you come to my office . . ."

**Correct.** He would like another piece of cake, and so would I.

**Correct.** He would always walk in the middle of the street after dark.

**Correct.** The president would often skip lunch altogether.

*Would* is also used in hypothetical situations and in indirect discourse.

**Correct.** If I were offered a trip to the moon, I would refuse.

**Correct.** If he should suddenly find himself in Lilliput, he would soon feel perfectly at home.

**Correct.** I said that I would try, and she agreed that she would help me.

## 30e Use of the Subjunctive Mode

Subjunctive forms (*be* instead of *am, are, is; were* instead of *was;* etc.) are used much less than formerly. In speech, the subjunctive has almost disappeared, except in formulas like "If I were you . . ." Informal writing often uses, and formal writing demands, the use of the subjunctive in the following instances:

Condition contrary to fact:

**Correct.** I wish that I *were* going.

**Colloquial.** I wish that I *was* going.

**Correct.** If I *were* you, I would refuse.

**Correct.** If this *were* a holiday, I would be out playing golf.

**Colloquial.** If this *was* a holiday, . . .

After *as if* or *as though:*

**Correct.** The dog acts as if he *were* frightened.

**Colloquial.** The dog acts as if he *was* frightened.

**Correct.** He acts as though he *were* drunk, and he probably is.

**Colloquial.** He acts as though he *was* drunk . . .

Indirect imperative:

**Correct.** The terms of the agreement demand that the dispute *be settled* out of court.

**Correct.** I insist that he *attend to* the matter today.

Motions and resolutions:

**Correct.** I move that the minutes *be approved.*

**Correct.** Resolved, that this question *be submitted* to a committee.

EXERCISE

Correct any errors in the use of verbs in the following sentences.

1. She wore a lavender dress, and her shoes, which once were white, were gray from lack of polish.
2. The professor said that the moon was approximately 239,000 miles from the earth.
3. For the reader who has never ran across advertising of this kind, a further explanation may be necessary.
4. Squeaky, our cat, would lay on the floor for hours and played with a ball of string.
5. I should have liked to have told her what I thought of her.
6. The dog begun to growl when I started to run down the walk.
7. The conductor, who was a pianist in his youth, showed us that he can still play.
8. I finally done the assignment, but the teacher said that I should of handed it in earlier.
9. If I had only chose physics as my major, I wouldn't have to write all these papers.
10. Before Noah finishes building the ark, it begun to rain hard.
11. It was a serious mistake to have written such a letter.

12. The book was laying right where we had laid it.
13. The water level began to raise, and by noon it had rose ten feet.
14. I recognized the girl who had spoke to me at the dance.
15. By midafternoon we had drank most of the water in the canteen.

## REVIEW EXERCISE

Correct all grammatical errors in the following sentences.

1. Most ski accidents are the result of someone being discourteous or thinking they are more skillful than they really are.
2. But along with increased speed comes many new problems in aircraft design.
3. My uncle was setting on the porch, right where we saw him three hours earlier.
4. The young person of high school age is apt to feel that if they do not conform, they will be ostracized.
5. Intercollegiate sports, even though the whole student body does not actively participate in it, provides recreation for most of the students.
6. Certain basic characteristics of man, such as his urge to gain power for himself, is a serious obstacle to a peaceful society.
7. I know of several people in my school whom I'm convinced scarcely opened a book in four years.
8. The trial of criminals in that country is very fair in that he is considered innocent until proven guilty.
9. I believe that coaches should clamp down on the members of the team so that he will gain their respect.
10. Within the boundaries of these islands lie a great variety of beautiful scenery.

11. My father has been a mining engineer for over forty years, and not once do I remember him going to work in anything other than work clothes.
12. Anyone with common sense can learn how to cook, can't they?
13. Every time any of us open a magazine, we read of new trouble abroad.
14. I knew all along that it was my duty to have reported the accident, but since nothing valuable had been broke, I decided to lay low.
15. According to a report just received, a bonus will be given to whomever exceeds their quota.
16. A horse is one of those animals which lives entirely on vegetable food.
17. His favorite reading matter are novels, preferably science fiction.
18. Extra work was assigned to we students who came into the class late.
19. The sergeant told Stan and I to report at nine the next morning.
20. If I had known what the square root of 225 was, I would of passed the test.

## Punctuation

**31.** END PUNCTUATION

**32.** THE COMMA

**33.** THE SEMICOLON

**34.** QUOTATION MARKS

**35.** THE APOSTROPHE

**36.** THE COLON

**37.** THE DASH

**38.** PARENTHESES AND BRACKETS

Rules for the use of punctuation marks state the common conventions accepted by writers and readers. In general, the conventions of punctuation are intended to make communication easier, but some rules are arbitrary and can be justified only on the ground of accepted practice. At best, punctuation is a minor aid to clarity in writing. A sentence which is badly constructed or poorly phrased cannot be saved by punctuation alone; it must be revised or phrased more accurately.

The explicit rules about which there is general agreement do not cover all the uses of punctuation marks. A good deal of punctuation is optional: a writer may use commas or not, depending on his taste or his intention, in such a sentence as the following:

> Eleven All-Americans would not in fact guarantee a good team.
>
> Eleven All-Americans would not, in fact, guarantee a good team.

Most readers would probably feel that setting off the *in fact* gives it a little more emphasis, and a writer who wanted this emphasis would probably use the commas. But either sentence is correct. On the other hand, there are many instances in which using a punctuation mark would be an unmistakable error. However, trying to frame rules telling when *not* to use punctuation would be an endless and fruitless task.

The following sections contain the rules which specify where punctuation marks are needed. Beyond this, you must use your judgment. If you are in doubt, and no positive rule covers the point, you will probably be safer to omit the punctuation mark.

# 31 END PUNCTUATION

## 31a Period

A period is used after a complete declarative or imperative sentence.

**Correct.** This is an example of a declarative sentence.

**Correct.** Use a period at the end of a sentence like this.

A period is also used after abbreviations, like *Dr.*, *Mr.*, *Ph.D.*, *etc.*, *A.D.*, *P.M.*, *Calif.*, *Inc.* For the proper use of abbreviations see Section **48.**

Three spaced periods (. . .), called ellipsis marks, are used to indicate the omission of a word or words from a quoted passage. If the omitted words come at the end of a sentence, a fourth period is needed.

**Correct.** We hold these truths to be self-evident: that all men . . . are endowed by their Creator with certain unalienable rights. . . .

Similarly, three or four periods are sometimes used in dialog and interrupted narrative to indicate hesitation and pauses. Beginning writers should use these with caution.

**Correct.** He inspired uneasiness. That was it! Uneasiness. Not a definite mistrust — just uneasiness — nothing more. You have no idea how effective such a . . . a . . . faculty can be.

— JOSEPH CONRAD, *Heart of Darkness*

## 31b Question Mark

A question mark is used after a direct question, like the following:

**Correct.** Who were the first Americans?

**Correct.** How many pages can you read in an hour?

**Correct.** Pointing to me, the sergeant said, "What's your name?"

An indirect question should be followed by a period, not a question mark.

**Correct.** He asked what had caused the delay.

**Correct.** I wonder how many people in the country read books nowadays.

A request which is phrased as a question for politeness' sake is followed by a period.

**Correct.** Will you please send me your latest catalog.

## 31c Exclamation Mark

An exclamation mark, made on the typewriter by an apostrophe with a period beneath it, is used at the end of a sentence, fragment, or interjection to indicate the extra stress which would be given to an emphatic spoken exclamation.

**Correct.** Help! Man overboard!

**Correct.** What a piece of work is man! How noble in reason! How infinite in faculty!

Though common in popular fiction and advertising, the exclamation mark is not much used in expository writing. Certainly it should not be used in an effort to lend force to a weak and flabby statement, nor to call attention to an intended irony.

# 32 THE COMMA

The chief uses of the comma are to separate coordinate sentence elements and to set off subordinate constructions in a sentence. That is, a single comma may be required to separate *x* from *y:* $\underline{\quad x \quad}$, $\underline{\quad y \quad}$. But two commas may be needed to set off *x* from the rest of the sentence: $\underline{\qquad}$, $\underline{\quad x \quad}$, $\underline{\qquad}$. In addition, a comma is occasionally used to prevent misreading: to separate words which might be erroneously grouped together by a reader.

## 32a Comma in Compound Sentences

Two independent clauses joined by a coordinating conjunction (*and, or, nor, but, for*) should be separated by a comma. Note that the comma is always placed before the conjunction.

**Correct.** A tape recorder gives very accurate reproduction, and it has the great advantage that it can be used at home as well as at the studio.

**Correct.** Hearne was still declaiming with great eloquence, but no one in the crowd was listening.

Very short independent clauses need not be separated by a comma if they are closely connected in meaning.

**Correct.** The gun went off and everyone jumped.

Coordinating conjunctions are often used to join the parts of a compound predicate: that is, two or more verbs with the same subject. In such a sentence a comma is not required to separate the predicates. However, if the two parts are long or imply a strong contrast, a comma may be used to separate them.

**Correct.** We covered the dark wood with gray paint and rubbed it down with steel wool.

**Correct.** Mr. Morgan discussed at length the strong points and weaknesses of each candidate, and concluded with a summary of his reasons for believing that Eliot would be elected.

**Correct.** To our surprise, the box neither sank to the bottom nor floated on the surface, but hung suspended in the water about halfway to the bottom.

When the clauses of a compound sentence are long and are also subdivided by commas, a stronger mark of punctuation than a comma may be needed to separate the clauses from each other. For this purpose a semicolon is regularly used.

**Correct.** Spectacles with gold or silver frames, the common type at the turn of the century, gave way to rimless or horn-rimmed glasses; and today the plastic frame, either clear or colored, has become the standard type among Americans, both men and women.

### EXERCISE

Give reasons for any commas or semicolons you would insert in the following sentences.

1. Seven legislators from the southern part of the state changed their votes and with their aid the bill was passed.
2. The student with a late paper may explain that he is just recovering from the flu or he may deplore the fact that his new glasses give him a headache and thus prevent him from writing.

3. Liberals are seldom violently partisan and are often accused of having no principles at all.
4. The truck pulled up at the roadside and the sergeant led us into the woods.
5. The new cars are certainly more powerful but it is doubtful that they are any safer.
6. Three of the editors argued that the article was biased and malicious and voted to reject it in spite of the distinguished reputation of the author.
7. You may correct the sentence by changing the participle to a dependent clause or you may omit the participial phrase altogether.
8. The teller at the bank, a man I had never seen before, looked dubiously at the check I offered him and even though I knew the check was good, I could feel a guilty look freezing on my face as his doubts increased.
9. All the housewife has to do is "add water and mix" or "drop contents into boiling water and cook for five minutes."
10. There was a time when agriculture was not controlled by middlemen but in the last hundred years the relations between farmer and consumer have changed completely.

## 32b Comma in a Series

The typical form of a series is *a*, *b*, and *c*. A series may contain more than three parallel elements, and any of the coordinating conjunctions may be used to connect the last two. The elements of the series are separated by commas from each other, but the series as a whole should not be separated from the rest of the sentence.

**Correct.** I subscribe to the *New Yorker*, the *Reporter*, and *Harper's Magazine*. [Series of nouns]

**Correct.** Do you like your steak rare, medium, or well done? [Series of adjectives]

**Correct.** Light entered the room through cracks in the walls, through holes in the roof, and through one small window. [Series of phrases]

**Correct.** Nitrogen, oxygen, carbon dioxide, and water vapor make up the mixture called air. [Series of nouns]

**Correct.** Vickers put down his pen, closed his checkbook, and sighed regretfully. [Series of predicates]

**Correct.** The rain was still falling, the reservoirs were filling up, and the District Engineer was considering opening the floodgates. [Series of independent clauses]

The comma before the last item in a series is omitted by some writers, but its use is generally preferred since it may help prevent misreading. The abbreviation *etc.* at the end of a series is always set off by commas.

**Correct.** A trunk checked on a railway ticket may contain personal possessions, clothes, toilet articles, books, etc., but not household goods.

If all the elements of a series are joined by coordinating conjunctions (*a and b and c*), no commas are necessary to separate them.

**Correct.** We packed her bag and bought her ticket and put her on the train.

## 32c Comma with Other Coordinate Elements

Adjectives modifying the same noun should be separated by commas if they are coordinate in meaning. Coordinate adjectives are those which could be joined by *and* without distorting the meaning of a sentence.

**Correct.** Railroads provide inexpensive, efficient transportation. [The adjectives are coordinate: *transportation which is inexpensive and efficient.*]

Sometimes, however, an adjective is so closely linked with the noun that it is thought of as part of the noun. Such an adjective is not coordinate with a preceding adjective.

**Correct.** I bought a large bath towel. [This does not mean *a towel which is large and bath. Bath* indicates the kind of towel; *large* describes the bath towel.]

Note that numbers are not coordinate with other adjectives and are not separated from them by commas.

**Correct.** We bought four large, rough bath towels. [*Four* and *large* should not be separated by a comma. But since the four bath towels were *large and rough*, a comma is used to separate these two coordinate adjectives.]

Coordinate words or phrases which are sharply contrasted are separated by commas.

**Correct.** I said *allusion*, not *illusion*.

**Correct.** The new party advocated government for the people, not by the people.

An idiomatic way of asking a question is to make a direct statement and add to it a coordinate elliptical question. Such a construction should be separated by a comma from the direct statement.

**Correct.** He promised to be there, didn't he?

**Correct.** You aren't seriously interested in that girl, are you?

Another idiomatic construction which requires a comma is the coordinate use of adjectives like *the more . . . , the more . . . .*

**Correct.** The harder the wood, the hotter the fire.

**Correct.** The more scientists learn, the more they have left to learn.

EXERCISE

Insert commas where they are required in the following sentences, and give a reason for each comma.

1. A rich aromatic pipe tobacco can be blended from burley Virginia and Latakia.
2. Painted surfaces should be washed with a detergent sanded lightly and covered with a thin coat of plastic varnish.
3. Everyone knows that the more you put into an activity the more you get out of it.
4. I painted the wall a rich deep forest green.
5. Playgrounds have been built in the downtown areas of New York Los Angeles and San Francisco.
6. For some years Mr. Jackson has lived in a big sprawling modern house on top of a hill.
7. I put the brushes in place wound the coil and adjusted the contact points.
8. You haven't signed the contract have you?
9. I believe that horse racing should be legalized because it would provide revenue increase employment and attract tourists to the state.
10. I judge a person of another race by what he says and how he acts not by the color of his skin.

## 32d Commas with Nonrestrictive Modifiers

This rule applies to dependent clauses, participial phrases, and appositives. A modifier is nonrestrictive when it can be omitted without changing the main idea of the sentence. Nonrestrictive modifiers give additional information about a word that has already been limited or which needs no limitation. A restrictive modifier, on the other hand, restricts the meaning of the word it modifies to one particular thing or group. If it is omitted, the main idea of the sentence is changed.

### Nonrestrictive Clauses and Phrases

Nonrestrictive clauses and phrases should be set off by commas. Note that two commas are required to set off a nonrestrictive modifier in the middle of a sentence; one comma is sufficient if the modifier is at the beginning or end of the sentence. Restrictive clauses and phrases should not be set off at all.

**Nonrestrictive clause.** My faculty adviser, *who had to sign the program card,* was very hard to find. [If the clause were omitted, some information would be lost, but the sentence would still make the same point: that my adviser was hard to find.]

**Restrictive clause.** A faculty adviser *who is never in his office* makes registration difficult. [Omitting the clause here changes the sense completely. The purpose of the clause is to limit the statement to a certain kind of faculty adviser — those who are never in their offices.]

**Correct.** The book was still lying on the kitchen table, where I had left it the night before. [Nonrestrictive clause]

**Correct.** The book was lying where I had left it. [Restrictive clause]

**Correct.** Hundreds of church bells, *ringing loudly after years of silence,* announced the end of the war. [Nonrestrictive phrase]

**Correct.** For six months there have been no deaths *caused by automobile accidents* in our city. [Restrictive phrase]

Notice how the meaning of a sentence may be altered by the addition or the omission of commas:

**Correct.** She has made a special study of the native women, who are monogamous. [Nonrestrictive clause. The sentence implies that all the native women were studied.]

**Correct.** She has made a special study of the native women who are monogamous. [Restrictive clause. The study deals with a special group, women who are monogamous.]

### EXERCISE

Insert commas in the following sentences to set off nonrestrictive clauses and participial phrases. In doubtful cases, explain the difference in meaning produced by the insertion of commas.

1. King Leopold of Belgium who was Queen Victoria's uncle also gave her a great deal of advice.
2. Many people who have never been to the United States think of it as a country of wealth and luxury where everyone lives on the fat of the land.
3. Some years ago I lived in a section of town where almost everyone was a Republican.
4. With the advent of the jet engine which is more efficient at high than at low altitudes aircraft could attain greater heights.
5. The physical endurance of a pilot flying at very high speeds is the only limitation which cannot be overcome.
6. The average student hoping to get a C without too much work should stay out of Economics 152.
7. We shall have to hire a caretaker if you can't find time to keep the place neat and orderly.
8. The packing plant where I worked all summer earning over $500 is in South San Francisco.
9. The new plane which is being designed is radically different from the old-fashioned propeller plane whose wing shape resembled a cross.
10. The average American woman tired of last year's clothes and seeking something new is an easy prey for the fashion designers who capitalize on herd psychology and the craving for novelty.

### Nonrestrictive Appositives

Appositives are usually nonrestrictive and hence are set off by commas. If, however, an appositive puts a necessary limitation upon its noun, it is restrictive and no punctuation is necessary.

**Nonrestrictive appositive.** On the wall was a topographic quadrangle, a detailed map published by the U.S. Geological Survey.

**Restrictive appositive.** The word *topographic* comes from a Greek noun meaning "a place."

Note that an appositive used to define a word is often introduced by the conjunction *or*. Such appositives are always set off by commas, to distinguish them from the common construction in which *or* joins two coordinate nouns.

**Correct.** The nursery specialized in primulas, or primroses.

**Correct.** We couldn't decide whether to order pansies or petunias.

Note that an abbreviated title or degree (*K.C.B.*, *USMC*, *M.D.*, *Ph.D.*) is treated as an appositive when it follows a proper name.

**Correct.** He introduced himself as James Weatherly, M.D., and added that he also held a Ph.D. from Columbia.

#### EXERCISE

The following sentences contain dependent clauses, participial phrases, and appositives which are to be set off by commas if they are nonrestrictive. Be able to justify your answers.

1. Workers in other fields of social science particularly sociology and psychology are rapidly inventing new techniques.

2. The term *deciduous* is used to indicate plants which shed their leaves each year.
3. Paris the world center of fashion determines what the average woman living in a Midwestern town will be wearing next year.
4. Mark Twain born and raised in Missouri was well qualified to describe river life in his most famous novel *Huckleberry Finn.*
5. The only shrub growing in the yard was an *Osmanthus* or sweet olive.
6. Not recognizing it at first I took it to be either a coffee berry or a kind of privet.
7. Two prominent alumni from St. Louis are Rev. Ralph Harrison D.D. and Captain Henry King USN.
8. The Olympic Games copied from the ancient Greek festival still retain a part of their original purpose the promotion of understanding and good will.
9. A student who has not yet discovered what he wants to major in should learn all he can about the world in which he must some day take his place.
10. Although the newspapers have printed guesses as to the amount of damage no official estimate will be possible until the floodwaters have receded.

## 32e Commas with Parenthetic Expressions

*Parenthetic* is a general term describing explanatory words or phrases which are felt to be intrusive and subordinate. That is, they interrupt the normal sentence pattern to supply additional, supplementary information, and they are accordingly set off by commas or other punctuation marks. In the widest sense of the term, nonrestrictive modifiers are a kind of parenthetic element. Many other sentence elements may become parenthetic if they are removed from their regular place and inserted so that they interrupt the normal order of a sentence.

For example, adjectives normally are placed before the words they modify: *Two tired, hungry boys came into camp.* If the adjectives are inserted elsewhere in the sentence, they become parenthetic and should be set off: *Two boys, tired and hungry, came into camp.* Similarly, it is possible to rewrite a sentence like *I have always believed that democracy is the most satisfactory form of government* so that one clause becomes parenthetic: *Democracy, I have always believed, is the most satisfactory form of government.*

**Correct.** The balance sheet, I am sorry to say, shows a considerable deficit.

**Correct.** The proposal made by the Bolivian government is not, in the opinion of most experts, likely to be accepted.

### Transitional Words and Phrases

Transitional words and phrases, like *however, moreover, indeed, consequently, of course, for example, on the other hand,* are usually set off by commas, especially when they serve to mark a contrast or the introduction of a new point. In short sentences where stress on the transitional word is not needed or desired, the commas are often omitted.

**Correct.** Moreover, the paper was late again this morning. It was so late, in fact, that I had to leave for the office without it. However I am not complaining.

**Correct.** The contract stated that construction should be completed by December 15. However, it was specified that the contractor should not be penalized for delay resulting from strikes.

**Correct.** The court ruled, consequently, that no damages could be collected.

Notice that *however* is sometimes used as a regular adverb, to modify a particular word rather than as a sentence modifier, and that when so used it is not set off by a comma.

**Correct.** However much he tries, he will not succeed. [Since *however* modifies *much*, it is not set off.]

### Dates and Addresses

Additional elements of dates and addresses and references are set off by commas. If only one element (day of month, year, city, etc.) appears, no punctuation is needed.

**Correct.** April 26 is his birthday.

**Correct.** New Jersey is his native state.

**Correct.** Act II is rather dull.

But if other elements are added, they are set off by commas.

**Correct.** April 26, 1944, is the date of his birth.

**Correct.** 233 West 118th Street, Detroit, Michigan, was given as the return address.

**Correct.** The quotation is from *King Lear*, II, ii, 2.

### Direct Address, Interjections, *yes* and *no*

Nouns used as terms of direct address, interjections, and the words *yes* and *no* should be set off by commas.

**Correct.** Mr. Bennett, will you read the next paragraph?

**Correct.** These figures, ladies and gentlemen, will prove my point.

**Correct.** Yes, I have answered the letter.

**Correct.** Oh, well, you can try again tomorrow.

### Quotation Expressions

Quotation expressions such as *he said* are set off by commas when used with a direct quotation.

**Correct.** "When I was a child," he said, "I had to walk two miles to school."

Do not put a comma after *he said*, etc., when the quotation following is indirect.

**Correct.** The boatswain said that the wheel was damaged.

**Correct.** They told us that they had escaped late at night.

When the quotation contains two independent clauses and the quotation expression comes between them, a semicolon may be required to prevent a comma fault. (See Section **11.**)

**Correct.** "I'm not going," he said; "it's too hot."

**Correct.** "I'm not going," he said. "It's too hot."

**Correct.** "I'm not going," he said, "and I'd advise you not to go."

(For other rules regarding the punctuation of direct quotations, see Section **34.**)

### Absolute Phrase

An absolute phrase should be set off by commas. An absolute construction consists of a participle with a subject (and sometimes a complement) grammatically unconnected with the rest of the sentence and usually telling when, why, or how something happened.

**Correct.** The floodwater having receded, people began returning to their homes.

**Correct.** I hated to leave home, circumstances being as they were.

#### EXERCISE

Insert commas where they are required to set off parenthetic elements in the following sentences.

1. Money is not to be sure the only problem that people worry about.

2. Yes I have lived in California most of my life, but I was born in Seattle Washington.
3. My uncle formerly one of the richest men in Berkeley promised to put me through college.
4. In the first place there is no evidence Mr. Jones that my client was driving a car in San Diego on July 14 1955.
5. Teaching of course has certain disadvantages salaries being what they are today.
6. "Come over here" said Mr. Newman "you can see the car from this window."
7. The study of Latin or any other foreign language for that matter helps to clarify English grammar.
8. My cousins tired and wet returned from their fishing trip at sunset.
9. Stricter laws it is said would be of no use without more machinery for their enforcement.
10. Portland Oregon was not as I remember it an unpleasant place for a boy to grow up in.

## 32f Commas with Introductory Clauses and Phrases

A dependent clause coming first in the sentence is usually set off by a comma. If a dependent clause follows the main clause, a comma is used when the clause is nonrestrictive. (See **32d.**)

**Correct.** If you have time, telephone me from the station. [Introductory adverbial clause, set off by a comma]

**Correct.** Telephone me from the station if you have time. [Restrictive adverbial clause following main clause]

**Correct.** Since the word *honor* is borrowed from Old French, it is not found before the Middle English period.

**Correct.** Phone me the minute you reach the airport, even if it means missing the limousine. [Nonrestrictive adverbial clause, set off by a comma]

An introductory verbal phrase (participial, gerund, or infinitive) is usually followed by a comma. A prepositional phrase of considerable length at the beginning of a sentence may be followed by a comma.

**Correct.** Seeking to improve the condition of the Irish people, Swift wrote a series of letters attacking Wood's halfpence. [Participial phrase]

**Correct.** Before sending his manuscript to the printer, Swift had it transcribed so that his handwriting would not be recognized. [Gerund phrase]

**Correct.** To understand Swift's behavior toward Vanessa, one must know something of his relations with Stella. [Infinitive phrase]

**Correct.** Soon after the end of the War of the Spanish Succession, Bolingbroke was impeached and fled to France. [Long prepositional phrase]

**Correct.** Within an hour the news was all over town.

## 32g Comma to Prevent Misreading

Use a comma to separate any sentence elements that might be incorrectly joined in reading and thus misunderstood. This rule supersedes all others. Clarity of expression is more important than conventional correctness, and commas which will prevent ambiguity are always in order.

**Misleading.** Ever since he has devoted himself to athletics.

**Clear.** Ever since, he has devoted himself to athletics.

**Misleading.** Inside the house was brightly lighted.

**Clear.** Inside, the house was brightly lighted.

**Correct.** Soon after, the minister entered the chapel.

**Correct.** To begin with, the study of the classics is traditional in England.

## 32h Unnecessary Commas

Using commas where they do not belong is a more flagrant error than omitting them where they might be expected. Leaving out a comma may be the result of carelessness, but putting one in the wrong place is positive evidence of ignorance. In any case, modern practice is to use less, rather than more, punctuation in narrative and expository prose. A good working rule for the beginner is to use no commas except those required by the preceding rules.

Listing all the circumstances in which a comma should not be used would be an endless task. Here are some examples of the kinds of serious errors due to excessive punctuation. In all the following sentences, the commas should be omitted.

**Incorrect.** His ability to solve the most complicated problems on the spur of the moment, never failed to impress the class. [The comma erroneously separates subject and predicate.]

**Incorrect.** The men who lived in the old wing of the dormitory, unanimously voted to approve the new rules. [If the clause is restrictive, no commas should be used; if the clause is nonrestrictive, two commas are required. Using one comma here is a glaring example of ignorance.]

**Incorrect.** After the meeting the Dean announced, that the new rules would go into effect at once. [The comma erroneously separates an indirect quotation from the rest of the sentence.]

**Incorrect.** We were so bored, that we left at ten o'clock. [The comma erroneously splits an idiomatic construction: *so bored that.*]

Do not put a comma before the first member or after the last member of a series, unless the comma is required by some other rule.

**Incorrect.** For breakfast I usually have, an egg, some toast, and coffee. [The comma after *have* separates the whole series from the rest of the sentence. It should be omitted.]

**Incorrect.** New York, New Orleans, and San Francisco, are supposed to be good "story" cities. [The comma after *San Francisco* erroneously separates the whole series from the rest of the sentence.]

**Correct.** New York, New Orleans, and San Francisco, in that order, are supposed to be the best cities for the setting of a story. [The comma after *San Francisco* is required to set off the parenthetic phrase *in that order*.]

## EXERCISE

Punctuate the following sentences. Be able to state a reason for each comma used.

1. I could readily understand for instance that primitive man who was ignorant and easily terrified might develop a group of medicine men who would govern tyrannically.
2. Modern man it seemed to me should have outgrown such an attitude and I was always surprised to find my fellow students seeking authoritative rule.
3. The Dean so far as I could tell shared my feeling but he made little effort to establish responsible democratic student government.
4. The instructor a precise fussy little man explained what the experiment was supposed to show and how we were to perform it.
5. Tucked away in a corner was a fine old brick fireplace which looked as though it had never been used.
6. In World War II all our fighter planes were propeller-driven employing an internal combustion engine with cylinders pistons and a crankshaft.
7. The hot sticky days of the summer make me feel that I could cheerfully leave Dubuque Iowa forever.

8. Three details which should always be specified in a contract for the sale of land are water rights mineral rights and general option rights.
9. The *Peninsula Herald* a newspaper published in Monterey California is a model of what a small-town paper should be.
10. The class agreed that the Noble Dog Miz Beaver little Grundoon and Albert were their favorite comic strip characters.
11. Hoping to earn some money by giving lessons or from performances of his compositions Mozart left for Paris on March 14 1778 and arrived there on March 23.
12. For many of us the time is fast approaching when we shall have to decide which branch of the service we prefer.
13. Although Dante and Boniface were both great Dante's power lay in his heart and intellect and in his poetic genius.
14. A grove of cypress trees wind-blown and shaggy with Spanish moss still grows on the headland as it did when Stevenson first explored the area.
15. Somervell the only son of a hard-working country doctor and a mother who had been trained as a school teacher was born in a quiet secluded farming town in Arkansas on August 21 1892.
16. For example you may have noticed that an oar appears to be bent when one end is in the water.
17. In 1936 the United States Canada Argentina and Australia shipped large quantities of wheat to Europe an area which consumes more grain than it produces.
18. Objects which burn readily in air burn with great brilliance in oxygen and objects which burn with difficulty in air burn readily in oxygen.
19. Another method of transferring property and with this I shall conclude the discussion is barter the direct exchange of goods without the use of money.
20. On March 14 1905 my father weary of trying to save money on a small salary left the Middle West and set out for Seattle Washington in the hope of making his fortune.

# 33 THE SEMICOLON

The semicolon indicates a greater break in the sentence than does the comma. Its most important use is to separate two independent clauses when no conjunction joins them. It is also used whenever a comma is not adequate to indicate a separation.

## 33a Semicolon between Principal Clauses

When the independent clauses of a compound sentence are not joined by a conjunction, a semicolon is required. The conjunctive adverbs (*so*, *therefore*, *however*, *hence*, *nevertheless*, *moreover*, *accordingly*, *besides*, *also*, *thus*, *still*, *otherwise*, etc.) are inadequate to join two independent clauses. A semicolon is required to separate two independent clauses not connected by a pure conjunction. Using a comma instead produces a run-together sentence. See Section **11.**

**Correct.** I do not say that these stories are untrue; I only say that I do not believe them.

**Correct.** In these remote villages the curfew still tolls the knell of parting day; the lowing herd still winds slowly o'er the lea.

**Run-together sentence.** I had hoped to find a summer job in the city, however, two weeks of job-hunting convinced me that it was impossible.

**Correct.** I had hoped to find a summer job in the city; however, two weeks of job-hunting convinced me that it was impossible.

**Correct.** From the high board, the water looked amazingly far away; besides, I was getting cold and tired of swimming.

**Correct.** The loan account book must be sent with each monthly payment; otherwise, there may be disputes as to the amount still owing.

If the clauses are short and closely parallel in form, commas are frequently used between them even if conjunctions are omitted.

**Correct.** The curtains fluttered, the windows rattled, the doors slammed.

As a means of combining sentences into compound sentences, the semicolon may easily be overworked. If a conjunction expresses the relationship between two sentences, use the conjunction. The semicolon should be reserved for use when the relationship between two statements is so clear that it is unnecessary to state it explicitly.

## 33b Semicolon When a Comma Is Not Adequate

Even when two independent clauses are joined by a coordinating conjunction, a semicolon may be used to separate them if the clauses are long or are subdivided by commas. The purpose of the semicolon in such a sentence is to make the break between the clauses greater than the breaks within the clauses.

**Correct.** The *Herald Tribune*, though officially a Republican paper, handled the story with scrupulous, if disdainful, objectivity; but many of the supposedly Democratic papers, to everyone's surprise, played up all the scandalous aspects of the case.

**Correct.** As a reward for his services to his country, the Duke was given pensions, special grants, and honorary offices; and a fund was created to erect a memorial in his honor.

A semicolon is used to separate elements in a series when the elements contain internal commas. That is, when a comma is not a strong enough mark of separation to indicate the elements of a series unmistakably, a semicolon is used instead.

**Ambiguous.** The committee consisted of Mr. Webster, the president of the bank, Mr. Elton, the manager of the water company, and the Mayor. [How many men on the committee?]

**Correct.** The committee consisted of Mr. Webster, the president of the bank; Mr. Elton, the manager of the water company; and the Mayor.

**Correct.** Supplementary material will be found in W. D. Taylor, *Jonathan Swift;* Ricardo Quintana, *The Mind and Art of Jonathan Swift;* and Bernard Acworth, *Swift.*

Be sure that semicolons separate coordinate elements. Using a semicolon to separate an independent clause and a subordinate clause is an error similar to writing a sentence fragment, and just as serious.

**Incorrect.** High school students have a tendency to conform to the manners and customs of the other students; rather than following their own individual tastes and inclinations.

**Correct.** High school students have a tendency to conform to the manners and customs of the other students, rather than following their own individual tastes and inclinations.

### EXERCISE

Explain the punctuation in the following sentences. In order to do so, it will be necessary to distinguish between principal clauses, subordinate clauses, and phrases.

1. There are no set rules which an actor must follow to become proficient in his art; however, there are certain prin-

ciples regarding the use of mind, voice, and body which may help him.

2. The book covered the life of Lotta Crabtree from birth to death; it painted her as one of the most colorful figures of early California.
3. Her forehead was wrinkled, her mouth was firm and tense, but her eyes had a dreamy, reminiscent look.
4. The unconscious sailor would then be taken to an outbound ship, to be sold to the captain at a price ranging from $100 to $300, depending on how pressed the captain was for men; and he would regain consciousness somewhere in the Pacific Ocean, without the slightest idea of where he was or where he was going.
5. Among the colorful figures in the book are Johnny Highpockets, a simple-minded settler; Charley Tufts, formerly a professor at Yale; and the author of the book himself.
6. Lord Warwick was a young man of very irregular life and perhaps of loose opinions, and Addison had very diligently tried to reclaim him; but his arguments and expostulations had no effect.
7. One experiment, however, remained to be tried; when he found his life near its end, he called for the young earl.
8. When Lord Warwick desired, with great tenderness, to hear his last injunctions, Addison told him, "I have sent for you that you may see how a Christian can die."
9. What effect this awful scene had on the earl I know not; he likewise died himself in a short time.
10. Jensen made three more visits to England: in January, 1922; in November, 1925; in April, 1927; and on the day preceding his death, March 21, 1931.

## EXERCISE

In the following sentences cross out semicolons which are unnecessary or incorrect and add semicolons where they are needed.

1. The second edition of the book, published in 1922, is relatively scarce and hard to find; but the third edition, published four years later, can be seen in almost any store selling old books.
2. In most respects the hotel is admirably located, it is near the corner of Fifth Avenue and 52nd Street, within walking distance of most mid-town points of interest.
3. I might ask here; "What is the most important thing in life?"
4. The sculptor can work for more than a week on the same clay model; because clay can be kept soft and workable by the application of wet towels.
5. The average person is not financially able to do a great deal of traveling to distant countries, and therefore he will probably never have the chance to see the places he reads about.
6. Sometimes I get so interested in a book that I stay up until I finish it; regardless of whether I have to go to class the next morning or not.
7. Since air is dissolved by water at the surface only, the shape of an aquarium is important, too small an opening may cause an oxygen deficiency.
8. I don't mean to criticize the hospitality of the University; actually when I go there I am always received most cordially.
9. On the postcard was a reproduction of a water color by John Piper, it showed the interior of Ingelsham Church.
10. "Get off at the next main intersection," said the bus driver, "the park entrance is two blocks to the right."

# 34 QUOTATION MARKS

Use quotation marks to enclose a direct quotation, but not an indirect quotation. A direct quotation is a part of a sentence which gives the exact words of a speaker. An indirect quotation is the writer's paraphrase of what someone said.

**Incorrect.** He said "that he was sorry." [This is an indirect quotation, since it does not give his exact words.]

**Correct.** He said that he was sorry.

**Correct.** He said, "I am sorry." [Since this gives his exact words, it is a direct quotation.]

The expression *he said* is never included within the quotation marks. If the actual quotation is interrupted by such an expression, both halves must be enclosed by quotation marks. (For punctuation of *he said* expressions, see page 250.)

**Correct.** "In that case," he said, "let's sit down and talk it over."

**Correct.** "I wish you'd join," Henderson said. "We need more men like you."

## 34a Quotations of More than One Sentence

If a quotation consists of several sentences, uninterrupted by a *he said* expression, use one set of marks to enclose the entire quotation. Do not enclose each separate sentence. If a quotation consists of several paragraphs, put quotation marks at the beginning of each paragraph and at the end of the last paragraph.

**Correct.** She said, "Is this the truth? Then I must tell my husband. He ought to know."

**Correct.** Poor Richard has a number of things to say about diet: "They that study much, ought not to eat so much as those that work hard, their digestion being not so good.

"If thou art dull and heavy after meat, it's a sign thou hast exceeded the due measure; for meat and drink ought to refresh the body and make it chearful, and not to dull and oppress it.

"A sober diet makes a man die without pain; it maintains the senses in vigour; it mitigates the violence of the passions and affections."

A quotation within a quotation is enclosed with single quotation marks. Be sure to conclude the original quotation with double marks.

**Correct.** The professor said, "The dictionary defines *inference* as 'a logical conclusion, or deduction.'"

## 34b Implied Speech

Quotation marks are frequently used for implied speech, but are not customarily used for unspoken thoughts.

**Correct.** He tried to cry, "She is there, she is there," but he couldn't utter the words, only the sounds.

— Jan de Hartog

**Correct.** It was a momentary liberation from the pent-up, anxious state I usually endured to be able to think: At least I'm not them! At least I'm not those heavy, serious, righteous people upstairs.

— Robert Lowry

## 34c Material Quoted from Another Writer

Quotation marks are used around material directly quoted from another writer, but not around a paraphrase of an author's ideas.

**Correct.** Bacon's aphoristic style can be illustrated by such sentences as these: "Studies serve for delight, for ornament, and for ability," or "Reading maketh a full man; conference a ready man; and writing an exact man."

**Correct.** Bacon believed that reading made a man learned, conversation made a man quick-witted, and writing made a man exact in thought and statement.

If you quote only a few words from a well-known writer and work them into your own sentence, quotation marks may be omitted.

**Correct.** As a small boy I often wondered when I was going to start enjoying those unalienable rights with which, so I was told, I had been endowed by my Creator: life, liberty, and the pursuit of happiness.

But quotation marks should be used if the audience may not recognize a quotation or if the limits of the direct quotation need to be indicated or if special emphasis is to be placed upon the quoted words.

**Correct.** Most news commentators make at least some faint pretense to logic, but our local announcer, like Shadwell, "never deviates into sense."

**Correct.** Although Milton's phrase "blind mouths" could be called a mixed metaphor, it is vivid and effective.

When a borrowed quotation runs to several lines of print, it may be set off by indenting and single-spacing. Quotation marks should not be used when the quoted material is so indicated.

**Correct.** Steinbeck's explanation of Mr. Pritchard's biological inadequacy is given in *Sea of Cortez:*

> Perhaps the pattern of struggle is so deeply imprinted in the genes of all life conceived in this benevolently hostile planet that the removal of obstacles automatically atrophies a survival drive. With warm water and abundant food, the animals may retire into a sterile, sluggish happiness.

A quotation of more than one line of poetry should be set off by indenting and single-spacing, without quotation marks. Be sure to keep the line lengths exactly as they are in the original.

**Correct.** Pope's philosophy is summed up in a famous couplet:

> And, spite of Pride, in erring Reason's spite,
> One truth is clear, WHATEVER IS, IS RIGHT.

## 34d Position of Other Marks with Quotes

At the end of a quotation, a period or comma is placed inside the quotation mark; a semicolon or colon is placed outside the quotation mark.

**Correct.** "Quick," said my cousin, "hand me the flashlight."

**Correct.** The bride and groom said, "I do"; the ladies in the audience wept.

**Correct.** I have only one comment when you say, "All men are equal": I wish it were true.

A question mark or exclamation mark goes inside the quotation mark if it applies to the quotation only, and outside the quotation mark if it applies to the whole sentence.

**Correct.** My father said, "Are you hurt?"

**Correct.** Did the invitation say "R.S.V.P."?

**Correct.** The captain said, "God help us!"

**Correct.** Above all, don't say weakly, "I can't"!

### 34e Titles of Books, Plays, etc.

Titles of books, poems, plays, musical compositions, etc., may be enclosed in quotation marks, but the preferred practice is to italicize titles of whole publications or works and to use quotation marks for the titles of chapters, articles, etc. Titles of paintings and other objects of art are regularly enclosed in quotation marks.

**Correct.** The sixth chapter of Ève Curie's *Madame Curie* is entitled "The Long Wait."

**Correct.** For the Vienna production of *Don Giovanni,* Mozart added the famous aria "Mi trado."

### 34f Quotes Not Used for Humor, Emphasis, or Slang

Do not use quotation marks for humor, for emphasis, or as an apology for slang. If occasionally you want to indicate that a word or phrase should be heavily stressed or deserves special attention, use italics. Humor or irony should be indicated by the context. Using quotation marks to call attention to an ironic or humorous passage is like poking your listener in the ribs when you have reached the point of a joke.

As to slang, if you use it at all, take full responsibility for it. Do not apologize for a phrase by putting it in quotation marks. If you are ashamed of it, don't use it. See Section **40c**.

#### EXERCISE

Insert quotation marks where they are necessary in the following sentences.

1. The Dean replied that he knew very well freshmen had trouble getting adjusted. But, he added, it doesn't usually take them eight months to find themselves.

2. I wonder, said Professor Ellis, if anyone can identify a quotation for me. It's from the end of a sonnet, and all I can remember is Like a lean knife between the ribs of Time.
3. President Woodbridge, according to the *Alumni Magazine*, believed that the chief values of a liberal education were nonmaterial; but on another page he was quoted, in the course of a speech delivered in Seattle, as saying a college education is essential for any man who does not plan to marry money.
4. The janitor — they call him custodian now — dragged the filing case in and grunted Where do you want it? When he had put it in the corner, I started to say Thank you, but he had disappeared.
5. I asked whether Professor Lawrence still began his first lecture by saying My name is Lawrence and I wish I were not here, as he always did when I was in college.
6. When I hear some of my colleagues saying In other words . . . or To put it another way . . ., I am reminded of Pope's couplet:

   Words are like leaves; and where they most abound,
   Much fruit of sense beneath is rarely found.

7. Take a chair, said my tutor, and have a cigarette. He picked up my paper. Tell me honestly, he said; is this the best you can do?
8. Madame Lenoir said, As my first number I will sing a song from Schubert's *Winterreise*, Der Leiermann.
9. In the poem Spring from Thomson's *The Seasons*, songbirds are referred to as gentle tenants of the shade.
10. When asked To what do you attribute your success?, Henderson always answered Sleeping late in the morning.

# 35 THE APOSTROPHE

The chief uses of the apostrophe are to indicate the possessive case of nouns and indefinite pronouns, to mark the omission of letters in a contracted word or date, and to indicate the plural of letters or numerals.

## 35a Possessive Case

Nouns and indefinite pronouns which do not already end in *s* form the possessive by adding an apostrophe and an *s*.

**Correct.** a man's hat — men's hats
Milton's poems — children's books
one's self-respect — Horace's odes

Plural nouns which end in *s* form the possessive by adding an apostrophe only.

**Correct.** boys' caps — ladies' clothes
a girls' school — the Joneses' house
the waitresses' uniforms — the Prentices' cottage

Singular nouns which end in *s* form the possessive by adding an apostrophe and an *s* if the *s* is to be pronounced as an extra syllable.

**Correct.** Keats's poems — Burns's songs
Mr. Thomas's house — King Charles's reign
a waitress's uniform — an actress's career

But if an extra syllable would be awkward to pronounce, the possessive is formed by adding the apostrophe only and omitting the second *s*.

**Correct.** Ulysses' voyages    Euripides' plays
Moses' life    an octopus' tentacles

Despite a long set of complicated rules for dealing with such words (Cf. *Webster's New Collegiate Dictionary*, Appendix on Punctuation), in actual practice usage is divided. Both *Dickens's* and *Dickens'* can be found in reputable publications. Note however that in all instances the apostrophe comes after the complete nominative form of the word.

**Correct.** Tennessee Williams' plays [never Tennessee William's plays]
Sophocles' tragedies [not Sophocle's tragedies]
Yeats's poems [not Yeat's poems]

The personal pronouns never require an apostrophe, even though the possessive case ends in *s*.

**Correct.** his, hers, its, ours, yours, theirs

In joint possession the last noun takes the possessive form. In individual possession each name should take the possessive form.

**Joint possession.** Marshall and Ward's St. Paul branch

**Individual possession.** John's, George's, and Harold's separate claims

In compound words the possessive form is usually added to the last word.

**Correct.** my mother-in-law's visit

Note also these preferred forms: *someone else's book; somebody else's opinion.*

The possessive case is not ordinarily used for inanimate objects. Instead use a phrase beginning with *of.*

**Awkward.** The barn's roof was sagging.

**Correct.** The roof of the barn was sagging.

There are many exceptions: expressions designating time or measure, such as *a day's journey, a stone's throw, five minutes' walk, two dollars' worth;* expressions implying personification, such as *for pity's sake, the law's delay;* and certain idiomatic expressions like *the earth's surface, heart's content, the rocket's velocity.*

## 35b Contractions

Use an apostrophe to indicate omitted letters in contracted words and dates.

| **Correct.** | haven't | doesn't | isn't | it's | o'clock |
|---|---|---|---|---|---|
| | have not | does not | is not | it is | of the clock |

**Correct.** the class of '53, the hurricane of '38

## 35c Plural of Letters and Numerals

The plural of letters and of numerals is formed by adding *'s.* The plural of a word considered *as a word* may be formed in the same way.

**Correct.** His *U's* were like *V's,* and his *2's* like *Z's.*

**Correct.** In this theme there are too many *he said's* and too many *and's.*

### EXERCISE

Insert apostrophes, or an apostrophe and *s,* where they are required in the following sentences.

1. Robert Burns poems are favorites of ours.

2. In spite of its reputation, Hughes restaurant is not popular with the students; its too expensive.
3. Dont take Charles promises too seriously.
4. In our reading of Shakespeares *A Midsummer Nights Dream*, Theseus part was read by the teacher.
5. He ordered fifty cents worth of ground beef at Ross market.
6. The mens dormitories are always open, but the girls residence halls close at midnight.
7. Members of the class of 26 wore sport shirts covered with letters, bright crimson Hs and Cs.
8. Brooks and Callahan store isn't as large as Otis department store.
9. The Davises car was parked on our driveway, right behind Travis hot rod.
10. Too many *ands* will weaken anyones writing.
11. Don't take anyone elses word for it; trust your own experience.
12. Keats poems are more like Tennysons than like Brownings.
13. A fifteen minutes walk every day may save five dollars worth of doctors prescriptions.
14. It used to be thought that *Titus Andronicus* was Thomas Kyds work, but scholars now agree that it is Shakespeares.
15. My brothers boat was not working, so we borrowed a launch belonging to the Willises.

# 36 THE COLON

The colon is a rather formal mark of punctuation, and it is not widely used in informal writing if a semicolon or dash will serve instead. The colon is primarily an introductory mark, and its proper uses are listed below.

## 36a Introducing a Formal List, a Long Quotation, or an Explanatory Statement

The principal use of the colon is to introduce a formal enumeration or list, a long quotation, or an explanatory statement.

**Correct.** There are three causes: poverty, injustice, and indolence.

**Correct.** In 1803 Thomas Jefferson said: "We have seen with sincere concern the flames of war lighted up again in Europe. . . ." [A long quotation follows.]

**Correct.** Blair regarded the demand for popular rights as a king might regard it: that is, as a mode of usurpation.

Note that a list introduced by a colon should be in apposition to a preceding word; that is, the sentence preceding the colon should be grammatically complete without the list.

**Undesirable.** We furnish: towels, sheets, pillow slips, dishes, cooking utensils, silverware.

**Correct.** We furnish the following articles: towels, sheets, etc.

**Correct.** We furnish the following: towels, sheets, etc.

**Correct.** The following articles are furnished: towels, sheets, etc.

## 36b Between Main Clauses

The colon may be used between two principal clauses when the second clause explains or develops the first.

**Correct.** Intercollegiate athletics continues to be big business, but Robert Hutchins long ago pointed out a simple remedy: colleges should stop charging admission to football games.

**Correct.** There is one strong reason why gambling should not be legalized: gambling establishments always attract gangsters and criminals.

## 36c After a Formal Salutation in a Business Letter, etc.

A colon is used after a formal salutation in a business letter.

**Correct.** Dear Sir:
Gentlemen:
My dear Mr. Harris:

A colon is used to separate hour and minutes in numerals indicating time.

**Correct.** The train leaves at 9:27 A.M., and arrives at St. Louis at 8:15 P.M.

In bibliographical references, a colon is used between the place of publication and the name of the publisher.

**Correct.** New York: Oxford University Press

Between the parts of a Biblical reference a colon may be used.

**Correct.** *Proverbs* 28:20

# 37 THE DASH

Since the dash (made on the typewriter by *two* hyphens) is a rather dramatic mark of punctuation, it should not be used indiscriminately in place of commas, semicolons, or periods. Its proper use is to indicate a stronger degree of separation than the comma. The overuse of dashes may suggest that the writer is careless, or that he does not know how to use the other marks of punctuation, or that he is striving to gain emphasis by the easy device of emphatic punctuation rather than by exact and vivid diction or effective sentence structure.

## 37a As a Separator

A dash is used, as a separator, to indicate that a sentence is broken off or to indicate a sharp turn of thought.

**Correct.** The Senator spoke of the need for economy in government, for aid to distressed farmers and industrialists, for — but you know the rest.

**Correct.** In the end Hawthorne simply "rescues" Coverdale by suppressing the conflicts that threaten to liberate him — and thereby, it might be added, destroying the novel.
— IRVING HOWE

## 37b To Set Off Parenthetic Elements

Dashes may be used to set off appositives or parenthetic elements when commas are insufficient.

**Correct.** Three ships — a yawl, a sloop, and a schooner — were anchored in the harbor. [If the commas were used to set off *a yawl, a sloop, and a schooner*, the sentence might be misunderstood to refer to six ships. The dashes make it clear that only three ships are meant.]

**Correct.** By the time the speech was over — it lasted almost two hours — I was dozing in my chair. [Since the parenthetic element is an independent clause, commas would be insufficient to set it off clearly.]

Modern writers often use a dash to emphasize an important or contrasting appositive.

**Correct.** The educated classes are learning to blame ideas for our troubles, rather than blaming what is a very different thing — our own bad thinking.

— LIONEL TRILLING

## 37c To Mark a Summarizing Statement

When a sentence begins with a list of substantives, a dash is commonly used to separate the list from the summarizing statement which follows.

**Correct.** To work, to play, to raise children, to move about freely in the country — we tend to take these rights for granted.

**Correct.** The chance to sit on a committee with no big issues to debate, the prospect of introducing bills which will never be reported, the opportunity to write speeches that will rarely be delivered — these are not horizons toward which an able man will strain.

—HAROLD LASKI

# 38 PARENTHESES AND BRACKETS

Parentheses, like dashes and commas, are used to enclose or set off parenthetic, explanatory, or supplementary material. Arbitrary rules indicating which marks to use cannot be laid down, but in general commas are the weakest marks, dashes are stronger, and parentheses are strongest. Commas are most frequently used, and are usually sufficient when the parenthetic material is very closely related in thought or structure to the rest of the sentence. If the parenthetic material is long or if it contains commas, dashes would customarily be used to set it off. Parentheses are most often used for explanatory or supplementary material of the sort which might be put in a footnote — useful information which is not essential. Parentheses are also used to enclose numbers which mark an enumeration within a sentence.

**Correct.** The individual combatant might say he is fighting (if you should ask him and he would honestly and seriously reply) because he has been drafted — drafted either by the Selective Service or the equally potent public opinion (however camouflaged under words like *duty, patriotism,* etc.).

— HARLOW SHAPLEY

**Correct.** His latest article ("Markets and Monopoly") was published in 1949.

**Correct.** In general, the war powers of the President cannot be precisely defined, but must remain somewhat vague and uncertain. (See Wilson's *Constitutional Government in the United States.*)

**Correct.** The types of noncreative thinking listed by Robinson are (1) reverie, or daydreaming, (2) making minor decisions, (3) rationalizing, or justifying our prejudices.

Brackets are used to enclose a word or words inserted in a quotation by the person quoting.

**Correct.** "It is clear [the message read] that the Muscle Shoals development is but a small part of the potential public usefulness of the entire Tennessee River."

— D. E. LILIENTHAL

**Correct.** "We know more about its state [the state of the language] in the later Middle Ages; and from the time of Shakespeare on, our information is quite complete."

The word *sic* (meaning *thus*) enclosed in brackets is sometimes inserted in a quotation after a misspelling or other error to indicate that the error occurs in the original.

**Correct.** He sent this written confession: "She followed us into the kitchen, snatched a craving [*sic*] knife from the table, and came toward me with it."

### EXERCISE

Study the use of colons, dashes, parentheses, and brackets in the following sentences.

1. And so far as they [those who go to college for social reasons] are concerned, the remedy is plain: a stern insistence on the part of the college authorities that they demonstrate a right to be there.

   — RICHARD BURTON

2. A sense of the value of time — that is, of the best way to divide one's time into one's various activities — is an essential preliminary to efficient work.

   — ARNOLD BENNETT

3. And watching the white clouds so bright against the intense blue, Ashurst, on his silver-wedding day, longed for — he knew not what.

— JOHN GALSWORTHY

4. It had never occurred to me that he was a real Communist (I had never, so far as I knew, met one) until, looking over the proofs of a forthcoming book, I read the assertion that he had been a Party member.

— BRADFORD SMITH

5. Clubs, fraternities, nations — these are the beloved barriers in the way of a workable world; these will have to surrender some of their rights and some of their ribs.

— E. B. WHITE

Insert colons, dashes, parentheses, and brackets as they are needed in the following sentences.

1. Each of its large rooms there were no separate cells in this prison housed some twenty prisoners.
2. I took part in a number of activities in high school the rally committee, dramatics, *Metate* staff the *Metate* is our annual, and glee club.
3. He had already joined the Quakers and was an occasional speaker the Quakers have no ordained ministers at their meetings in Philadelphia.
4. According to an inscription on the flyleaf, the book had been owned by Alburt *sic* Taylor.
5. The writers covered during the semester were Pope, Swift, Gay, Mandeville, James Thomson the man who wrote *The Seasons*, not the later James Thomson, Addison, and Steele.
6. This religious sect permits dancing but forbids some other seemingly innocent recreations card playing, for example, is banned as being the next thing to gambling.
7. According to the *Mason Report* Stearns testified as follows "I made his John Brown's acquaintance early in January, 1857, in Boston."

8. The midnight programs at the Owl Theater feature horror films, science-fiction thrillers, movies of strange monsters from the sea you know the kind of thing.
9. Three new cars a station wagon and two sedans held the whole party.
10. The musicians according to the program they were Gypsies played some sentimental tunes by Victor Herbert.

## REVIEW EXERCISES

### 1

Punctuate the following sentences. Be ready to give a reason for any mark of punctuation you use.

1. This incident illustrates a very important reason for being physically fit fitness may make the difference between life and death
2. I want to see Rome and its ancient ruins London where so many historical events have taken place and Paris which is filled with great art treasures
3. In the new house the kitchen the bathroom and the utility rooms will have plain wood floors
4. Under the system just established a student from a family which cannot afford to send a child away to college will have a chance for a scholarship especially if he is interested in science or engineering
5. Reading gives enjoyment to many friendless lonely people but it will not encourage them to go out and make friends
6. Despite the protests of so-called humanitarians scientists who are doing physiological research require experimental animals to work on
7. Many years ago I read the novel *Gone with the Wind* a lengthy story of the Civil War
8. Man lives in groups small animals live in groups even plants sometimes live in groups

9. The following men will report to the Infirmary Wednesday October 3 at 4 30 for medical examinations Appleby Peter Catlin Bill Hadley Charles Stevenson Robert
10. Jan was born in Vienna Austria on January 14 1934 in a fashionable residential area
11. The student if he is lucky enough to pass the test may register for the next course in the sequence
12. In the Dark Ages a man was born a serf lived as a serf and died a serf his sons inherited their father's place in society and their sons could expect nothing better
13. With Prince Albert the prime minister said we have buried our sovereign
14. Sam blew through a straw into a glass of water for an ocean effect rang bells slammed doors and beeped into a long wooden whistle all without cracking a smile
15. The inhabitants of Washington DC must endure hot sticky weather for most of the summer
16. Only the soft continuous thumping of the engine breaks the stillness while behind the ship the long white wake gleams in the darkness
17. Dr Kings book says that there is no longer any danger of epidemics in Western Europe but I think he neglects the possibility of new diseases developing
18. Most people today accustomed to the increasing benefits afforded by the federal government would disagree with the authors statement That government is best which governs least
19. The average college graduate is bound to have some knowledge of the common arts painting music architecture literature
20. The chief trees found on the hills are scrub oaks live oaks sugar pine and pinyon trees and along the San Antonio and Nacimiento Rivers willows and cottonwoods grow thickly
21. Admiral Byrd the first man to fly over the South Pole did so on November 28 1929

22. In his book Mr Carnegie says If you lose an argument you lose it and if you win an argument you also lose it
23. To be more specific let us compare two carrier-based naval fighter aircraft the Hellcat of World War II and the Panther which fought in Korea
24. Boys are like that Dad said dont worry so much
25. Philosophers differ widely among themselves as to the nature of truth however they all agree that such a thing as truth exists even though it cannot certainly be discovered

**2**

Punctuate the following paragraphs and be ready to give a reason for each mark used.

**1.** In the past poets may have felt the pity of struggling against destiny the sadness of death taking off the young and the beautiful the bitterness of injustice but they were also influenced by the poverty and hopelessness of the common man by the fatal bars of privilege by slavery and grinding toil and hunger. If the happy ending was only an aspiration to people in the past a life free from pressing want is an actuality of the present American economy for such numbers of people that our atmosphere is charged with confidence. The background against which tragedy was written in the past does not exist here and if we do not create great tragedies it may be because they are not necessary for us. The individual who cannot understand tragedy in the arts may become incapable of facing anything serious in his own life but this does not mean that the popular arts are under any compulsion to be largely tragic in tone. An aesthete and an intellectual of the first order has even been skeptical of the uses of tragedy "Because Aeschylus and Sophocles were great poets Santayana writes does it follow that life would be cheap if it did not follow their fables? The life of tragic heroes is not good it is misguided unnecessary and absurd." In this respect the executives of Hollywood seem to adhere to the life of reason more closely than their critics.

— GILBERT SELDES, *The Great Audience* [1]

[1] From *The Great Audience* by Gilbert Seldes. Reprinted by permission of The Viking Press, Inc.

**2.** I could tell without turning who was coming. There wasnt a big flat-footed clop-clop like horses make on hard-pack but a kind of edgy clip-clip-clip. There was only one man around here would ride a mule at least on this kind of business. That was Bill Winder who drove the stage between Reno and Bridgers Wells. A mule is tough all right a good mule can work two horses into the ground and not know it. But theres something about a mule a man cant get fond of. Maybe its just the way a mule is just as you feel its the end with a man whos that way. But you cant make a mule part of the way you live like your horse is its like he had no insides no soul. Instead of a partner youve just got something else to work on along with the steers. Winder didnt like mules either but thats why he rode them. It was against his religion to get on a horse horses were for driving

Its Winder Gil said and looked at Davies and grinned. The news gets around dont it

I looked at Davies too in the glass but he wasnt showing anything just staring at his drink and minding his own thoughts

Winder wouldnt help Davies any we knew that. He was edgy the same way Gil was but angry not funning and you couldnt get at him with an idea

Gabe Hart was with him on another mule. Gabe was his hostler a big ape-built man stronger than was natural but weak-minded not crazy but childish like his mind had never grown up. He was dirty too he slept in the stables with his horses and his knees and elbows were always out of his clothes and his long hair and beard always had bits of hay and a powder of grain chaff in them. Gabe was gentle though not a mean streak in him like there generally is in stupid very strong men

— WALTER VAN TILBURG CLARK, *The Ox-Bow Incident*[2]

**3.** Let us consider Dr Parkman for a moment. It was he a Harvard man himself who had given the very land on which the then new Medical College stood. Moreover he had endowed the Parkman Chair of Anatomy then occupied by Dr Oliver Wendell Holmes. The Parkmans had been prominent from what even by Boston stand-

[2] From *The Ox-Bow Incident* by Walter Van Tilburg Clark, copyright 1940 by Walter Van Tilburg Clark. Reprinted by permission of Random House, Inc.

ards were ancient times. His brother the Rev Francis Parkman was a well-known divine whose son of the same name was on the verge of achieving fame as an historian. All of the Parkmans were well-to-do and the doctors wealth was such that his son who never earned a penny in his life was to leave five million dollars for the care and improvement of Boston Common

The usually staid Boston press threw all its genteel standards out of the window and went into a dither. Police arrested scores of obscure persons. And then though neither police nor public knew of it an astonishing incident occurred. Professor John White Webster made a call on the Rev Francis Parkman. The professor said that he had had what he termed an interview with the missing man in the Medical College on Friday afternoon the day of the doctors disappearance November 23 1849 at which time he had paid Doctor Parkman the sum of $483. The latter had then said the professor left the college

John White Webster was 56 years of age a graduate of Harvard Medical. Since 1824 he had taught chemistry at Harvard and since 1827 had held the Erving Chair of Chemistry and Mineralogy. The Websters lived in Cambridge had four pretty daughters and were noted for the hospitality they lavished on faculty members and wives

— STEWART HOLBROOK, "Murder at Harvard,"
*The American Mercury*

4. Ben Wister yelled at his mules and the barge began to move. In immediate response came other yells wilder and louder. Down the slope from the Inn gamboling in the moonlight rushed Harry Wurts his head decorated with maple leaves. He had somehow possessed himself of a harmonica which he blew rather than played. Reaching the tow path he jumped on board safely

After him pell-mell hallooing and whooping came Dick Nyce and Mark Irwin. Mark flung himself plainly with intention short of the stern and struck the water with a prodigious splash

Throw him the anchor shouted Harry. Blow the man down. Mark came to the surface gave a roar and struck out swimming after the barge but he made little progress and soon he touched bottom and clambered streaming up the bank. Dick Nyce on the tow path was doubled up helpless convulsed with laughter so Mark rushed at him and pushed him in

The damn fools said Joe Jackman. Boy are they going to feel good tomorrow

It could be seen that his sentiment was generally shared but Harry Wurts throwing his maple leaves overboard said That's what I say Only why wait till tomorrow? Sit near Joe and feel bad right now

By way of dismissing these monkey-shines the mandolin sounded under the awning and several voices began to sing Last night I was dreaming of thee Love was dreaming

Harry Wurts hearing it groaned and covered his ears but the older people liked it and the volume increased. The barge glided on the bow ripples running silver the moon behind lifting higher above the narrow water. At farm houses across the fields the aroused dogs barked and barked as the singing floated to them faintly moving back toward Childerstown

— James Gould Cozzens, *The Just and the Unjust*[3]

**5.** For the residents of Long Beach California May 22 1953 was a day of civic self-satisfaction. President Eisenhower had just signed what is somewhat inaccurately known as the Tidelands Oil Act a measure effectively relinquishing all Federal claims to the submerged lands "within the historic boundaries" of the coastal states. It was a complex piece of legislation reflecting complex and bitterly contested legal and political arguments but to most of the three hundred thousand citizens of Long Beach its meaning was simple and wonderful the city was almost as rich as the Aga Khan

It is estimated that the oil reserves in the submerged lands within the historic boundary of the State of California a minimum of three miles seaward from the shoreline at low tide are worth more than $10 billion at current prices. About a fifth of this total or roughly $2 billion worth lies under submerged lands granted to Long Beach in 1911 for what seemed then their only possible use harbor development. After the discovery of the great oil pool under the harbor many years later the state supreme court of California ruled that the 1911 grant included mineral rights because it hadn't excluded them. In 1951 the state legislature went even further giving the city per-

[3] From *The Just and the Unjust* by James Gould Cozzens. Reprinted by permission of the publishers, Harcourt, Brace and Company, Inc.

mission to spend oil and gas revenues for capital improvements other than harbor development. What could be more natural then than to assume that the new Congressional action had removed any doubt concerning the city's title to the potential two billion? What question could there be that as a result of the decision Long Beach was about to enter upon an almost taxless municipal millennium

Well somewhere mayors are smiling and somewhere councilmen shout but there is no joy in Long Beach. A surprise ruling of the state supreme court early last spring took away fifty per cent of the oil wealth and all of the accompanying dry-gas revenues. And state legislators have been threatening to take what remains. The state and Long Beach happy hand-holding partners when they trooped to Washington with the big oil companies to fight the Federal grab are now glaring at each other over Long Beach newspaper headlines about the state grab

— HALE CHAMPION, "Battle Royal for Oil" [4]

[4] From *The Reporter*, December 29, 1955. Reprinted by permission.

## Diction

**39.** USE OF THE DICTIONARY

- **a.** Abbreviations and symbols in a dictionary
- **b.** Information found in a dictionary

**40.** GOOD USAGE: LEVELS OF USAGE

- **a.** Levels of standard English
- **b.** Substandard English
- **c.** Slang
- **d.** Errors in idiom

**41.** EXACT DICTION

- **a.** Specific words
- **b.** Colorless verbs
- **c.** Jargon
- **d.** Exact connotation

**42.** EFFECTIVE DICTION

- **a.** Pretentious language
- **b.** Trite rhetorical expressions
- **c.** Technical language
- **d.** Appropriate figures of speech
- **e.** Awkward repetitions

**43.** GLOSSARY OF WORDS COMMONLY MISUSED

# 39 USE OF THE DICTIONARY

Like all languages, English is continually changing. New words are added as names are required for new inventions, discoveries, and ideas: *meson*, *penicillin*, *transistor*, *motel*, *radar*, *apartheid*. Old words acquire new meanings as they are used in new ways: *half life* (physics), *snow* (television), *stylus*, *cartridge* (high-fidelity recording). Some old words disappear as the need for them vanishes; a whole vocabulary dealing with horse-drawn vehicles is probably on its way out. Words gain or lose prestige: *strenuous* and *mob* are now standard words, although they were once considered slang. *Aryan* acquired such disreputable associations through its use by the Nazis that most writers avoid it today.

A dictionary is an attempt to record the current uses and meanings of words. Large unabridged dictionaries include a history of the past meanings of words, biographical and geographical data, rules for pronunciation, spelling, and punctuation, and a variety of other useful information. The large dictionaries, found in any college library, include:

*The Oxford English Dictionary*. 12 volumes and Supplement. Oxford: Clarendon Press, 1933. (This is the standard historical dictionary of the language; it traces and illustrates the development of each word from its earliest appearance to the present.)

*Webster's New International Dictionary*. Second Edition. Springfield, Mass.: G. & C. Merriam Co., 1954.

*New Standard Dictionary*. New York: Funk & Wagnalls Company, 1952.

Unabridged dictionaries are invaluable for occasional reference, but too bulky for constant use. More practical for the student to own is one of the following abridged desk dictionaries. All are reliable, but some strong and weak points are noted below.

*Webster's New Collegiate Dictionary.* Springfield, Massachusetts: G. & C. Merriam Co., 1956. (Conservative and authoritative. Lists meanings in chronological order, so that the ordinary sense of a word is not always readily discernible. Separate alphabetical sections for biographic and geographic names.)

*Webster's New World Dictionary.* Cleveland: The World Publishing Company, 1953. (Simplified definitions. Clear and full etymologies. Liberal policy toward informal and colloquial English. Simplified key to pronunciation, with equivalents in the International Phonetic Alphabet.)

*American College Dictionary.* New York: Harper and Brothers, 1948. (Stresses American usage. Gives basic meanings of a word first. Simplified key to pronunciation. An awkward system of abbreviations makes the etymologies difficult to follow.)

*New College Standard Dictionary.* New York: Funk & Wagnalls Co., 1950.

*The Winston Dictionary.* College Edition. Philadelphia: The John C. Winston Co., 1945.

*Thorndike-Barnhart Comprehensive Desk Dictionary.* New York: Doubleday & Company, Inc., 1951.

## 39a Abbreviations and Symbols in a Dictionary

To use a dictionary effectively, you must understand the abbreviations and symbols it uses. These are explained in the introductory section. Here are entries from three collegiate dictionaries:

Spelling and Syllabication

Part of Speech

**im·ply′** (ĭm·plī′), *v. t.;* IM·PLIED′ (-plīd′); IM·PLY′ING. [OF. *emplier,* fr. L. *implicare.*] **1**. *Obs.* To infold. **2**. To involve in substance, or by fair inference, or by construction of law, when not expressly stated; to contain by implication; as, war *implies* fighting. **3**. To express indirectly; to hint or hint at. **4**. Of words or phrases, to involve as a meaning or meanings. — **Syn.** See INCLUDE: SUGGEST.

Synonyms

By permission. From Webster's New Collegiate Dictionary
Copyright, 1949, 1951, 1953, 1956
by G. & C. Merriam Co.

Pronunciation

Etymology

**im·ply** (im-plī′), ***v.t.*** [IMPLIED (-plīd′), IMPLYING], [ME. ***implien;*** OFr. ***emplier;*** L. ***implicare*** < ***in-***, in + ***plicare,*** to fold], 1. to have as a necessary part, condition, or effect; contain, include, or involve naturally or necessarily: as, drama ***implies*** conflict. 2. to indicate without saying openly or directly; hint; suggest; intimate: as, his attitude ***implied*** boredom. 3. [Obs.], to enfold; entangle. —***SYN***. see **suggest.**

Meanings

Usage Label

From *Webster's New World Dictionary of the American Language,* College Edition, Copyright 1957 by The World Publishing Company.

Inflected Forms

**im·ply** (ĭm plī′), *v.t.,* **-plied, -plying. 1.** to involve as a necessary circumstance: *speech implies a speaker.* **2.** (of words) to signify or mean. **3.** to indicate or suggest, as something naturally to be inferred, without express statement. **4.** *Obs.* to enfold. [ME *implie(n),* t. OF: m. *emplier,* g. L *implicāre* enfold, entangle, involve]

Reprinted by courtesy of the publishers from *The American College Dictionary,* copyright 1947–1957 by Random House, Inc. (textbook edition by Harper & Brothers).

## 39b Information Found in a Dictionary

### Spelling and Syllabication

When more than one spelling is given, the one printed first is usually to be preferred. Division of the word into syllables follows the conventions accepted by printers.

### Pronunciation

A key to the symbols used to indicate pronunciation of words is printed on the front or back inside cover of the dictionary. Some dictionaries also run an abbreviated key to pronunciation at the bottom of each page or every other page. Word accent is shown by the symbol (′) after the stressed syllable.

### Part of Speech

Abbreviations (explained in the introductory section of the dictionary) are used to indicate the various grammatical uses of a word: e.g., **imply,** *v.t.* means that *imply* is a transitive verb. Note that some words can be used as several different parts of speech. *Forfeit*, for example, is listed first as a noun, and its various meanings in this use are defined. Then its meaning when used as an adjective is given, and finally its meaning as a transitive verb.

### Inflected Forms

Forms of the past tense and past participle of verbs, the comparative or superlative degree of adjectives, and the plural of nouns are given whenever there might be doubt as to the correct form or spelling.

### Etymology

The history of each word is indicated by the forms in use in Middle or Old English, or in the language from which the word was borrowed. Earlier meanings are often given.

### Meanings

Different meanings of a word are numbered and defined, sometimes with illustrative examples. Some dictionaries give the oldest meanings first; others list the common meanings of the word first, and rarer, earlier meanings last.

### Usage Labels

Descriptive labels, often abbreviated, indicate the level of usage: Obsolete, Colloquial, Slang, Dialectal, etc. Sometimes usage labels indicate a special field, rather than a level of usage: e.g., Poetic, Irish, Chemistry, etc. If a word has no usage label, it may be assumed to be in common use on all levels of speech and writing. Note that foreign words which are not yet naturalized and hence should be written in italics are indicated by a special symbol (‖) or (‡), or by a label: *French*, *Italian*, etc.

### Synonyms

Words that have nearly identical or closely related meanings often need careful discrimination to indicate the precise connotation of each. A full account of the distinctions in meaning between synonyms (for example, *suggest*, *imply*, *hint*, *intimate*, and *insinuate*) is given at the end of the entry for the basic word. Cross references to this word are given for its synonyms.

## EXERCISES

### 1

In looking up the meanings of words, try to discover within what limits of meaning the word may be used. Read the definition as a whole; do not pick out a single synonym and suppose that this and the word defined are interchangeable. After looking up the following words in your dictionary, write sentences which will unmistakably illustrate the meaning of each word.

| | | |
|---|---|---|
| anachronism | irony | precocious |
| duress | materiel | retroactive |
| eminent | misanthropy | sabotage |
| fetish | mundane | sinecure |
| hedonist | neologism | sophistication |
| imminent | nepotism | taboo |
| increment | ostentatious | tempera |
| innocuous | philanthropy | travesty |

**2**

Look up each of the following words both in an unabridged dictionary and in an abridged one, and write a report showing how much more discriminatingly and clearly the larger volume explains the use of each word than the smaller one does. State the exact title, the publisher, and the date of both dictionaries.

| | | | |
|---|---|---|---|
| Bible | Christian | court | idealism |
| catholic | color | evolution | liberal |

**3**

How may the etymologies given by the dictionary help one to remember the meaning or the spelling of the following words? (Note that when a series of words has the same etymology, the etymology is usually given only with the first word of the series.)

| | | |
|---|---|---|
| agnostic | denouement | malapropism |
| alibi | homogeneous | peer (noun) |
| capitol | hyperbole | privilege |
| cohort | insidious | sacrilegious |
| colleague | isosceles | sarcasm |
| concave | magnanimous | subterfuge |

### 4

Some dictionaries have a separate section listing all abbreviations in common use; others put abbreviations used in the dictionary in one list and include other abbreviations in the main alphabetical arrangement. Look up the following abbreviations and be ready to state in class what they mean:

| | | |
|---|---|---|
| *at. wt.* | *E.T.A.* | *LL.D.* |
| *CAA* | *ff.* | *OHG.* |
| *colloq.* | *K.C.B.* | *Pb* |
| *e.g.* | *l.c.* | *q.v.* |

### 5

Consult the dictionary for the distinctions in meaning between the members of each of the following pairs of words:

| | |
|---|---|
| *neglect* and *negligence* | *contagious* and *infectious* |
| *ingenuous* and *ingenious* | *wit* and *humor* |
| *fewer* and *less* | *eminent* and *famous* |
| *admit* and *confess* | *criticize* and *censure* |
| *instinct* and *intuition* | *farther* and *further* |

### 6

In each sentence, choose the more precise of the two italicized words. Be able to justify your choice.

1. The decadent Roman civilization was a *feminine, effeminate* civilization.
2. Her charming innocence is *childlike, childish.*
3. The problem is to assure the farm workers *continuous, continual* employment.
4. He is *continuously, continually* in trouble with the police.
5. I am quite *jealous, envious* of your opportunity to study in Europe.

6. She is so *decided, decisive* in her manner that people always give in to her.
7. If we give your class all of these privileges, we may establish *precedents, precedence* which may be unwise.
8. She always makes her health her *alibi, excuse* for her failures.
9. Many in the class were *disinterested, uninterested* and went to sleep.
10. He had always impressed me as cold and *forbidding, foreboding.*

### 7

Find the precise meaning of each word in the following groups, and write sentences to illustrate that meaning.

1. abandon, desert, forsake
2. hate, loathe, despise
3. ludicrous, droll, comic
4. silent, reserved, taciturn
5. work, labor, toil, drudgery
6. meager, scanty, sparse
7. knack, talent, genius
8. anxious, eager, avid
9. expect, anticipate, hope
10. famous, renowned, notorious

# 40 GOOD USAGE: LEVELS OF USAGE

Modern linguistics has largely discarded the terms *good* and *bad*, *correct* and *incorrect*, to describe English usage. But linguists still speak of "standard" and "substandard" English, to indicate the difference between the usage of educated persons and that of the illiterate or semiliterate. Within these two large divisions, a number of levels are recognized.

Standard English:
- Formal and Technical
- Informal (or General)
- Colloquial

Substandard English:
- Dialectal
- Slang
- Illiterate (or Vulgate)

A dictionary labels all substandard words, or uses of words, which it includes. But standard words are labeled only to show special limitations in their use. Some of the common labels for standard words are the following:

*Colloquial.* Characteristic of the familiar conversation of the educated.

**Example.** One reporter did a *take-off on* the President.

*Obsolete.* No longer in general use, but found in older works of literature.

**Example.** Mice and rats, and such small *deer* . . . [i.e., any small animals.] — SHAKESPEARE

*Archaic.* Going out of use, too old-fashioned for ordinary contexts.

> **Example.** Dry clashed his *harness* [armor] in the icy caves . . . — TENNYSON

*Poetic.* Used in poetry rather than in ordinary prose.

> **Example.** *Oft* in the stilly night . . .

*Law.* A legal term not in general use.

> **Example.** *Tort,* a wrongful act not involving a breach of contract.

*Zoology.* A technical term used by scientists.

> **Example.** When *endoderm* is applied to embryonic structures it is equivalent to *hypoblast.*

*Scottish.* Limited chiefly to Scotland.

> **Example.** *dour,* in the sense of "stern and severe."

Notice that most standard words are not labeled at all and that dictionaries do not distinguish between the Formal and Informal levels.

## 40a Levels of Standard English

Formal English is usually written and is used in scholarly articles, official documents, formal letters, and any context calling for scrupulous propriety.

Informal or General English is the language, both written and spoken, used by the educated classes in carrying on the everyday business of the country. It is the level used in most books, magazines, newspapers, and ordinary business communications.

Colloquial English is the language of familiar conversation among educated people. It occurs frequently in informal writing and is usually considered Standard English, though it would be inappropriate in formal or semiformal contexts.

It is impossible to draw sharp lines between the levels of Standard English. Relative differences, however, can be indicated. *Exhausted* and *fatigued* are more formal than *tired; interred* is more formal than *buried; acquire* is more formal than *get; purchase* is more formal than *buy. Hunch* used as a verb is Standard Informal English. Used as a noun (to have a hunch that . . .) it is colloquial; it would be used freely in educated speech and often in informal writing to avoid the very formal *premonition* or *foreboding. Size up* is colloquial; *look over* is informal; *inspect* and *examine* might be used in either informal or formal contexts; *scrutinize* is definitely formal and is rarely heard and not often used in writing.

Study the following groupings of approximate synonyms:

| FORMAL | INFORMAL | COLLOQUIAL |
|---|---|---|
| comprehend | understand | catch on |
| altercation | quarrel | row |
| wrathful, irate | angry | mad |
| goad, taunt | tease | needle |
| predicament | problem | jam, fix |
| exorbitant | high | steep |

The basic principle of good usage is to fit the level of your language to the situation and to the reader. If you are writing an obituary or a formal letter of application, substandard English would be as inappropriate as a T shirt at a funeral. If you are writing a handbook of information for newcomers at a summer camp, formal English would be as incongruous as a starched shirt at a clambake. During the past fifty years, the center of common usage has moved away from the Formal level toward the Informal and Colloquial. Especially in magazines and newspapers, good writers are more apt to use colloquialisms and even slang rather than risk the stilted pompousness of Formal English in a commonplace context. Nevertheless, it is still important to be able to distinguish between Colloquial, Informal, and Formal usage, since an educated person may need to use all of these levels on occasion.

#### EXERCISE

With the aid of a dictionary and your own linguistic judgment, classify the following Standard English words as Formal, Informal, or Colloquial.

1. nebulous, vague
2. flaccid, limp
3. crank, card (eccentric or droll person)
4. square (to settle, or repay)
5. square meal
6. square one's shoulders
7. old maid, spinster
8. hide, secrete
9. enigma, puzzle
10. grimace, make a face at
11. contend with, fight, combat
12. sock, hosiery
13. cram, study
14. cranky, irascible
15. jack up the price
16. criticize, ridicule, ride

### 40b Substandard English

All substandard words which the dictionary includes are labeled, but it must be remembered that many illiterate, profane, or slang terms do not appear in the dictionary at all. The common labels for substandard words are the following:

*Dialect.* A word common to a particular region and not used throughout the country. Such words are not necessarily substandard in the regions where they are found, and sometimes they are useful additions to the local vocabulary. But they should not be used when equivalent words in national use are available.

**Examples.** *lagniappe* (Creole country), *side meat* (South), *stoop*, meaning "porch" (Midwest).

*Illiterate*, or *Vulgar*. Found chiefly in the speech of the uneducated. Not to be used in writing except in dialogue.

**Example.** *hain't*, *ain't*, *sot* in his ways.

*Slang*. Words with a forced, exaggerated, or humorous meaning, often originating among groups of people who wish to set themselves off from the average, respectable citizen. (See **40c**.)

Invented words coined without authority from words in good standing and not yet generally accepted are substandard and should be avoided in writing. Advertising copywriters are continually inventing new words (visit our *sleepwear* department, our *whisper-weight* wool dress, to be *accessorized* casually, *Torque Flite*) which have little chance of gaining general acceptance. Occasionally a coined word may justify itself:

> Churchill's chief strength was his basic *John Bullishness*.

But a beginning writer had better not risk such barbarisms as the following:

> Hitler tried to subdue his opponents with a deliberate policy of terrorism and *torturism*.

Other examples of Substandard English will be found in the Glossary of Words Commonly Misused, Section **43.**

## 40c Slang

To call a man whose ideas and behavior are unpredictable and unconventional "a screwball" and to describe his ideas as "for the birds" apparently satisfies some obscure human urge toward irreverent, novel, and vehement expression. Some slang terms remain in fairly wide use because they are vivid ways of expressing an idea which has no exact standard equivalent: *stooge*, *lame duck*, *shot* of whiskey, a bridge *shark*. Such words have a good chance of becoming accepted as Standard English. *Mob*, *banter*, *sham*, and *lynch* were all once regarded as slang terms.

A good deal of slang, however, reflects nothing more than the user's desire to be different, and such slang has little chance of being accepted into the language. Newspaper columnists and sports writers often use a flamboyant jargon intended to show off their ingenuity or cleverness. For centuries criminals have used a special, semisecret language, and many modern slang terms originate in the argot of the underworld: *gat*, *scram*, *squeal* or *sing* (confess), *bump off*. Teen-agers and hot jazz addicts develop a constantly changing slang which seems intended mainly to distinguish the user as a member of a select group or inner circle.

Whatever the motive behind it, slang should be used with discretion. Its incongruity in a sober, practical context makes it an effective way of achieving force and emphasis:

**Acceptable slang.** This book is so intelligently constructed, so beautifully written, so really acute at moments—and so *phony*.

But most slang terms are too violent to fit comfortably into ordinary, everyday writing.

**Objectionable slang.** We, the undersigned students, are not *crabbing* about the disciplinary measures drawn up by the Council; our *gripe* is that we are not adequately represented on the Council.

Furthermore, slang goes out of fashion very quickly, through overuse, and dated slang sounds more quaint and old-fashioned than formal English. *Tight* has worn well, but *spifflicated* now sounds depressingly dowdy, and *boiled*, *crocked*, *fried*, and *pie-eyed* may soon be museum pieces.

The chief objection to the use of slang is that it so quickly loses any precise meaning. Calling a person *a drip* or *a creep* conveys nothing but your feeling of dislike. *Swell* and *lousy* are the vaguest kind of terms, lumping all experience into two crude divisions, pleasing and unpleasing. Try to get several people to agree on the precise meaning of *egghead* and you will realize how vague and inexact a term it is. The remedy is to analyze your meaning and specify it. What exactly are the qualities which lead you to classify a person under the loose term *egghead?*

If, despite these warnings, you must use slang in serious writing, do it deliberately and accept the responsibility for it. Do not attempt to excuse yourself by putting the slang term in quotation marks. If you are ashamed of a slang term, do not use it.

## 40d Errors in Idiom

An idiom is an expression peculiar to the language and not explainable by the principles of logic or the ordinary meanings of the individual words. Why do we say that a person is *on duty*, *in trouble*, or *at play?* The only answer is that these combinations are idiomatic. How can a foreigner who knows the words *take*, *in*, *up*, *down*, and *over* deduce the meanings of *take in* (comprehend), *taken in* (fooled), *intake*, *take up* (begin to consider), *take down* (humiliate), *take over*, and *overtake?* He can't. These are idioms, and they must be learned individually.

Idiom requires that some words be followed by arbitrarily fixed prepositions. Something may be *required of* all students, *compulsory for* all, *necessary to* all, or *obligatory on* all. Here are some idiomatic uses of prepositions:

agree *to* (a proposal); *on* (a procedure); *with* (a person)
angry *at*, *about* (a thing); *with* (a person)
argue *with* (a person); *for* or *against* or *about*, not *on* (a measure)

correspond *to* or *with* (a thing); *with* (a person)
differ *from* expresses unlikeness; differ *with* expresses divergence of opinion

This book differs from the other in giving more details.
I differ with you about the importance of athletics.

independent *of*, not *from*
interest *in*, not *for*
listen *to*, not *at* (but: listen *at* the door)
possessed *by* or *with* (an idea); *by* (a spirit); *of* (goods)
*with regard to* or *as regards*, not *with regards to* nor *in regards to*
stay *at* home, not stay *to* home
superior *to*, not *than*
try *to*, not try *and* (except colloquially)
wait *on* (a customer); *for* (a person or thing); *at* (a place)

Idiom demands that certain words be followed by infinitives, others by gerunds. For instance:

| Infinitive | Gerund |
|---|---|
| able to go | capable of going |
| like to go | enjoy going |
| eager to go | cannot help going |
| hesitate to go | privilege of going |

If two idioms are used in a compound construction, each idiom must be complete. (See also Section **21.**)

**Wrong.** He had no love or confidence in his employer.

**Correct, but awkward.** He had no *love for*, or *confidence in*, his employer.

**Better.** He had no love for his employer and no confidence in him.

**Wrong.** I shall always remember the town because of the good times and the friends I made there.

**Correct.** I shall always remember the town because of the *good times I had* and the *friends I made* there.

EXERCISE

Correct the violations of English idiom in the following sentences.

1. I had to confess that I agreed on most of Mr. Wilson's arguments.
2. After such a bad beginning, the whole game developed into rather of a farce.
3. On the boat I acquired a rudimentary knowledge and keen interest in chess.
4. Casement windows were unacceptable, on account of we wanted to put screens on the outside.
5. The example and conversation of a friend may also be influential on changing a person's religious beliefs.
6. Oriental peoples in general have a great respect and deference to their elders.
7. We studied the Gulf Indians, of which the Cherokees were affiliated.
8. Palmerston's chief fault as Prime Minister was his neglect to have the Queen's approval to all dispatches before he released them.
9. Ned was angry at me because my grades were superior than his.
10. I differ from you with regards to the importance of intercollegiate athletics.

# 41 EXACT DICTION

Choose words which say precisely what you mean. A reader has the right to expect that you mean exactly what your words say. Before copying the final draft of a paper, go over it carefully to see that the words exactly express your meaning. It is not enough to make sure that you can be understood; you ought to make sure that you cannot be misunderstood.

## 41a Specific Words

Choose specific rather than general terms, unless there is a good reason for being general. A general term like *food* is a name for a whole group of specific things — from vegetable soup to T-bone steak to strawberry shortcake. If you want to make a statement about all foods, the general term is appropriate: "Food is becoming more and more expensive." But do not use the general term when concrete details and specific words are called for.

**Vague and general.** For dinner we had some really good food.

**Improved.** For dinner we had barbecued steaks and sweet corn.

Note that *specific* and *general* are relative, not absolute terms. In the following list, running from specific to more general, any of the four terms might be used to refer to a famous tree growing on the campus:

**Specific.** Charter Oak (one particular tree)

**Less specific.** oak (includes thousands of trees)

**More general.** tree (includes oaks, pines, palms, etc.)

**More general.** plant (includes trees, flowers, bushes, etc.)

*Tree* is more specific than *plant*, but more general than *oak*.

A good rule to follow is to make your language as specific as possible. General terms are commonly overused, either because the writer's thoughts are vague and general or because the writer is too lazy to find the exact word to express what he has in mind. Specific and concrete words create definite and vivid pictures in the reader's mind. A habit of using them will help you to say *exactly* what you mean.

**Vague and abstract.** My father showed his disapproval.

**Concrete and specific.** My father growled, "Stop that!"

**Vague.** One member of the city government has failed in the performance of his duties.

**Specific.** Assemblyman Case has attended only one meeting of the City Council in the last six months.

Note that a specific statement may require no more space than a vague, indefinite one.

**General and wordy.** One of our family has recently made a start on a career of authorship.

**Specific.** Last week my brother Ed finished writing his first novel.

## EXERCISES

### 1

Give several specific or concrete words for each general or abstract word. For example: *cloth: velvet, satin, taffeta, linen, burlap.*

**Nouns.** *fruit, vehicle, bird, goodness*

**Verbs.** *to look, to walk, to talk, to laugh*

**Adjectives.** *unpleasant* taste, *cold* day, *young, dark, colored*

**2**

Make the following sentences more specific and concrete:

1. Since the weather was uncomfortable, we didn't do much of anything.
2. Something was wrong with the elevator, so we had a hard time getting up to the office.
3. At an early age, a friend of ours found himself handicapped by ill health.
4. I saw a play the other night, but I didn't think it was very good.
5. Litmus paper is used to show the nature of a solution.
6. It looked as though a boat out on the bay was having trouble.
7. At one meal we had my favorite food.
8. This family likes to demonstrate its financial standing by wearing imported clothing.
9. The expedition encountered a serious difficulty, which delayed its departure for some time.
10. The first night in camp, one of the fellows played a trick on us which was not too pleasant.

## 41b Colorless Verbs

Make your verbs work. In the sentence "He made a hasty exit," the verb is abstract, and the adjective and noun "hasty exit" carry what meaning the sentence has. Choose a more exact and forceful verb: "He rushed from the room," or "He jumped out the window."

Verbs like *occur, took place, prevail, exist* have legitimate uses, but they are often colorless, used merely to complete a sentence.

**Weak.** In the afternoon a sharp drop in the temperature took place.

**Improved.** In the afternoon the temperature dropped sharply.

**Weak.** Throughout the meeting, an atmosphere of increasing tension prevailed.

**Improved.** Throughout the meeting, the tension increased.

Copulative verbs (*be*, *seem*, *appear*, etc.) completed by an adjective or participle are usually weaker than concrete verbs.

**Weak.** He was occasionally inclined to drink too much.

**Improved.** Occasionally he drank too much.

Do not, in an effort to avoid flat and colorless verbs, go to the opposite extreme and use verbs which are too explosive for their context.

**Exaggerated.** Her angry words pounced out upon him.

**Exaggerated.** He heaved, "Great day, this."

Unnecessary use of the passive voice produces weak sentences. The passive voice is appropriate when the doer of an action is unknown or irrelevant to the statement.

**Correct.** Three purses and eight parcels *were left* in municipal buses last week. They *may be claimed* at the office.

**Correct.** Chicken and green peas *were served* at the banquet.

Usually, however, the doer of an action *is* important, and the subject of the verb should name him.

**Weak.** The picnic was enjoyed by everybody.

**Improved.** Everybody enjoyed the picnic.

**Weak and awkward.** Every night Mr. Richardson's lawn had to be watered by me.

**Improved.** Every night I had to water Mr. Richardson's lawn.

### EXERCISE

Supply forceful verbs or verb forms in the following sentences.

1. Whenever he hears a loud noise, my dog tends to give a jump and tremble all over.
2. It was soon discovered by the new settlers that life in the colonies was not utopian.
3. In some high schools there is a very definite lack of emphasis on the development of a program in remedial English.
4. To get the effect of sharpness and pungency in a salad dressing, careful measurement of the right proportions of ingredients is important.
5. The old-fashioned system of formal lecturing was present in about half of my freshman classes.
6. During the summer, week-end guests are to be found filling every corner of our house on the lake.
7. Great flocks of birds could be seen rising from the beach as we approached.
8. Jewelry and cameras seemed to be the chief interest of the robbers, but money was not passed up by them, either.
9. Most of the desert resorts at the foot of the mountains have been confronted by disastrous winter floods.
10. After I had explained matters, the floorwalker was full of elaborate apologies.

## 41c Jargon

Avoid jargon: for example, writing "adverse climatic conditions" when all you mean is "bad weather." Some writers feel that simple, natural language is dull and commonplace and prefer high-sounding synonyms or generalities. Official reports — of educators, social scientists, government commissions or advisory committees — are often written in stilted, roundabout, abstract language, and the style is sometimes imitated by students who feel that what they have to say is not impressive enough to stand on its own feet. So they dress up their ideas in formal, abstract, "official" language, with the vague hope of sounding authoritative and profound. Actually, to an intelligent reader, they sound silly and pretentious.

Certain key words betray the writer of jargon. He has an unhealthy fondness for *factor*, *case*, *basis*, *in terms of*, *in the nature of*, *with reference to*, *elements*, *objectives*, *personnel*. This last word, remarks the London *Times*, is usually applied to persons who do not go, but proceed. "They do not have, they are (or more often are not) in possession of. They do not ask, they make application for. . . . They cannot eat, they only consume; they perform ablutions; instead of homes they have places of residence in which, instead of living, they are domiciled. They are not cattle, they are not ciphers, they certainly are not human beings: they are personnel." The following sentence is also quoted by the *Times* as an example of jargon:

> The unity of view of the participants in the conversations has been established regarding the exceptional importance at the present time of an all-embracing collective organization of security on the basis of indivisibility of peace.

See if you can put it into English.

**Jargon.** Plant personnel are requested to extinguish all illuminating devices before vacating the premises.

**Improved.** Employees are asked to turn out all lights before leaving the plant.

## EXERCISE

Improve the following sentences by eliminating jargon.

1. A slackening in the tempo of business and recreational activities is highly advisable in the case of an individual who has attained the age of fifty.

2. Participation in interscholastic athletics is unfortunately limited to students whose performance in a given sport is already of so outstanding a nature that little more can be expected in the way of improvement.
3. The establishment of a fixed stipend as a child's weekly allowance affords valuable training in the intelligent handling of monetary matters.
4. Difficulty of movement of motoring personnel through congested metropolitan areas presents the most troublesome aspect of modern highway planning.
5. I feel certain that you are aware that I am not in accord with the favorable attitude which represents the views of a majority of the committee regarding the desirability of increasing salaries.
6. The use of a heavy lubricant will render the mechanism of the clock inoperative.
7. Please make every effort to establish contact with Colonel Gaylord and ascertain his views in relation to the acceptability of our proposal to utilize a detachment of soldiers as part of the parade.
8. In the case of the passenger plane shot down over Bulgaria, this type of incident could be responsible for tragic consequences of international significance.
9. My high school instructors must have had access to and knowledge of my previous academic accomplishment, and from this they could have deduced the nature of my difficulties.
10. All the imaginary countries described by Gulliver show Swift's affirmative attitude toward the sectioning of people into social groups in terms of upper and lower classes.

## 41d Exact Connotation

Choose words with the exact connotation required by the context. In addition to their *denotation* (literal meaning), words have a *connotation*, a fringe of associations and overtones which makes them appropriate to certain situations but not to others. *House*, *home*, and *domicile* all have the same denotation — a place of residence. But their connotations are quite different: *house* emphasizes the physical structure; *home* suggests family life, warmth, comfort, affection; *domicile* has strictly legal overtones.

The connotation of each word must be appropriate to the context. It would not be possible to write a sentimental song entitled "House, Sweet House," nor would it seem fitting to call the official residence of the President of the United States "The White Home." Similarly, the word *skull* is appropriate in a medical book or ghost story, but its connotations make it unsuitable in an advertisement for men's clothing: not "a hat to suit each type of *skull*" but "a hat to suit each type of *head*."

One learns the connotations of a word by seeing the word in different contexts. *Trip* usually appears in a context which indicates a short distance ("to the city," for example); *journey* is used for travel over long distances ("to Australia"). Your dictionary distinguishes the connotations of many near-synonyms, and special dictionaries of synonyms, like Roget's *Thesaurus* or *Webster's Dictionary of Synonyms*, are available in any library.

## EXERCISES

### 1

Explain the difference in connotation between the words in the following pairs:

1. violin, fiddle
2. horse, steed
3. mutter, mumble
4. mariner, sailor
5. awkward, clumsy
6. split, cleave
7. infant, baby
8. perturbed, agitated
9. marsh, swamp
10. pester, bother

## 2

For the following words, find synonyms whose connotations fit under the headings listed below:

| *Commonplace, neutral* | *Vulgar, derogatory* | *Colloquial, slang,* etc. | *Elevated, poetic* |
|---|---|---|---|
| girl | slut | skirt | maiden |
| | hussy | jane | damsel |
| boy | | | |
| food | | | |
| money | | | |
| complain | | | |
| dog | | | |
| go away | | | |
| ship | | | |
| eat | | | |
| automobile | | | |

## 3

Revise the following sentences, substituting words with connotations appropriate to the context.

1. Evelyn was a serious student of dramatic art and spent all her spare time going to shows.
2. On hot afternoons we went down to the lake to engage in natation.
3. Three scientists are studying the junk discovered in an excavation of an Indian mound.
4. A good many people disliked the proposal, but nobody kicked about it.
5. I had no trouble getting the horse to go forward, but it was almost impossible to make him recede.
6. Aunt Tilly was a sight; she was less than five feet tall, but excessively corpulent.

## 4

Improve the diction of the following sentences.

1. As for religious differences, I consider them grossly unimportant.
2. The speaker deplored the narrowmindedness and inflexibility that occurs with many educators and scientists.
3. A country of beautiful landscapes and picturesque villages is thought of by me when I think of France.
4. When Eastern colleges refused admission to women, the women initiated their own colleges.
5. The Nazis turned passion and prejudice into political power, and therefore cruelty became a natural output.
6. The fact that women are paid less than men doing similar work is an example of their degradation in our society.
7. In the near future trips around the world will be able to be made in a few hours.
8. The reputation for integrity enjoyed by the legal profession today appears to be one of its most favorable items.
9. Throughout the pages of history one finds the importance of economic pressure.
10. Anyone affiliated with this club who shall fail to make prompt payment of his monthly dues shall be deemed liable to expulsion.
11. My cousin came home in a sorry state as a result of an unfortunate accident.
12. Medicine is one trade that absolutely requires a college education.
13. No industrial plant can function effectually without trained employees.
14. The basic fundamental behind our theory of government is the belief that every individual should be permitted maximum activity in terms of legal guarantees against restrictions on free choice of belief and behavior.
15. His young appearance fascinated me.

16. When the meat inspection law was passed, we were freed from the unwholesome quality of canned meat.
17. In most women's colleges, a great deal of men are on the faculty.
18. Polytheism gradually disappeared until now only a faint trace exists in the world.
19. On my first day in the biology lab, I was horrified to find a disgusting object placed before me, which I was supposed to dissect.
20. Because the United States and Great Britain failed to face the problem in its infancy, we are now affronted with a serious choice of policies.
21. At last, after almost two centuries, the immortal words "All men are created equal" have come into practice.
22. If you have money, you will be respected irregardless of how dopey you may be.
23. The total amount of crimes committed in California seems to be considerable.
24. The Coast Guard is some different when compared to the other branches of the service.
25. The Dean asked if I was cognizant of the fact that two more cuts would eventuate in my flunking the course.

# 42 EFFECTIVE DICTION

In addition to being exact, your diction should be effective; that is, you should try to make it easy and pleasant for a reader to grasp what you are saying. If a reader must struggle with an awkward, pretentious, or repetitious style, he is apt to be prejudiced against you. Avoid antagonizing your audience; keep your diction natural and sincere, be direct and concise, use fresh, unhackneyed phrases, and avoid needless technical language.

## 42a Pretentious Language

Written prose is usually somewhat more formal than the spoken language, but according to current taste, expository writing should not be ornate or pretentious. A reader is apt to lose faith in the sincerity of the writer who decorates his sentences.

**Pretentious.** The heavens were dark save for the myriad twinkling of God's candles, the stars, which glittered like the eyes of snakes through the bitter chill of air as cold as outer space.

**Improved.** The night was clear and bitterly cold.

Anyone who prefers the ornate sentence to the simple statement is the natural prey of the advertising copywriter and the used-car salesman. Rich ornament may be appropriate on a jewel box, but it is a nuisance on the tools with which we earn a living.

One motive which leads to pretentious diction is a straining for novelty. Beginning writers often cherish the delusion that originality is achieved by avoiding ordinary words and substituting ingenious paraphrases.

| Ordinary Word | Strained Circumlocution |
|---|---|
| spade | implement for agricultural excavation |
| dog | faithful canine friend |
| codfish | denizen of the deep |
| basketball player | casaba-heaver |
| hit the ball | smacked the horsehide |

Such awkward expressions are sometimes used in an attempt to avoid repeating an ordinary word. Frequent repetition may be annoying, but it is better to repeat than to sound pretentious. For example, the word *edifice* should not be used merely to avoid repeating *house:*

**Bad.** After inspecting the house thoroughly, I decided that I would never buy such a poorly constructed *edifice.*

**Improved.** After inspecting the house thoroughly, I decided that I would never buy a house which was so poorly constructed.

**Needless circumlocution.** If it has this effect on a healthy skin, it will have a worse effect on an inflamed cuticle.

**Improved.** If it has this effect on a healthy skin, it will have a worse effect on an inflamed skin.

Foreign words and phrases, likewise, are apt to suggest that the writer is displaying his own superior knowledge. They are permissible when there is no English equivalent to convey the exact meaning, as in *blitzkrieg, a priori, laissez faire, slalom.* But foreign phrases like the following should be avoided, since English equivalents are available.

| Needless Foreign Phrase | English Equivalent |
|---|---|
| *entre nous* | between us |
| *joie de vivre* | enjoyment of life |
| *faux pas* | social blunder |
| *sub rosa* | secret or secretly |
| *Sturm und Drang* | storm and stress |

Rich and figurative language is not necessarily bad in itself. But it must be very good to be good at all, and it should be limited to appropriate contexts. It is better to be simple and unpretentious than to produce what the *New Yorker* sardonically calls "rich, beautiful prose."

**Pretentious.** Inexpensive pigments are certain to lose their lustrous hues upon exposure to the burning rays of summer.

**Improved.** Cheap paint will fade when exposed to bright sunlight.

**Pretentious.** I have ofttimes wondered, weary amidst the manifold confusions of urban existence, what would be my sensations could I awaken early some morn in the humble cottage where I first drew my breath.

**Improved.** When I am tired of the confusion of city life, I often wonder what it would be like to wake up some morning in the house where I was born.

## EXERCISE

Revise the following sentences to eliminate pretentious diction and unnecessary circumlocutions.

1. The shelves of the bookstore were richly laden with printed monuments of the past, in which immortal thoughts are embalmed in print.
2. If I were allowed to choose between buses and streetcars, I would cast my vote in favor of the latter means of conveyance.
3. How well I remember the halcyon days of summer, spent in blissful innocence on the shores of the lake or lounging neath the corrugated-iron roof of Schultz's Auto Repair Shop.
4. At the faculty meeting yesterday, the question of football was discussed. Those members of that learned aggregation who opposed the gridiron game succumbed at the final vote.

5. Out of the gathering gloom now spilling from the western horizon like ink from an overturned bottle of writing fluid, a gleaming jewel gradually resolved itself into a white tugboat illuminated by the ultimate rays of the departing sun.

## 42b Trite Rhetorical Expressions

"Hungry as bears" may originally have been effective, but it has been worn out by constant repetition. If it has any effect at all, it is to make one's writing sound stale and tired. Frank Sullivan, the *New Yorker's* cliché expert, has been collecting trite expressions for years without exhausting the supply. The list below illustrates the kind of hackneyed expression you should guard against.

abreast of the times
acid test
agony of suspense
all nature seemed clothed in
all too soon
among those present
as luck would have it
beat a hasty retreat
bitter end
blushing bride
bolt from the blue
breathless silence
briny deep
checkered career
cold as ice
crystal clear
deep, dark secret
depths of despair
do justice to a meal
doomed to disappointment
dull, sickening thud
each and every
easier said than done
fair sex
goes without saying
green with envy
herculean efforts
in this modern day and age
last but not least
long-felt want
mother nature, *or* mother earth
nestled among the hills
news leaked out
order out of chaos
partake of refreshments
poor but honest
proud possessor of
quick as a flash
reigns supreme
render a solo
sigh of relief

slow but sure
sought his downy couch
speculation was rife
tendered his resignation
the worse for wear
tiny tots
tired but happy
undercurrent of excitement
untiring efforts
wee small hours
wended their way
working like Trojans

Avoid hackneyed quotations, literary allusions, and proverbs, such as:

the light fantastic toe
truth is stranger than fiction
method in his madness
sadder but wiser
variety is the spice of life
the best laid plans of mice and men
all work and no play
never put off till tomorrow what you can do today
make hay while the sun shines
all is not gold that glitters
where ignorance is bliss, 'tis folly to be wise
music hath charms

The best way to eliminate trite phrases from your writing is to sharpen your awareness of them, so that you are not apt to write them unconsciously. The clichés in the following passage show how easy it is to fall unthinkingly into stereotyped diction.

Mr. Arbuthnot — They have not kept nor do they intend to keep . . . They have undermined the foundations . . . They constitute a threat to our democratic institutions . . . And I say to you, my fellow-Americans . . .

Q — Mr. Arbuthnot, I can tell what you're up to. . . . You're being a campaign orator again.

A — That's right. . . . Guess what kind of disclosures I plan to reveal in my speech at Wichita next week.

Q— What kind?

A— Mounting disclosures of graft and corruption.

Q— Where?

A— In high places. You know, of course, what my favorite brand of faith is.

Q— No. What?

A— An abiding faith. In the destiny of our g-reat democracy.

Q— Do you still prefer your indifference callous?

A— Yes, and my national debts astronomical, my corruption shameful, my courage invincible, my violations flagrant, and my appeals ringing. . . .

Q— Your abuse is reckless, I suppose.

A— No. The other side's abuse is reckless. I do not indulge in personalities. I confine myself to solemn obligations, political expediency, disloyal elements, supreme goals, historic roles, honest toil, headlong plunges, glowing words, empty phrases, giant strides, sordid business, secret understandings, eternal vigilance, staggering costs, paramount issues, valiant sons, jaundiced critics, painful necessities, governmental folly, and the great heart land of the South, also the great heart lands of the North, East, and West. . . .

Q— Whom are you going to call upon in your speeches?

A— Americans in every walk of life, irrespective of party.

Q— And where do you speak from?

A— I speak from the heart when I say to you that my candidate is a man unafraid, a man in whom there is no guile, who is equal to the task, whose name is a household word, who has worked untiringly, who is one of the outstanding, who has embarked on a career, who has not failed his country, who is a consistent advocate of, who has answered the call, and who will resist every attempt to encroach. . . .

Q— How does your man stand, Mr. Arbuthnot?

A— On his own two feet. . . . He faces facts, or grim reality. He will lead us out of the morass. His deeds will be writ large. His words will be engraved.

Q— Where?

A— On the hearts of his countrymen.

Q— Therefore you, as a stump speaker, do what?

A— Therefore, my friends, I take great pleasure. It is my firm belief. I can unhesitatingly say. And I need not remind you. Yet I cannot agree.

Q— Whom can't you agree with?

A— I cannot agree with those who. Yet there *are* those who. I defy them.

Q— How do you speak when you defy those who?

A— I speak not as a Republican or a Democrat but as an American.

— FRANK SULLIVAN

## 42c Technical Language

In writing addressed to specialists, technical terms are appropriate. But writing aimed at a general audience should avoid technical terms which are not commonly understood, even though more words are required to say the same thing in plain English. It may sometimes be necessary to use technical expressions because no others are available. In such a case, be sure to explain the meanings for the nontechnical reader.

**Too technical.** The book gives an elaborate account of the construction and validation of the English placement test for college freshmen, with a study of the predictive significance of this examination, and also discusses the adequacy of bases for the homogeneous grouping in freshman English.

**Improved.** The book explains in detail how the English placement test for college freshmen was constructed and checked for reliability and validity. (Reliability means consistency of performance; a reliable test will give nearly the same results when administered a second time to the same students. Validity means that the test measures the kind of knowledge or ability that it was intended to measure.) The booklet goes on to discuss the accuracy with which the test will predict the future performance in English classes of the students who take it. Finally, it criticizes the various methods and standards by which students are assigned to high, middle, or low sections in the freshman English course.

## 42d Appropriate Figures of Speech

A figure of speech is a comparison, either stated or implied, between two things which are unlike except in one particular. Figures of speech are used to give color and vividness to writing, and they should be fresh, reasonable, consistent, and suited to the context in which they appear.

**Effective figure of speech.** Arthur gave the old English sheepdog a prod, and it moved shapelessly from the room like an enormous decayed chrysanthemum.

—MICHAEL INNES

In a search for fresh comparisons, do not go too far afield. Voracious appetite is characteristic of the man-eating shark, but a shark would not be a suitable figure of speech in a serious description of a baby crying for its bottle or a girl eating at a roadside tavern after a dance. Strained or incongruous comparisons may be deliberately used for humorous effect. But when they appear in serious writing, farfetched figures of speech are apt to make the reader laugh at you, instead of with you.

**Deliberate incongruity.**

And like a lobster boiled, the morn
From black to red began to turn.

**Strained figure.** The little lake, like a tired child, snuggled down among its hills and went to sleep. [What is there in common between a lake and a tired child?]

**Incongruous metaphor.** The brakeman got some oil for the wheel at the next station, and thus the hotbox was nipped in the bud. ["Nipped in the bud" means that something is checked before it can develop, and hence it is logically correct here. But the comparison is from gardening, and the picture it calls up is incongruous with that of a brakeman pouring oil into a hot journal box.]

**Inappropriate figure.** The empty stalls of the cowshed were like a desolate garden in late November. [The elevated and poetic comparison "like a desolate garden in late November" is inappropriate to anything so homely as the stalls of a cowshed.]

Even though a figure of speech is consistent and appropriate in itself, it may be incongruous with the literal sense of an adjoining figure, and the mixing of the two may be ludicrous.

**Mixed figure.** This young attorney is rapidly gaining a foothold in the public eye. [Either of these metaphors is satisfactory by itself: "gaining a foothold" is drawn from mountain climbing; "in the public eye" personifies the public. But together they call up an unfortunate picture of the young attorney digging his toe into the eye of the public.]

**Mixed figure.** The freshman algebra course is a rocky and difficult road to travel, but whether we like it or not, we are required to wade through it.

**Mixed figure.** The probe of the grand jury has netted five corrupt officials.

**Improved.** The probe of the grand jury has revealed five corrupt officials. [*Or,* The dragnet of the grand jury has caught five corrupt officials.]

## EXERCISE

In the following sentences explain the literal as well as the figurative sense of each figure of speech. Revise the sentences which contain inappropriate or incongruous figures.

1. The underprivileged people of Asia were fertile soil awaiting only the spark of Communist doctrine.

2. Psychologists tell us that lack of love is the backbone of all feelings of insecurity.
3. Hitler was as vile an insect as ever crawled across the pages of history.
4. Western culture has spread from place to place as a forest fire spreads from tree to tree, but today the tide may be turning.
5. Hotspur at this point is a man torn between two fires.
6. The Gadsden Purchase was but a drop of land in the ocean of the vast continent.
7. When Albert supplanted him, Lord Melbourne sank into the depths of happy memories of his golden past.
8. His smiling face and helping hand was extended to all around him.
9. Lena's love for Heyst gave her a reason for living and filled an empty spot in her outlook on life.
10. Applied political science branches out and engulfs the study of how the theorist and the practical politician can work together for the common good.

## 42e Awkward Repetitions

Reading a paper aloud is the best way to detect the unpleasant echo produced by needless repetition of a word or sound. Sometimes a word or phrase is deliberately repeated, and the writer capitalizes on the echo for emphasis or to make a meaning clear. Deliberate repetition of a word may also be preferable to straining after synonyms. But the echo caused by the needless repetition of a word or phrase is disturbing.

**Deliberate repetition.** Harriet came to spend the last week in May with us, and strangely enough the last week in May was the only time George could come for a visit.

**Awkward repetition.** He said that the orders said that uniforms must be worn.

**Improved.** He said that the orders required uniforms to be worn.

**Needless repetition.** Probably the next problem that confronts a parent is the problem of adequate schooling for his children.

**Improved.** The parent's next problem is providing adequate schooling for his children.

Particularly awkward is the repetition of a word which has two different meanings in the sentence.

**Awkward repetition.** Since a year had passed since Winchester's death, the family put away its mourning.

**Improved.** A year had passed since Winchester's death, and the family put away its mourning.

**Awkward repetition.** The object of the expedition was to investigate the object which had fallen from the sky.

**Improved.** The purpose of the expedition was to investigate the object which had fallen from the sky.

Noticeable repetition of sounds or other poetic devices is out of place in ordinary prose.

**Objectionable rhyme.** Then came the time for heartbreaking leave-taking.

**Objectionable repetition of sound.** To keep up the display, the fountains were kept playing night and day.

**Objectionable alliteration.** Ridgeway set a new record by flying farther and faster than anyone had formerly flown.

**Objectionable repetition of vowel sounds.** The owner sold the whole row of old homes.

Combinations of sounds which are difficult to pronounce should be avoided in writing, as in speech.

**Cacophonous.** Our statistics show that she should sell seven sets a day.

## EXERCISE

The following sentences contain examples of ineffective diction — pretentious language, trite phrases, inappropriate figures of speech, and awkward repetitions. Revise the sentences to make the diction more effective.

1. The Alcan Highway is an imperishable monument to the brave men who fought the good fight against a hostile environment and blazed the trail through a howling wilderness.
2. A plumber needs to know more than just plumbing if he is to install new plumbing fixtures in an old house.
3. To achieve good health, a person must build on the foundation of his native endowment, expanding it and training it for harmonious functioning.
4. A pinball game was much too tame for Tom.
5. Above me towered the sheer walls and towers of Manhattan, and in my ears was the roar of the multifarious activities necessary to the well-being of *homo sapiens.*
6. Democracy in the countries of Eastern Europe is slowly being strangled by a lack of contact with democratic ideas.
7. When the news leaked out, all our family was in an agony of suspense except Uncle Charles, who was as cool as a cucumber.
8. Once the balance of a family becomes off-balance, the family is never the same.
9. In suburban areas today, a typical case of diphtheria is as rare as a flawless diamond.
10. From the rock-bound coast of Maine to the sun-warmed sands of California, adventurous spirits who brave the briny deep wear Jensen's swimsuits.
11. The only guest still left was the lady who had sat on my left at dinner, and she left soon after.
12. *A Midsummer Night's Dream*, as produced last night at the high school auditorium, was a sumptuous vision of

ethereal splendor and a triumphant tribute to the genius of the director and the cast.

13. Matters that require decision by the city manager should be discussed in private by the aforementioned executive and the appropriate department head.
14. At every public meeting the senator was the center of attraction; his fame increased by leaps and bounds, and all his rivals were green with envy.
15. The improvement in electronic calculating machines has gone so far that the machines can now perform calculations that are beyond the ability of a human calculator.
16. Let's us try to make sure that, however short of funds the club may be, that we will never admit a member just because he has dough.
17. For most students, adequate education finances are apt to be of an inadequate nature.
18. From here I can hear every noise that annoys an earnest student.
19. In this modern day and age, the discovery of atomic energy will lead a path to many new inventions.
20. An understanding of the Oriental mind in terms of Eastern philosophy and literature would contribute materially to reducing the barriers and bridging the gap between East and West, and cancelling the possibility that never the twain shall meet.

### EXERCISE

Assuming that the following piece of writing should be written in effective Standard English, point out and correct expressions which are inappropriate.

Although his first novel, *Lucky Jim*, enjoyed a considerable success, Kingsley Amis pulled a blooper in his second effort in the fiction line. *Lucky Jim* narrates in risible detail the misadventures of a slap-happy lecturer in an English university, who is constantly precipitating himself into embarrassing predicaments, both amatory and academic. A born schnook, Jim has entered on an academic career *faute de mieux*. He takes no real interest in teaching or research; the height of his ambition is a steady job with adequate remuneration. In order to achieve this end, it is essential to butter up the Professor of History, at least until he recommends the appointment which will insure Jim permanent tenure. The Professor is a pompous old windbag, whose memory is failing and whose motives are beyond the comprehension of mortal man. In addition, he is a fiend for chamber music, madrigals, and other highbrow forms of artistic endeavor.

One of the funniest scenes in the book is the account of a house party, which features a motley crowd of early English music fans. In the natural course of events, Jim tries to fake his part in a madrigal, with disastrous results. As luck would have it, he then proceeds to ignite the bedclothes, ruin an antique table, and antagonize the Professor's wife. He woos and wins a member of the fair sex, taking her away from the Professor's son. When all is said and done, the book might be described as high farce, and it is very funny.

The second novel, *That Uncertain Feeling*, is another kettle of fish. Ostensibly a humorous criticism of marital relations, it wavers between seriousness and hokum. The attempts at psychological analysis barely scratch the surface, and the so-called humor is either grotesque slapstick or pure corn. The only thing which reminds one of the author of *Lucky Jim* is the clear, acid style.

# 43 GLOSSARY OF WORDS COMMONLY MISUSED

Note that the label *colloquial* means that a word is frequently used in speech and may be found in very informal or familiar writing. A good working principle is to avoid colloquialisms in serious writing unless you have a special reason for using them.

**A.D.** Means *in the year of our Lord.* Inaccurate when appended to the name of a *century.* Should not be appended to a date self-evidently modern. When used, should precede the date and should not be preceded by a preposition.

INACCURATE. The sixth century A.D.
CORRECT. The sixth century after Christ.
CORRECT. Arminius died A.D. 21.

**Above.** The use of *above* as an adjective is best confined to legal documents; it is out of place in ordinary writing.

POOR. The above remarks should be taken seriously.
BETTER. These remarks should be taken seriously.
CORRECT. The lines quoted above prove the point.

**Accept.** See **Except.**

**Ad.** Colloquial abbreviation for *advertisement.* Write the word in full.

**Affect.** Means to *influence;* as *War is almost sure to affect trade seriously.* Often confused with *effect. Effect* (verb) means *to bring to pass;* as *He will effect a reconciliation. Effect* (noun) means *result;* as *The drug had a fatal effect.*

**Aggravate.** Means *to intensify* or *to make worse;* as *The shock aggravated his misery.* In the sense of *annoy, irritate, arouse the anger of,* it is colloquial.

**Ain't.** An illiterate contraction of *am not, is not,* or *are not.*

**Alibi.** Means, in legal usage, an assertion that one was in another place at the time of the commission of a certain act. Colloquial when used to mean *excuse.*

CORRECT. His alibi was that he was in New York when the robbery was being committed in Los Angeles.

**All right.** Not spelled *alright, allright,* or *all-right.*

**All the.** *All the farther, all the higher, all the faster,* or similar expressions should not be used mistakenly for *as far as,* etc.

WRONG. That was all the farther we went that day.
CORRECT. That was as far as we went that day.

**Allude.** Means *to refer indirectly. Refer* means an open, direct mention. *When he alluded to profiteers, we knew whom he meant. Later he referred to two men by name.*

**Already, all ready.** Distinguish *already,* meaning *by this time,* from *all ready,* which means *completely ready. The hotel was already full. They were all ready to go.*

**Alternative.** Strictly, means *choice between two things: One alternative was to jump from the window; the other was to be burned to death.* Now widely used to mean a choice between more than two things.

**And etc.** Never put *and* before *etc. Etc.* is an abbreviation of Latin *et* (and) plus *cetera* (others). See **Etc.**

**Anyplace, every place, no place, someplace.** Colloquialisms for *anywhere, everywhere, nowhere, somewhere. Anyplace* is most widely used.

**Anywheres.** Dialectal for *anywhere.*

**As.** A provincialism if used in place of *that* or *whether.* *I don't know that* [not *as*] *we can go.*

**At about.** Prefer *about.*

REDUNDANT. He came at about three o'clock.
CORRECT. He came about three o'clock.

**Avail.** *Of no avail* is properly used only with some form of *be* or other linking verbs.

UNIDIOMATIC. He tried, but of no avail.
CORRECT. His attempt was of no avail.

**Badly.** Colloquially used for *a great deal* or *very much* with verbs signifying *want* or *need.*

COLLOQUIAL. I want badly to see you.
PREFERRED IN WRITING. I want very much to see you.

**Balance.** Colloquial when used in the sense of *remainder,* except of a balance at the bank.

COLLOQUIAL. One was an Italian; the balance were Greeks.
PREFERRED IN WRITING. One was an Italian; the rest [*or* the others] were Greeks.

**Besides.** Means *additionally* or *in addition to.* Not to be confused with *beside,* which is always a preposition meaning *by the side of,* as *beside the house.*

**Between.** In the literal sense *between* applies to only two objects, and *among* to more than two; but *between* is often used with more than two objects. "It is still the only word available to express the relation of a thing to many surrounding things severally and individually . . ." NEW ENGLISH DICTIONARY.

**Blame . . . on.** Colloquially used instead of *blame . . . for.*

COLLOQUIAL. You needn't blame it on me.
MORE FORMAL. You needn't blame me for it.

**Bunch.** Colloquial for *group* or *party.*

**But.** See **Hardly.**

**But what.** A colloquialism sometimes used for *that.*

COLLOQUIAL. I don't doubt but what he is lying.
PREFERRED IN WRITING. I don't doubt that he is lying.

**Can't hardly.** See **Hardly.**

**Complected.** A barbarism for *complexioned.*

WRONG. A light-complected girl.
RIGHT. A light-complexioned girl.

**Considerable.** A colloquialism when used as a noun.

COLLOQUIAL. He lost considerable in the fire.
PREFERRED IN WRITING. He lost a good deal of property in the fire.

**Contact.** Chiefly, and correctly, used as a noun. It is widely used to mean *consult, meet, confer,* but many people find this use objectionable.

DUBIOUS. I did not contact any of my old friends during the vacation.
PREFERRED. I did not see any of my old friends during the vacation.

**Contemplate.** Should not be used with a preposition.

BAD. He contemplated on [*or* over] a trip to Alaska.
CORRECT. He contemplated a trip to Alaska.

**Continual.** Not synonymous with *continuous,* according to modern usage. *Continual* means *occurring in close succession, frequently repeated;* as *Continual hindrances discouraged us. He coughs continually. Continuous* means *without cessation, continuing uninterrupted;* as *Continuous opposition discouraged us. He slept continuously for ten hours.*

**Could of.** See **Of.**

**Data, phenomena, strata.** Plural, not singular forms, and so used in formal writing. But the use of *data* with a singular verb is increasing in informal writing.

FORMAL. These data have been taken from the last Census Report.

INFORMAL. This data has been taken from the last Census Report.

**Different.** Usually followed by *from*, but also by *to*, especially in England, and by *than*. The constructions with *to* and *than* have long literary usage to support them, but are considered incorrect by many.

DOUBTFUL. His method is different than the one I use.
IMPROVED. His method is different from the one I use.

**Don't.** A contraction of *do not*. Therefore unacceptable when used with a subject in the third person singular.

SUBSTANDARD. He don't know.
STANDARD. He doesn't know.

**Due to.** An adjective modifier, and should, therefore, modify a substantive, not a verb. It is confused with *owing to*, *because of*, *on account of*, which have become prepositions and which, therefore, can introduce phrases modifying verbs.

UNDESIRABLE. The forces were divided, due to a misunderstanding.

IMPROVED. The forces were divided through [*or* because of] a misunderstanding.

IMPROVED. The division of the forces was due to a misunderstanding.

**Each other.** Strictly used as referring to only two, as distinguished from *one another*, which refers to more than two; but the expressions are used interchangeably in informal writing.

**Effect.** See **Affect.**

**Either, neither.** Preferably used to designate one of two persons or things; less desirably, one of three or more.

LESS DESIRABLE. I asked Leahy, Mahoney, and McGinty, but neither of them was willing.

PREFERABLE. I asked Leahy, Mahoney, and McGinty, but none of them was willing.

*Either* requires a singular verb; *neither* should in formal writing be used with a singular verb, but the plural idea suggested by the negative has led to accepted use of a plural verb.

CORRECT. Either of the boxes is large enough.

ACCEPTABLE. Neither of the boxes are large enough.

**Enthuse.** Common in speech, but to be avoided in writing.

COLLOQUIAL. Everyone was enthused about the idea.

PREFERRED IN WRITING. Everyone was enthusiastic about the idea.

**Equally as good.** A confusion of two phrases: *equally good* and *just as good as*. Use either of the two phrases in place of *equally as good.*

CORRECT. Their radio cost much more than ours, but ours is equally good.

CORRECT. Our radio is just as good as theirs.

**Etc.** Avoid the vague use of *etc.;* use it only to dispense with useless repetition or to represent terms that are entirely obvious.

UNDESIRABLE. She was more beautiful, witty, virtuous, etc., than any other lady.

PREFERABLE. She was more beautiful, witty, and virtuous than any other lady.

**Every bit.** Colloquial for *in every way, quite.*

**Every place.** See **Anyplace.**

**Except** (verb) means *to exclude;* as *He alone was excepted from the amnesty. Except* (preposition) means *with the exception* (i.e., *exclusion*) *of;* as *All's lost except honor. Except* is not to be confused with *accept*, which means *to receive.*

**Expect.** Should not be used for *suppose.*

COLLOQUIAL. I expect it's time for us to go.
PREFERRED IN WRITING. I suppose it's time for us to go.

**Extra.** Not to be used in the sense of *unusually,* as *an extra fine day.*

**Factor.** Means *a force or agent coöperating with other forces or agents to produce a certain result;* as *Industry and perseverance were factors in his success.* Should be used with intelligent regard to its meaning.

INEXACT. Being ducked in the lake is an inevitable factor in the freshman's experience.
CORRECT. Being ducked in the lake is an inevitable part of the freshman's experience.

**Farther, further.** In careful usage *farther* indicates distance; *further* indicates degree and also means *additional.* Both are used as adjectives and as adverbs: *a mile farther, further disintegration, further details.*

**Fellow.** A colloquialism when used as the equivalent of *man* or *boy.*

COLLOQUIAL. Many of the fellows are wearing sport shirts.
PREFERRED IN WRITING. Many of the men are wearing sport shirts.

**Fine** (1). Means *refined, delicate, free from impurity, of excellent quality: fine cutlery, fine dust, fine sense of honor, fine gold.* Widely but somewhat loosely used and overused as an epithet of approval: *a fine fellow, a fine ship.*

**Fine** (2). Colloquial when used as an adverb to mean *well* or *very well: The motor works fine.*

**Firstly.** Most writers prefer *first,* even when followed by *secondly, thirdly,* etc.

**First-rate.** May be used as an adjective but only colloquially as an adverb.

CORRECT. It is a first-rate building.
COLLOQUIAL. He plays tennis first-rate.

**Fix** (1). Colloquial for *situation* or *condition.*

**Fix** (2). Colloquial in the United States for *repair* or *arrange.* The expression *fix up* used in one of these senses is likewise a colloquialism.

**Flunk.** Colloquial for *fail.* Generally to be avoided in writing.

**Former, latter.** Properly used to designate one of two persons or things, not one of three or more. (See **Either, neither.**) For designating one of three or more, say *first* or *last.*

**Gentleman, lady.** These terms are properly used to indicate persons of cultivation, refinement, or good social standing. To indicate sex differences in compound words use *man* and *woman.*

CORRECT. Men's clothing, cleaning woman, repairman, saleswoman.

**Get.** *Get to* (*go*), *get across, get by with, get over* are colloquialisms. *Get next to, get on to, get away with, get left* are slang. Consult an unabridged dictionary for the many uses of *get.*

**Good.** An adjective; should not be used as an adverb meaning *well.*

WRONG. Do it good this time.
CORRECT. Do it well this time.

**Got.** The perfect tense is colloquial in the sense of possession. It is correct in the sense of *obtained.*

COLLOQUIAL. Have you got a knife with you?
PREFERRED IN WRITING. Have you a knife with you?
CORRECT. Have you got what you wanted?

*Got* is also colloquial in the sense of *must.*

COLLOQUIAL. I have got to hurry.
PREFERRED IN WRITING. I must hurry.
PREFERRED IN WRITING. I have to hurry.

**Gotten.** The older form of the past participle of *get.* Still used in the United States, but being replaced by *got,* except in expressions like *ill-gotten gains.*

**Had have** or **had of.** Often incorrectly used for *had.*

INCORRECT. If he had have [*or* had of] tried, he would have succeeded.
CORRECT. If he had tried, he would have succeeded.

**Had ought.** See **Ought.**

**Hardly, scarcely, only, but.** These words all convey the idea of negation. Hence they should not be used with another negative.

WRONG. It was so misty that we couldn't hardly see.
CORRECT. It was so misty that we could hardly see.
WRONG. There isn't but one store.
FORMAL. There is but one store.
INFORMAL. There is only one store.

**Honorable.** See **Reverend.**

**Hung.** With reference to the death penalty, *hanged* is preferred to *hung.*

UNDESIRABLE. He was found guilty and hung.
CORRECT. He was found guilty and hanged.
CORRECT. We hung the flag on the balcony.

**In, into.** *In* is generally used for *place in which,* and *into* for *place into which.*

UNIDIOMATIC. He went in the bank.
CORRECT. He went into the bank.
CORRECT. He was in the bank.

**Individual.** Should not be used indiscriminately for *person.* Properly used to mean *individual person.*

CORRECT. He made a general address to the class, and also gave special advice to the individuals in the class.
LOOSE. He is a tall, gaunt individual.
CORRECT. He is a tall, gaunt person.

**Infer.** Means to reach a conclusion by reasoning from facts or premises. Never to be used instead of *imply*, which means *to suggest* or *to hint.*

INEXACT. Does your statement infer that I am wrong?
CORRECT. I infer, as my statement implies, that you are wrong.

**Inferior.** See **Superior.**

**Inside.** Does not require *of* following. Say simply *inside.*

CORRECT. They were trapped inside the walls.

**Inside of.** A colloquial Americanism for *within*, in time expressions.

COLLOQUIAL. It will disappear inside of a week.
PREFERRED IN WRITING. It will disappear within a week.

**Just.** A colloquialism when used as an intensive.

COLLOQUIAL. I shall be just delighted to come.
PREFERRED IN WRITING. I shall be delighted to come.

**Kind, sort.** Are singular, and should therefore be modified by a singular demonstrative adjective.

INCORRECT. I don't like those kind [*or* those sort] of photographs.
CORRECT. I don't like that kind [*or* that sort] of photographs.

**Kind of, sort of** (1). Should not be used in writing to modify verbs or adjectives. Say *somewhat*, *somehow*, or *rather*. Often it is better to use no adverb.

BAD. People who kind of chill you . . .
CORRECT. People who somehow chill you . . .
BAD. The man who does nothing but study gets sort of dull.
CORRECT. The man who does nothing but study grows dull.

**Kind of, sort of** (2). Should not be followed by *a* or *an*.

COLLOQUIAL. What kind of a house is it? It is a sort of a castle.
PREFERRED IN WRITING. What kind of house is it? It is a sort of castle.

**Latter.** See **Former.**

**Lay.** Often confused with *lie*. *Lay* is a transitive verb meaning *to put*, or *place*, *something*. It always takes an object. Its principal parts are *lay*, *laid*, *laid*.

*Lie* is intransitive and means *to recline*. Its principal parts are *lie*, *lay*, *lain*. When in doubt, try substituting the verb *place*. If it fits the context, you want some form of *lay*.

CORRECT. I lie down every afternoon.
CORRECT. I lay the paper by his plate every morning.
CORRECT. I lay down yesterday after dinner.
CORRECT. I laid the paper by his plate yesterday.
CORRECT. I have lain here for two hours.
CORRECT. I have laid the paper by his plate many times.

**Leave, let.** Do not use *leave* in the sense of *permit* or *let*.

WRONG. Leave him go.
CORRECT. Let him go.

**Less.** Should not be used in place of *fewer*. *Less* refers to amount; *fewer* refers to number.

WRONG. Less men were hurt this year than last.
CORRECT. Fewer men were hurt this year than last.
CORRECT. You will need less butter with this recipe.

**Let's.** Contraction of *let us*. Should be used only where *let us* can be used.

WRONG. Let's don't leave yet.
CORRECT. Let's not leave yet.

**Liable.** Not properly used in the sense of *likely* except in designating an injurious or undesirable event which may befall a person or thing.

UNDESIRABLE. We are liable to have a clear day tomorrow.
CORRECT. We are likely to have a clear day tomorrow.
CORRECT. We are liable to have a flood if the rain continues.

**Like.** Should not be used to introduce a clause. Use *as* or *as if.*

COLLOQUIAL. He acted like the rest did.
PREFERRED IN WRITING. He acted as the rest did.
PREFERRED IN WRITING. He acted like the rest.
COLLOQUIAL. I felt like I had done something generous.
PREFERRED IN WRITING. I felt as if I had done something generous.

**Locate.** A colloquialism for *settle.* Correct when used with an object.

COLLOQUIAL. He located in Ohio.
PREFERRED IN WRITING. He settled in Ohio.
PREFERRED IN WRITING. He located his factory in Lima.

**Lot, lots, a whole lot.** Colloquialisms for *much, many, a great deal.*

COLLOQUIAL. Lots of students have part-time jobs.
PREFERRED IN WRITING. Many students have part-time jobs.

**Mad.** Means *insane.* Colloquial or childish when used to mean angry.

**May of.** See **Of.**

**Mean.** Means *lowly* or *base.* Colloquial when used to mean *cruel, vicious, unkind,* or *ill-tempered.* Slang when used to mean *excellent* or *formidable;* as *He serves a mean ball.*

**Messrs.** The plural of *Mr., Messrs.,* should never be used without a name or names following it.

**Might of.** See **Of.**

**Most.** Colloquial when used to mean *almost.*

COLLOQUIAL. Most everyone was invited.
PREFERRED IN WRITING. Almost everyone was invited.

**Mrs.** *Mrs.* may be followed by the husband's surname, by the husband's Christian name (or initials) and surname, or by the woman's Christian name and the husband's surname. The husband's *title*, if stated at all, should be put in another part of the sentence.

CORRECT. Mrs. Boughton, Mrs. John C. Boughton, Mrs. Mary Boughton.

**Much.** See **Very.**

**Must of.** See **Of.**

**Myself.** Colloquial as a substitute for *I* and *me.*

COLLOQUIAL. They received help from Mary and myself.
PREFERRED IN WRITING. They received help from Mary and me.

**Neither.** See **Either.**

**Nice.** Has the primary meaning of *keen* and *precise in discrimination*, or *delicately* or *precisely made;* as *a nice judge of values, a nice distinction in meaning.* It may also mean *pleasant* or *agreeable*, but in this sense it is overused. Prefer adjectives that more exactly express the meaning.

**No place.** See **Anyplace.**

**Notorious.** Means *of bad repute;* as *a notorious gambler.* Not to be used for *famous, celebrated*, or *noted.*

**Nowhere near.** A colloquialism for *not nearly.*

COLLOQUIAL. There is nowhere near enough for all of us.
PREFERRED IN WRITING. There is not nearly enough for all of us.

**Nowheres.** Dialectal for *nowhere.*

**Of.** *Could of, may of, might of, must of, should of*, and *would of* are illiterate corruptions of *could have, may have, might have, must have, should have*, and *would have.*

**Off of.** *Of* is superfluous.

REDUNDANT. Keep off of the grass.
PREFERRED. Keep off the grass.

**Only.** See **Hardly.**

**Or.** Should not be correlated with *neither;* use *nor.*

BAD. Neither the long arctic night or any other cause . . .
IMPROVED. Neither the long arctic night nor any other cause . . .

**Ought.** The combination of *ought* with *had* is a vulgarism.

SUBSTANDARD. You hadn't ought to have entered.
PREFERRED IN WRITING. You ought not to have entered. You should not have entered.

**Outside of** (1). *Of* is usually superfluous. Say simply *outside.*

**Outside of** (2). *Outside of* should not be used in writing for *aside from, except for.*

COLLOQUIAL. Outside of this mistake, it is very good.
PREFERRED IN WRITING. Aside from this mistake, it is very good.

**Over with.** *With* is superfluous. *The regatta is over.* (Not *over with.*)

**Party.** Means *a person or group of persons taking part* (*in some transaction*). Colloquial when used to mean simply *person.*

CORRECT. He was party to the plot.
CORRECT. The parties to the marriage were both young.
COLLOQUIAL. The party who wrote that article must have been a scholar.
PREFERRED IN WRITING. The person who wrote that article must have been a scholar.

**Per cent.** Use *per cent* only after a numeral. *Per cent* means literally *by the hundred* and should therefore be used when there is an exact numerical statement. *Percentage* means, loosely, a *part* or *proportion of a whole.*

DOUBTFUL. A large per cent were Chinese.
CORRECT. Twenty per cent were Chinese.
CORRECT. A large percentage were Chinese.

The words *per cent* should be used rather than the sign %. In strictly commercial writing, however, the sign is used, but only after numerals.

**Phenomena.** A plural noun. The singular form is *phenomenon.*

**Phone.** A colloquialism. Widely used, but not yet proper in formal discourse.

**Piece.** A provincialism when used in the sense of *distance* or *short distance.*

**Plenty** (1). Dialectal when used as an adjective before a noun. Say *plenty of.*

DIALECTAL. We have plenty time.
CORRECT. We have plenty of time.

**Plenty** (2). Colloquial when used as an adverb meaning *very, quite.*

COLLOQUIAL. His playing is plenty good.
PREFERRED IN WRITING. His playing is very good.

**Poorly.** Colloquial when used to mean *not well, in poor health.*

COLLOQUIAL. She has been poorly for many years.
PREFERRED IN WRITING. She has been in poor health for many years.

**Put in.** A colloquialism for *spend* or *occupy.*

COLLOQUIAL. I put in three hours in trying to memorize the speech.
PREFERRED IN WRITING. I spent three hours, etc.

**Quite.** Means (*a*) *wholly;* as *The stream is now quite dried up;* or (*b*) *greatly, very;* as *We could see it quite distinctly.* Questionable when used in the sense of *rather.*

**Quite a few.** Colloquial for *a good many* or *a considerable number.*

**Quite a little.** Colloquial for *a considerable amount* or *a good deal.*

**Raise.** Often confounded with *rise.* Remember that *raise* means *to cause something to rise.* Therefore *raise* must always have an object. Remember the principal parts of each verb:

| | | |
|---|---|---|
| I rise | I rose | I have risen |
| I raise | I raised | I have raised |

CORRECT. I rise at six o'clock every morning.

CORRECT. I raise flowers for sale.
CORRECT. I rose at six o'clock.
CORRECT. I raised flowers for sale.
CORRECT. I have risen at six o'clock for years.
CORRECT. I have raised flowers for years.

**Real.** Substandard when used for *very*. Not *real hot*, but *very hot*.

**Reverend, Honorable.** In formal contexts should be preceded by *the*, and should never be followed immediately by a surname.

VULGAR. Rev. Carter
FORMAL. The Reverend Mr. Carter
INFORMAL. Reverend Amos Carter

**Right along.** Colloquial. Write *continually* or *frequently*.

COLLOQUIAL. I hear from him right along.
PREFERRED IN WRITING. I hear from him frequently.

**Same.** Not in good use as a pronoun except in legal documents.

CRUDE. We will repair the engine and ship same [*or* the same] to you next week.
CORRECT. We will repair the engine and ship it to you next week.

**Say.** Colloquial in the sense of *give orders*, with an infinitive as object.

COLLOQUIAL. The guard said to go back.
PREFERRED IN WRITING. The guard ordered us [*or* told us] to go back.

**Scarcely.** See **Hardly.**

**Set.** A transitive verb often confounded with *sit*, an intransitive verb. Remember the principal parts of each verb:

| | | |
|---|---|---|
| I sit | I sat | I have sat |
| I set | I set | I have set |

The use of *set* without an object, as expressing mere rest, is a vulgarism; say *sit*, *stand*, *lie*, *rest*, or *is set*.

WRONG. The vase sets on the mantel.
CORRECT. The vase stands [*or* rests] on the mantel.

*Setting hen* is an idiomatic expression in good usage.

**Shape.** Should not be used loosely to mean *manner*, *condition*, *state*.

COLLOQUIAL. He is in good shape for the debate.
PREFERRED IN WRITING. He is in good condition [*or* thoroughly prepared] for the debate.

**Should of.** See **Of.**

**Show.** Colloquial for *play*, *opera*, *moving picture*.

**Show up.** A colloquialism when used intransitively in the sense of *appear*, *attend*, *come*, or *be present;* and slang when used transitively in the sense of *expose*.

**Sit.** See **Set.**

**Size up.** Colloquial for *observe*, *scrutinize*, *estimate*, *evaluate*.

**Some** (1). A colloquialism when used as an adverb meaning *a little*, *somewhat*.

COLLOQUIAL. I worked some last winter. I am some better today.
PREFERRED IN WRITING. I did some work last winter. I am somewhat better today.

**Some** (2). Slang when used as an intensifying adjective; as *That is some car you are driving.* A word conveying the precise meaning should be substituted.

**Someplace.** See **Anyplace.**

**Sort.** See **Kind.**

**Superior, inferior.** Should not be limited by a *than* phrase, but by a *to* phrase.

WRONG. It was superior from every point of view than the lathe previously used.
CORRECT. It was superior from every point of view to the lathe previously used.

**Sure.** Substandard when used for *certainly, undoubtedly, surely.*

**Suspicion.** Incorrectly used as a verb.

SUBSTANDARD. I did not suspicion that he was coming.
CORRECT. I did not suspect that he was coming.

**Take and.** Sometimes used redundantly.

REDUNDANT. It will stay if you take and put it on right.
IMPROVED. It will stay if you put it on right.

**Take sick.** Dialectal for *become sick.*

**This here, these here, that there, those there.** Vulgarisms. Say *this, these, that,* or *those.*

**Through.** Colloquial when used as in the following sentence:

COLLOQUIAL. He is through writing.
PREFERRED IN WRITING. He has finished writing.

**Transpire.** Means *to give forth* or *to become known;* as *In spite of their efforts at concealment, the secret transpired.* Stilted and pompous when used to mean *happen, occur.*

**Try and.** Long used for *try to,* but should be avoided in writing. *I must try to* [not *try and*] *find a job.*

**Unique.** Means the only one of its kind. Often, but unadvisedly, used to mean *unusual, outstanding.*

**Up.** Do not attach a superfluous *up* to verbs unless you are sure that by so doing you can make your expression more effective.

SUPERFLUOUS. He opened up the box and divided the money up among the men.
IMPROVED. He opened the box and divided the money among the men.

**Very** and **much** with past participles. A past participle that has not yet become an adjective should not be immediately preceded by *very* but by *much, greatly, seriously,* or some other intensive. A past participle that has become an adjective may be preceded by *very.*

IDIOMATIC. I am very much interested in the work. Not *very interested*. [*Interested* is a past participle.]
IDIOMATIC. He was a very tired boy. [*Tired* is an adjective.]

**Want** (1). Should not be followed by a clause.

SUBSTANDARD. I want you should be happy.
CORRECT. I want you to be happy.

**Want** (2). *Want in, want out, want through* are localisms.

DIALECTAL. Do you want in?
STANDARD. Do you want to come in?

**Want for.** Omit the superfluous *for* after *want.*

PROVINCIAL. I want for you to get some water.
IMPROVED. I want you to get some water.

**Ways.** Colloquial in such expressions as *a little ways.* In writing, the singular is preferred: *a little way.*

**Where to, where at.** The prepositions are usually redundant.

COLLOQUIAL. Where are you going to?
PREFERRED IN WRITING. Where are you going?

**Whose.** In modern usage, the possessive case of *who* only, though originally also of *which,* and still sometimes so used to avoid awkward circumlocution.

DUBIOUS. Soon we came to a swamp, on whose bank stood a hunter's cabin.
PREFERABLE. Soon we came to a swamp, on the bank of which stood a hunter's cabin.
ACCEPTABLE. The dealer refused to take the three paintings whose colors had faded.

**Would have.** Often incorrectly used in *if* clauses instead of *had.*

WRONG. If he would have stood by us, we might have won.
CORRECT. If he had stood by us, we might have won.

**Write-up.** Slang for *a report, a description, an account.*

# Spelling

## 44. SPELLING

- **a.** Trouble spots in words
- **b.** Similar words frequently confused
- **c.** Spelling rules
- **d.** Hyphenated words
- **e.** Words commonly misspelled

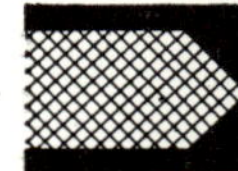

# 44 SPELLING

Misspelling of common words is regarded by the general public as a sure sign of a lack of education. College graduates cannot afford to be poor spellers. They need not be, since most misspelling is a habit and habits can be changed with a little effort.

The first step is to make a list of words which you misspell. Have someone give you a series of spelling tests on the words listed in Section **44e**. These are all common words frequently misspelled. Difficult words like *asphyxiate* or *symbiosis*, which occur infrequently in ordinary writing, need not be learned, since you can consult a dictionary for the spelling of any word which is obviously difficult.

Add to the list words which are misspelled on your themes, and study the list. Look carefully at the letters of each word, pronounce the word a syllable at a time, write the word repeatedly to fix the pattern in your mind and muscles. Invent mnemonic devices — pictures, jingles, associations — to help you remember particular spellings. For example, a student might remember the distinction between *capital* and *capitol* by associating capit*A*l with W*A*shington and capit*O*l with d*O*me. Learn the more common prefixes and suffixes, and analyze words to see how they are formed. For example,

disappoint = dis + appoint
dissatisfied = dis + satisfied
misspelling = mis + spell + ing
really = real + ly

unnecessary = un + necessary
undoubtedly = un + doubt + ed + ly
studying = study + ing
government = govern + ment
carefully = care + ful + ly
incidentally = incident + al + ly

See how many words in the list of Words Commonly Misspelled (**44e**) can be analyzed into a root word with prefixes or suffixes. If you find exceptions, look for an explanation in the Spelling Rules (**44c**).

When you have finished the final draft of a paper, proofread it carefully before you hand it in. It is no excuse to say that you knew the correct spelling of a word but that your pen slipped. Misspellings due to typographical errors or general carelessness are still misspellings.

## 44a Trouble Spots in Words

Common words are almost always misspelled in the same way. That is, a particular letter or combination of letters is the trouble spot, and if you can remember the correct spelling of the trouble spot, the rest of the word will take care of itself. Learn to look for the trouble spots in words and concentrate on them. *Receive*, like *deceive*, *perceive*, and *conceive*, is troublesome only because of the *ei* combination; if you can remember that it is *ei* after *c*, you will have mastered these words. To spell *beginning* correctly, all you need to remember is the double *n*.

Careful pronunciation may help you to avoid errors at trouble spots. In the following words, the letters in italics are often omitted. Pronounce the words aloud, exaggerating the sound of the italicized letters:

| | | |
|---|---|---|
| accident*al*ly | Feb*r*uary | li*a*ble |
| can*d*idate | gener*al*ly | lib*r*ary |
| ever*y*body | lab*o*ratory | liter*a*ture |

| | | |
|---|---|---|
| occasion*al*ly | reco*g*nize | su*r*prise |
| proba*b*ly | soph*o*more | temper*a*ment |
| quan*t*ity | stric*t*ly | us*u*ally |

Many people add letters incorrectly to the following words. Pronounce the words, making sure no extra syllables creep in at the spots indicated by italics.

| | | |
|---|---|---|
| a*thl*etics | en*tr*ance | mischie*vous* |
| disas*tr*ous | heigh*t* | remem*br*ance |
| drow*ned* | hin*dr*ance | simil*ar* |
| el*m* | ligh*tn*ing | um*br*ella |

Trouble spots in the following words are caused by a tendency to transpose the letters italicized. Careful pronunciation may help you to remember the proper order.

| | | |
|---|---|---|
| child*re*n | p*er*form | pre*j*u*d*ice |
| hund*re*d | p*er*spiration | p*re*scription |
| irre*lev*ant | p*re*fer | trag*edy* |

## 44b Similar Words Frequently Confused

Learn the meaning and spelling of similar words. Many errors are caused by confusion of such words as *effect* and *affect.* It is useless to spell *principal* correctly if the word that belongs in your sentence is *principle.* The following list distinguishes briefly between words which are frequently confused.

| | | | |
|---|---|---|---|
| accept | *receive* | affect | *to influence* (verb) |
| except | *aside from* | | |
| access | *admittance* | effect | *result* (noun) |
| excess | *greater amount* | effect | *to produce* (verb) |
| advice | noun | aisle | in church |
| advise | verb | isle | *island* |

| | |
|---|---|
| all ready | *prepared* |
| already | *previously* |
| allusion | *reference* |
| illusion | *misconception* |
| altar | *shrine* |
| alter | *change* |
| alumna | a woman |
| alumnae | women |
| alumnus | a man |
| alumni | men |
| angel | *celestial being* |
| angle | *corner* |
| ascent | *climbing* |
| assent | *agreement* |
| berth | *bed* |
| birth | *being born* |
| boarder | *one who boards* |
| border | *edge* |
| breath | noun |
| breathe | verb |
| capital | *city* |
| capitol | *building* |
| choose | present |
| chose | past |
| clothes | *garments* |
| cloths | *kinds of cloth* |
| coarse | *not fine* |
| course | *path, series* |
| complement | *to complete* |
| compliment | *to praise* |
| confidently | *with confidence* |
| confidentially | *secretly* |
| conscience | *sense of right and wrong* |
| conscious | *aware* |
| corps | *squad* |
| corpse | *dead body* |
| costume | *dress* |
| custom | *manner* |
| council | *assembly* |
| counsel | *advice* |
| descent | *slope* |
| decent | *proper* |
| desert | *wasteland* |
| dessert | *food* |
| device | noun |
| devise | verb |
| dairy | *milk room* |
| diary | *daily record* |
| dual | *twofold* |
| duel | *fight* |
| formally | *in a formal manner* |
| formerly | *previously* |
| forth | *forward* |
| fourth | *4th* |
| ingenious | *clever* |
| ingenuous | *frank* |
| its | *of it* |
| it's | *it is* |

| | | | |
|---|---|---|---|
| later | *subsequent* | respectfully | *with respect* |
| latter | *second of two* | respectively | *as relating to each* |
| lead | *metal* | | |
| led | past tense of verb *lead* | shone | cf. *shine* |
| | | shown | cf. *show* |
| loose | adjective | stationary | adjective |
| lose | verb | stationery | noun |
| peace | *not war* | their | possessive |
| piece | *a portion* | there | *in that place* |
| | | they're | *they are* |
| percent | *part of a hundred* | to | go *to* bed |
| percentage | *rate* | too | *too* bad, me *too* |
| | | two | *2* |
| personal | adjective | weather | *rain* or *shine* |
| personnel | noun | whether | *which of two* |
| principal | *most important* | who's | *who is* |
| principle | *basic doctrine* | whose | possessive |
| quiet | *still* | you're | *you are* |
| quite | *entirely* | your | possessive |

## 44c Spelling Rules

Spelling rules apply to a relatively small number of words, and unfortunately almost all rules have exceptions. Nevertheless, some of the rules may help you to spell common words which cause you trouble, especially those words formed with suffixes. For a complete list of rules, see the section "Orthography" in *Webster's New Collegiate Dictionary*.

It is as important to learn when a rule may be used as it is to understand the rule itself. Applied in the wrong places, rules will make your spelling worse, instead of better.

### Final Silent *E*

Drop a final silent *e* before suffixes beginning with a vowel. Keep a final silent *e* before suffixes beginning with a consonant.

| | |
|---|---|
| hope + ing = hoping | hope + ful = hopeful |
| love + able = lovable | nine + teen = nineteen |
| stone + y = stony | arrange + ment = arrangement |
| guide + ance = guidance | late + ly = lately |
| plume + age = plumage | pale + ness = paleness |
| white + ish = whitish | white + wash = whitewash |

SOME EXCEPTIONS:

| | | | |
|---|---|---|---|
| dyeing | hoeing | gluey | awful |
| ninth | truly | duly | wholly |
| noticeable | peaceable | courageous | outrageous |

The *e* is retained in such words as *noticeable* and *courageous* in order to keep the soft sound of *c* and *g*.

#### EXERCISE

Following the rule just given, write the correct spelling of each word indicated below.

| | |
|---|---|
| use + ing | pale + ing |
| use + ful | manage + ment |
| argue + ment | peace + able |
| guide + ance | write + ing |
| hope + ful | advantage + ous |
| outrage + ous | refuse + al |
| nine + teen | waste + ful |
| pale + ness | hope + less |
| immediate + ly | absolute + ly |
| please + ure | sure + ly |

### Doubling Final Consonant

When adding a suffix beginning with a vowel to words ending in one consonant preceded by one vowel, notice where the word is accented. If it is accented on the last syllable or if it is a monosyllable, double the final consonant.

| | |
|---|---|
| pre**fer** + ed = preferred | **ben**efit + ed = benefited |
| o**mit** + ing = omitting | **prof**it + ing = profiting |
| oc**cur** + ence = occurrence | **dif**fer + ence = difference |
| red + er = redder | **trav**el + er = traveler |

Note that in some words the accent shifts when a suffix is added.

| | |
|---|---|
| re**fer**red | **ref**erence |
| pre**fer**ring | **pref**erence |

There are a few exceptions to this rule, like *transferable* and *excellent;* and a good many words that should follow the rule have alternate spellings: either *worshiped* or *worshipped; traveling*, *traveler* or *travelling*, *traveller.*

#### EXERCISE

Make as many combinations as you can of the following words and suffixes. Give your reason for doubling or not doubling the final consonant. Suffixes: *able*, *ible*, *ary*, *ery*, *er*, *est*, *ance*, *ence*, *ess*, *ed*, *ish*, *ing*, *ly*, *ful*, *ment*, *ness*, *hood.*

| | | | | |
|---|---|---|---|---|
| occur | scrap | ravel | man | libel |
| happen | red | kidnap | vassal | will |
| begin | equip | hazard | sum | skill |
| god | commit | read | stop | expel |
| shrub | equal | rid | clan | rival |
| glad | profit | level | avoid | jewel |

### Words Ending in *Y*

If the *y* is preceded by a consonant, change *y* to *i* before any suffix except *ing*.

lady + es = ladies    lonely + ness = loneliness
try + ed = tried    accompany + es = accompanies
study + ing = studying

The *y* is usually retained if it is preceded by a vowel:

valleys    monkeys    displayed

SOME EXCEPTIONS: *laid, paid, said.*

#### EXERCISE

Add suffixes to the following words. State your reason for spelling the word as you do.

| | | | | |
|---|---|---|---|---|
| mercy | relay | hardy | bounty | medley |
| duty | study | wordy | jockey | galley |
| pulley | essay | fancy | modify | body |

### *IE* or *EI*

When *IE* or *EI* is used to spell the sound *EE*,
Put *I* before *E*
Except after *C*.

| | | | |
|---|---|---|---|
| ach*ie*ve | gr*ie*ve | retr*ie*ve | c*ei*ling |
| bel*ie*f | n*ie*ce | sh*ie*ld | conc*ei*t |
| bel*ie*ve | p*ie*ce | shr*ie*k | conc*ei*ve |
| br*ie*f | p*ie*rce | s*ie*ge | dec*ei*t |
| ch*ie*f | rel*ie*f | th*ie*f | dec*ei*ve |
| f*ie*ld | rel*ie*ve | w*ie*ld | perc*ei*ve |
| gr*ie*f | repr*ie*ve | y*ie*ld | rec*ei*ve |

SOME EXCEPTIONS: *ei*ther, l*ei*sure, n*ei*ther, s*ei*ze, w*ei*rd.

## 44d Hyphenated Words

A hyphen is used, under certain circumstances, to join the parts of compound words. Compounds are written as two separate words (*city hall*), as two words joined by a hyphen (*city-state*), or solid as one word (*cityfolk*). In general, the hyphen is used in recently made compounds and compounds still in the process of becoming one word. Because usage varies considerably, no arbitrary rules can be laid down. When in doubt consult the latest edition of an unabridged dictionary. The following "rules" represent the usual current practice.

### Compound Adjectives

Words used as a single adjective *before* a noun are usually hyphenated.

| | |
|---|---|
| coal-black hair | three-inch board |
| bright-eyed child | matter-of-fact statement |
| strong-minded woman | hit-or-miss driver |
| far-reaching results | so-called gadget |
| well-educated teachers | old-fashioned house |

When these compound adjectives *follow* the noun, they usually do not require the hyphen.

**Correct.** The snow-covered mountains lay ahead.

**Correct.** The mountains are snow covered.

When an adverb ending in *ly* is used with an adjective or a participle, the compound is not usually hyphenated.

**Correct.** highly praised organization, widely advertised campaign.

### Prefixes

When a prefix still retains its original strength in the compound, a hyphen is used. In most instances, however, the prefix has been absorbed into the word and should not be separated by a hyphen. Contrast the following pairs of words:

ex-president, excommunicate
vice-president, viceroy
pre-Christian, preconception
pro-British, procreation

Note that in some words a difference of meaning is indicated by the hyphen:

She recovered her strength.
She re-covered her quilt.

### Compound Numbers

A hyphen is used in compound numbers from twenty-one to ninety-nine.

**Correct.** twenty-six, sixty-three, *but* one hundred thirty.

### Hyphen to Prevent Misreading

To avoid ambiguity, a hyphen may be necessary.

**Ambiguous.** A detail of six foot patrolmen was on duty.

**Clear.** A detail of six foot-patrolmen was on duty.

**Ambiguous.** She is a normal school student.

**Clear.** She is a normal-school student.

### EXERCISE

Should the compounds in the following sentences be written solid, with a hyphen, or as two words? Consult a recent edition of a good dictionary.

1. We need an eight foot rod.
2. All the creeks are bone dry.
3. He gave away one fourth of his income.
4. The United States is a world power.

5. He was our go between.
6. She is very good looking.
7. The younger son was a ne'er do well.
8. Let us sing the chorus all together.
9. They are building on a T shaped wing.
10. She is getting a badly needed rest.
11. Are you all ready?
12. The leak was in the sub basement.
13. He was anti British.
14. She does her work in a half hearted manner.
15. I don't like your chip on the shoulder manner.
16. She always was old fashioned.
17. A high school course is required for admission.
18. I do not trust second hand information.
19. He is as pig headed a man as I ever knew.
20. He will not accept any thing second rate.

## 44e Words Commonly Misspelled

The following list is composed of some ordinary words that are often misspelled. If you learn to spell correctly those which you usually misspell, and if you will look up in a dictionary words which are obviously difficult or unfamiliar, your spelling will improve remarkably.

Have a friend test you on these words — fifty at a time. Then concentrate on the ones you miss. To help you remember correct spellings, trouble spots are italicized in many of the following words.

ab*s*ence
absor*p*tion
ab*su*rd
abund*a*nt
ac*a*demic
accident*al*ly
a*c*co*mm*odate
accumulate
accurate
ach*ie*vement
a*c*quainted
a*c*quire
a*c*ross
a*dd*ition*al*ly
a*dd*ress
ad*e*quat*e*ly
a*gg*ravate
airplane
allotment
allo*tt*ed
all right

already
a*l*toge*t*her
a*l*ways
am*a*t*eu*r
among
anal*y*sis
a*nn*ua*ll*y
apology
app*a*ratus
apparent
appear*a*nce
app*e*tite
appreciate
approp*r*iate
ar*c*tic
arg*u*ment
arithm*e*tic
arrangement
arti*cle*
ascend
association
a*thl*etic
attack*ed*
attend*a*nce
audience
av*ai*l*a*ble
awkward
bargain
basic*all*y
becom*i*ng
begi*nn*ing
bel*ie*ve
ben*e*fi*t*ed
bound*a*ry
brill*ia*nt
Brit*ai*n
bus*i*ness
calend*a*r
candidate
ca*r*eer
cat*e*gory
cemet*e*ry
cert*ai*n
chall*e*nge
chang*ea*ble
chan*gi*ng
Christ*ia*n
column
com*i*ng
commission
commi*tt*ee
comparatively
compet*e*nt
comp*eti*tion
conc*ei*t
con*c*entrate
conde*mn*
confid*e*nce
conqu*e*r*o*r
conscientious
con*scious*
consider
consist*e*nt
contemp*o*r*a*ry
contin*uous*
contro*ll*ed
conven*ie*nce
coo*ll*y
cop*ie*s
court*eous*
crit*ic*ism
de*a*lt
dec*ei*ve
dec*is*ion
def*i*nitely
des*c*end*a*nt
d*e*scribe
d*e*scri*p*tion
d*e*sir*a*ble
d*e*sp*ai*r
desp*e*rate
diction*a*ry
different
di*ff*icult
di*n*ing room
di*s*a*pp*ear
di*s*a*pp*oint
disas*tr*ous
dis*ci*pline
disease
dis*s*atisfied
dis*si*pate
d*i*vide
doct*o*r
dying
*e*ffect
ei*ghth*
eliminate
emba*rr*a*ss*
em*ph*asize
entir*e*ly
en*tr*ance
envi*ron*ment
equi*pp*ed
especially
etc. (*et cetera*)
exa*gg*erate
exc*ee*d

excell*e*nt
exception*al*ly
exercise
exist*e*nce
e*xo*rbitant
expen*s*e
exp*e*rience
expl*a*nation
famili*ar*
fa*sc*inate
feasible
February
fictitious
fina*ll*y
for*ei*gn
f*o*rty
fr*ie*nd
ga*u*ge
gover*nm*ent
gramm*a*r
g*u*ard
har*a*ss
hard*en*ing
heig*ht*
hin*dr*ance
hum*o*rous
hurr*ie*dly
h*y*pocris*y*
i*ll*iterate
imagination
i*m*itation
i*mm*ediat*e*ly
incident*al*ly
incred*ibl*y
independ*e*nt
indispens*a*ble
inf*i*nit*e*
initiative
intell*i*gence
in*te*rest
*i*nvolve
irre*l*e*v*ant
i*rr*esist*i*ble
itself
j*e*al*ou*sy
knowle*d*ge
lab*o*ratory
laid
l*e*d
l*ei*sure
library
li*c*en*s*e
literature
lon*e*liness
l*o*se
lux*u*ry
mag*az*ine
maint*e*nance
manufactur*e*r
marr*ia*ge
math*e*matics
ma*tt*ress
m*e*ant
medieval
mer*e*ly
mini*a*ture
munici*pal*
murm*u*r
m*y*ster*iou*s
ne*c*e*ss*ary
n*ei*ther
nin*e*teen
notic*e*able
now*a*days
nucleus
obst*a*cle
o*cc*a*s*ion*al*ly
o*cc*u*rr*ed
occurr*e*nce
o*m*i*ss*ion
omi*tt*ed
opinion
opportunity
opt*i*mism
or*i*gin
paid
pam*ph*let
para*ll*el
paralyzed
parl*i*ament
particularly
par*t*ner
pastime
p*er*form
p*er*haps
permanent
permiss*i*ble
persist*e*nt
personnel
p*er*suade
ph*y*sical
pleas*a*nt
politic*ia*n
po*ss*e*ss*
poss*i*ble
practic*al*ly
prece*d*ing
predomin*ant*

pre*j*udice
prep*a*ration
prev*a*l*e*nt
prim*i*tive
priv*i*l*e*ge
probably
proc*e*dure
proc*ee*d
pro*f*e*ss*ion
pro*f*ess*o*r
promin*e*nt
pron*u*nciation
pr*o*ve
psychology
p*u*rsue
qui*zz*es
rea*ll*y
rec*ei*ve
recognize
re*c*o*mm*end
refe*r*ence
refe*rr*ed
rel*ig*i*o*us
reminis*c*e
rep*e*tition
represen*t*ative
rhythm
r*i*diculous
sacr*i*fice
saf*e*ty
scene
sched*ule*
secretary
s*ei*ze
sen*s*e
sep*a*rate
s*e*rgeant
sever*e*ly
shi*n*ing
s*ie*ge
simil*a*r
sincer*e*ly
soliloquy
soph*o*more
specim*e*n
sp*ee*ch
sto*pp*ing
stren*uou*s
stretch
stud*y*ing
su*cc*eed
su*pp*ress
surprise
suscept*i*ble
syllable
sympathize
temper*a*ment
tend*e*ncy
th*o*rough
together
tra*g*edy
transfe*rr*ed
tr*u*ly
typical
tyranny
undoubt*ed*ly
un*n*e*c*e*ss*ary
unti*l*
using
usua*ll*y
vengeance
village
vill*ai*n
w*ei*rd
wri*t*ing

## EXERCISES

### 1

Write the infinitive, the present participle, and the past participle of each of the following verbs (e.g., *stop*, *stopping*, *stopped*):

prefer
profit
drag
slam
begin
equip
hop
differ
recur
acquit
commit
confer

## 2

Write the following words together with the adjectives ending in *able* derived from them (e.g., *love, lovable*):

| | | |
|---|---|---|
| dispose | compare | imagine |
| move | console | cure |
| prove | blame | measure |

## 3

Write the following words together with their derivatives ending in *able* (e.g., *notice, noticeable*):

| | | |
|---|---|---|
| trace | marriage | damage |
| service | charge | peace |
| change | place | manage |

## 4

Write the singular and the plural of the following nouns (e.g., *lady, ladies*):

| | | | |
|---|---|---|---|
| baby | remedy | treaty | turkey |
| hobby | enemy | delay | decoy |
| democracy | poppy | alley | alloy |
| policy | diary | attorney | corduroy |
| tragedy | laundry | journey | convoy |

## 5

Write the first and third persons present indicative, and the first person past, of the following verbs (e.g., *I cry, he cries, I cried*):

| | | | |
|---|---|---|---|
| fancy | spy | vary | worry |
| qualify | reply | dry | pity |
| accompany | occupy | ferry | envy |

### 6

Study the following words, observing that in all of them the prefix is not *diss*, but *dis*:

| | |
|---|---|
| dis + advantage | dis + obedient |
| dis + agree | dis + orderly |
| dis + approve | dis + organize |
| dis + interested | dis + own |

### 7

Study the following words, observing that in all of them the prefix is not *u*, but *un:*

| | |
|---|---|
| un + natural | un + numbered |
| un + necessary | un + named |
| un + noticed | un + neighborly |

### 8

Study the following words, distinguishing between the prefixes *per* and *pre*. Keep in mind that *per* means *through*, *throughout*, *by*, *for;* and that *pre* means *before.*

| | | |
|---|---|---|
| perform | perhaps | precept |
| perception | perspective | precipitate |
| peremptory | perspiration | precise |
| perforce | precarious | precocious |
| perfunctory | precaution | prescription |

### 9

Study the following adjectives, observing that in all of them the suffix is not *full*, but *ful:*

| | | |
|---|---|---|
| peaceful | forceful | healthful |
| dreadful | shameful | pitiful |
| handful | grateful | thankful |
| graceful | faithful | cupful |

## 10

Study the following words, observing that in all of them the ending is not *us*, but *ous:*

| | | |
|---|---|---|
| advantageous | specious | fastidious |
| gorgeous | precious | studious |
| courteous | vicious | religious |
| dubious | conscious | perilous |

## 11

Study the following words, observing that in all of them the suffix *al* precedes *ly*.

| | | |
|---|---|---|
| accidentally | terrifically | exceptionally |
| apologetically | specifically | elementally |
| pathetically | emphatically | professionally |
| typically | finally | critically |

## 12

Study the following words, observing that the suffix is not *ess*, but *ness:*

| | | |
|---|---|---|
| clean + ness | plain + ness | stern + ness |
| drunken + ness | stubborn + ness | keen + ness |
| mean + ness | sudden + ness | green + ness |

## 13

Study the following words, observing that the suffix is not *able*, but *ible*.

| | | |
|---|---|---|
| accessible | discernible | imperceptible |
| admissible | eligible | impossible |
| audible | feasible | incompatible |
| compatible | flexible | incredible |
| contemptible | forcible | indefensible |
| convertible | horrible | indelible |

intelligible
invincible
invisible
irresistible
legible
perceptible
permissible
plausible
possible
reprehensible
responsible
sensible
susceptible
tangible
terrible

**14**

Study the following groups of words:

| *ain* | | *ian* | |
|---|---|---|---|
| Britain | curtain | barbarian | guardian |
| captain | fountain | Christian | musician |
| certain | mountain | civilian | physician |
| chieftain | villain | collegian | politician |

**15**

Study the following groups of words:

| *ede* | | *eed* |
|---|---|---|
| accede | precede | exceed |
| antecede | recede | proceed |
| concede | secede | succeed |

**16**

Fill the blanks with *principal* or *principle*. *Principle* is always a noun; *principal* is usually an adjective. *Principal* is also occasionally a noun: *the principal of the school, both principal and interest.*

1. The ______ will be due on the tenth of the month.
2. His refusal was based on ______.
3. This is my ______ reason for going.
4. The ______ has asked that we hold our meeting tomorrow.
5. He did not even know the first ______ of the game.
6. Can you give the ______ parts of the verb?

## 17

Fill the blanks with *affect* or *effect:*

1. I do not like her ______ed manner.
2. An entrance was ______ed by force.
3. The ______ upon her is noticeable.
4. The law will take ______ in July.
5. It was an ______ive remedy.
6. The hot weather will ______ the crops.
7. There was no serious after______.
8. She ______ed ignorance of the whole matter.

## 18

Fill the blanks with *passed* or *past. Passed* is the past tense or past participle of the verb *pass; past* can be an adjective, noun, adverb, or preposition.

1. We ______ your house.
2. She went ______ me.
3. He whistled as he ______ by.
4. He is a man with a ______.
5. He is a ______ master at the art of lying.
6. He is ______ his prime.
7. Many years ______ before he returned.
8. It is long ______ bedtime.

## 19

Fill the blanks with:

*a*) *Its* (pronoun in the possessive case) or *it's* (contraction of *it is*)

1. ______ raining.
2. The cat has had ______ supper.
3. The clock is in ______ old place again.
4. ______ now six years since the accident.
5. I think that ______ too late to go.

*b*) *Your* (pronoun in the possessive case) or *you're* (contraction of *you are*)

1. ______ mistaken; it is ______ fault.
2. ______ position is assured.
3. ______ to go tomorrow.
4. I hope that ______ taking ______ vacation in July.

*c*) *There* (adverb or interjection), *their* (pronoun in the possessive case), or *they're* (contraction of *they are*)

1. It is ______ turn.
2. ______ ready to go.
3. ______, that is over with.
4. ______ car was stolen.
5. ______ back from ______ trip.

*d*) *Whose* (pronoun in the possessive case) or *who's* (contraction of *who is*)

1. ______ turn is it?
2. There is the man ______ running for mayor.
3. ______ responsible for this?
4. ______ book is this?
5. He is one ______ word can be trusted.
6. ______ ready to go?
7. Bring me a copy of ______ *Who*.

**20**

Circle the italicized word which is spelled correctly in each of the following sentences. Consult Section **44b** if necessary.

1. Everyone is going *accept, except* me.
2. People came to him every day for *advice, advise*, and he was always ready to *advice, advise* them.
3. At so high an altitude it was hard to *breath, breathe*.
4. His *breath, breathe* came in short gasps.

5. One of the sights of Washington, D.C. is the *Capital, Capitol.*
6. Albany is the *capital, capitol* of New York.
7. Before dinner I had time to change my *clothes, cloths.*
8. The tickets were sent with the *complements, compliments* of the manager.
9. The country was as dry and dreary as a *desert, dessert.*
10. The shack in which we *formally, formerly* lived is still standing.
11. It's *later, latter* than you think.
12. The winners were *lead, led* up onto the stage.
13. Button the money in your pocket so you won't *lose, loose* it.
14. Business letters should be written on good *stationary, stationery.*
15. I don't care *weather, whether* it's raining or shining.
16. After a long argument, we *preceded, proceeded* to the next item of business.
17. I'm not *all together, altogether* sure that I like the *bare, bear* hills of Mexico.
18. My uncle invented a *device, devise* for applying shoe polish directly from the container.
19. I hope to *hear, here* from you soon after you reach *their, there* house.
20. According to the new ordinance, no dogs are *aloud, allowed* on the streets.

## Mechanics

45. MANUSCRIPT

46. CAPITAL LETTERS

47. WRITING NUMBERS

48. ABBREVIATIONS

49. USE OF ITALICS

50. SYLLABICATION

# 45 MANUSCRIPT

Before a paper is handed in it should be carefully edited and corrected. An instructor has no way of knowing whether an error — in spelling, for example — is a result of ignorance or of hasty typing and careless editing. Do not expect him to give you the benefit of the doubt. The following rules are designed to make your paper easier to read.

## 45a Paper, Ink, and Penmanship

Paper should be $8\frac{1}{2} \times 11$ inches in size, unless your instructor specifies some other kind. It should be unruled if you type your themes. If you use ruled paper for handwritten themes, the lines should be widely spaced to prevent crowding. Themes should be either typed or written in ink — black or blue-black; pencil is difficult to read. Write legibly. An instructor or an editor cannot do full justice to a manuscript if he has to puzzle it out, one word at a time. Do not crowd your writing. Leave enough space between consecutive lines to permit editing. Write each word as an entity without gaps between the letters. Do not decorate letters with unnecessary flourishes; use plain forms. Simple, clear handwriting which can be easily read predisposes the reader in your favor. Conversely, handwriting which must be deciphered word by word makes it almost impossible for a reader to appreciate what you have written.

## 45b Arrangement on the Page

Observe the following conventions for arrangement of material.

1. Write on one side of the sheet only.
2. Leave a generous margin — at least an inch and a half — at the left side of each page and at the top. Leave about an inch of margin at the right side and at the bottom.
3. In typewritten manuscript, double-space the lines except in footnotes or in quotations set apart on the page. In handwritten manuscript, leave an equivalent space between lines.
4. Number all pages except the first in the upper right-hand corner. Use Arabic numerals, not Roman.
5. Indent uniformly for paragraphs. The usual indentation for typewritten manuscript is five spaces. Indent about an inch in handwritten manuscript.
6. Center the title at least two inches from the top of the page, or on the first line if you use ruled paper. Leave extra space between the title and the first line of the composition.

## 45c Arrangement of Quotations

Observe the following conventions in reproducing quotations.

1. A quotation of only a few words may be incorporated into the text.

**Correct.** Not all Augustan writers agreed with Pope's definition of wit as "nature to advantage dressed."

2. An extended quotation of verse or prose is usually set off from the body of the text by these methods:
   *a.* It begins on a new line.
   *b.* It is usually separated from the text by extra spacing.

*c*. In typewritten manuscript it is usually single spaced.

*d*. In handwritten manuscript it is usually given a wider margin than the text and is enclosed in quotation marks. In typewritten manuscript where it is clearly differentiated from the text by single spacing, the margin often remains the same and the quotation marks are usually omitted.

**Correct.**

```
     Lord Chesterfield's opinion of women is in-

dicated by the following quotation:

Women, then, are only children of a larger growth;
they have an entertaining tattle, and sometimes
wit; but for solid, reasoning good sense, I never
in my life knew one that had it, or who reasoned
or acted consequentially for four-and-twenty hours
together.

In the light of this undisguised contempt, it is

all the more remarkable that his son....
```

3. A quotation of poetry should be divided into lines exactly as the original is divided. If an entire line of verse cannot be written on one line of the page, the part left over should be indented.

**Correct.**

> 'Tis mute, the word they went to hear on high Dodona
>   mountain,
> When winds were in the oakenshaws, and all the cauldrons
>   tolled.

4. The text following a quotation should begin on a new line, indented if it begins a new paragraph, or flush with the left-hand margin if it continues the paragraph containing the quotation.

**Correct.**

In his essay called "Drift," Walter Lippmann writes of those who dream of the past:

> The weary man sinks back into the past, like a frightened child into its mother's arms. He glorifies what is gone when he fears what is to come. That is why discontented husbands have a way of admiring the cakes that mother used to bake.

It is only those, Mr. Lippmann says, who are at home in the world who find life more interesting as they mature.

## 45d Correcting the Manuscript

If a reading of your final draft shows the need of further alterations or revisions, make them unmistakably clear. It is not necessary to recopy an entire page for the sake of one or two insertions or corrections. Copying is necessary only when there are so many corrections as to make the page difficult to read or messy in appearance.

Words to be inserted should be written above the line, and their proper position should be indicated by a caret (^) placed below the line. Words so inserted should not be enclosed in parentheses or brackets unless these marks would be required if the words were written on the line. To transfer a group of words to another place in a sentence, do not encircle them and try to indicate by lines and arrows the new position. Rather, cancel the words, and insert them in the proper place. Cancel words by drawing a line through them. Parentheses or brackets should never be used for this purpose.

# 46 CAPITAL LETTERS

The general principle is that proper nouns are capitalized; common nouns are not capitalized. A proper noun is the name of a particular person, place, or thing: *Einstein, Texas, New Orleans, the Capitol, the United States Senate, Mount Hood.* A common noun is a more general term which can be used as a name for a number of persons, places, or things: *scientist, doctor, state, city, government building, legislative body, mountain.*

Note that the same word may be used as both a proper and a common noun.

**Correct.** There are dozens of lakes in California, but only one Lake Tahoe.

**Correct.** When I finished high school, I entered college. After graduating from Lincoln High School, I entered Grinnell College. Since I intended to major in history, I enrolled in History 22. My naive idea of deans and college presidents was changed when I met the Dean of Men at the President's reception.

Abbreviations are capitalized when the words they stand for would be capitalized: *U.S.N., ROTC, op. cit.,* 9 *a.m.,* NBC.

## 46a Proper Nouns

Capitalize proper nouns and the adjectives derived from them. Proper nouns include the following types:

1. Days of the week, and months
2. Organizations such as political parties, governmental bodies and departments, societies, institutions, clubs, churches, and corporations

**Correct.** The Socialist Party, the House of Representatives, the Department of Labor, the Red Cross Society, the Home for the Friendless, the Rotary Club, the Methodist Church, the Standard Oil Company

3. Members of such organizations: Socialists, Rotarians, Methodists, Catholics
4. Historical events and periods: the Fall of Rome, the Middle Ages, the Renaissance
5. Geographical areas: the South, the Midwest
6. Race and language names: French, English, Indian, Negro
7. Many words of religious significance: the Lord, the Son of God, the Trinity, the Saviour
8. Names of members of the family when used in place of proper names: *a letter from Mother telling about my brother's new job*
9. In biological nomenclature, the names of genera but not of species: Homo sapiens, *Salmo irideus*
10. Stars, constellations, and planets, but not the earth, sun, or moon unless in a list of astronomical names

## 46b Titles of Persons

Capitalize titles of persons when they precede proper names. When used without proper names, titles of officers of high rank should be capitalized; other titles should not.

**Correct.** Senator Benton, Professor Olson, Admiral Graves, Uncle John. Both the President and the Attorney General endorsed the candidacy of our congressman. The postmaster of our town appealed to the Postmaster General.

### 46c Titles of Books, Plays, Compositions, etc.

Capitalize the first word and the important words of the titles of books, plays, articles, musical compositions, pictures, and other literary or artistic works. The unimportant words are the articles *a*, *an*, and *the;* conjunctions; and prepositions.

**Correct.** *The Cloister and the Hearth*, *A Tale of Two Cities*, *The Merchant of Venice*, *The Ring and the Book*, *Seven against Thebes*, Beethoven's *Fifth Symphony*, Botticelli's "The Birth of Venus."

In hyphenated titles, capitalize both words if the second part of the compound is a noun. If the second part is an adjective or an adverb, capitalize only the first word of the compound.

**Correct.** *Walking-Stick Papers*, *The House on Forty-ninth Street*, *Eighteenth-Century Poetry*, *French for English-speaking Tourists.*

### 46d First Word of Sentences and Direct Quotations

Capitalize the first word of every sentence and of every direct quotation. Note that a capital is not used for the part of a quotation that follows an interpolated expression like "he said" unless that part is a new sentence.

**Correct.** "Keep your line tight," said my father, "and hold the tip of the rod up."

**Correct.** "Keep your line tight," said my father. "You can't hook a fish with a slack line."

**Correct.** My father said, "Keep your line tight."

A series of short questions or sentences following a colon need not be capitalized, but the first may be.

**Correct.** There were the same old stupid questions: What is the capital of the state? on what river is it located? what is its population? what are the chief products?

The first word of an unquoted sentence following a colon is capitalized only when the sentence is long or independent in meaning.

**Correct.** Here is the old question of campaign funds: If I take money from a group of men who have an interest in changing the income tax law, I take it with the knowledge that those men will expect me to remember their interest when new legislation is being considered.

**Correct.** There is one chief reason for concern: consumer credit is overexpanded.

## 46e Lines of Poetry

Capitalize the first word of every line of poetry. Do not capitalize, however, when the first part of a line is omitted or when the poem itself does not use a capital.

**Correct.**

. . . and vile it were
For some three suns to store and hoard myself,
And this grey spirit yearning in desire
To follow knowledge like a sinking star,
Beyond the utmost bound of human thought.

## 46f Salutation and Close of Letters

Capitalize the first and last words in the salutation of a letter, but only the first word in the complimentary close.

**Wrong.** Dear sir: Yours Sincerely,

**Correct.** Dear Sir: My dear Sir: Yours sincerely, Very truly yours,

## EXERCISE

What words in the following sentences should be capitalized? Why?

1. A canary-colored studebaker convertible was driving north on fountain avenue.
2. Although the wife of doctor gibbs was a southerner, the doctor himself came from New England.
3. Although many of the natives can speak spanish, they prefer their own indian dialect.
4. A novel experiment in american education was announced on monday by the yale school of law and the harvard school of business administration.
5. "I'm going out to the country club," said skipper; "want to come along?"
6. Although technically a veteran, he had served in the coast guard for only two weeks toward the end of the first world war.
7. It was spring; in fact, it was the beginning of may.
8. The douglas fir, often sold under the name oregon pine, is neither a fir nor a pine.
9. He makes these regional divisions: the east, the old south, the middle west, and the far west.
10. When I left high school I intended to major in economics, but in college I became interested in science and graduated as a biology major.
11. Buddhists, christians, jews, and moslems attended the conference, which was held at ankara, the capital of turkey.
12. Both the rotarians and the lions meet in the private dining room of the piedmont inn.

# 47 WRITING NUMBERS

Numbers appearing in tabular form are always represented by figures, but numbers used as part of an ordinary sentence are sometimes spelled out and sometimes written as figures. There is some variation in usage among publishers, but the following rules are generally accepted. For consistency, all related numbers in one context should be treated similarly. Do not use figures for some and words for others.

## 47a Spelling Out Numbers

Numbers that can be expressed in one or two words should be spelled out. Other numbers are usually expressed in figures.

**Correct.** Uncle Tom will be seventy-one tomorrow.

**Correct.** The class consisted of ten boys and twenty-two girls.

**Correct.** Nearly two thousand people had gathered by ten o'clock.

**Correct.** Altogether, we sold 364 tickets.

**Correct.** The state faces a deficit of twenty million dollars.

Spell out numbers that begin a sentence, even though they would ordinarily be represented by figures. If such a number is awkwardly long, recast the sentence so that the number does not come first.

**Correct.** Two hundred fifty dollars was the list price.

**Correct.** Ten Downing Street is the most famous address in London.

**Correct but awkward.** Nineteen hundred fourteen marked the end of an era.

**Improved.** The year 1914 marked the end of an era.

## 47b Use of Figures for Dates and Addresses

The day of the month and the year should be expressed in figures, except at the beginning of a sentence and in very formal social notes. If the year is omitted, the day of the month may be spelled out or written in figures. House numbers are normally written in figures. Street numbers may be written as figures or spelled out.

**Correct.** On November 10, 1931, I was born at 547 East 10th Street (or East Tenth Street).

**Correct.** We plan to leave on the 4th of August (or the fourth of August).

Note that the letters *st*, *nd*, *rd*, and *th* are regularly used with figures representing street numbers, but need not be added to figures following the name of the month.

**Correct.** He lives on 42nd Street.

**Correct.** That year the 10th of April fell on Monday.

**Correct.** The next year Easter fell on April 10.

## 47c Other Uses of Figures

Use figures for long numbers, page and chapter numbers, time expressed by A.M. and P.M., percentages, decimals, and technical numbers.

**Correct.** The tank contained 1,375 gallons.

**Correct.** Read Chapter 12, which begins on page 236.

**Correct.** I usually worked from 10 P.M. to 6 A.M.

**Correct.** I usually worked from ten at night to six in the morning.

**Correct.** The total rainfall from the storm was .62 inch.

**Correct.** You will receive 5 per cent of the profits.

**Correct.** The 42nd parallel. Longitude 59° 12′ W. A 60-watt bulb.

## 47d Sums of Money

After a dollar sign ($), always use figures. If a number is short it may be spelled out and followed by *dollars* or *cents.* When a series of sums is listed, use figures and abbreviations.

**Correct.** The bill for painting two rooms was $124.45.

**Correct.** I paid six dollars for a ticket.

**Correct.** These were my expenses: hotel, $7.00; meals, $8.00; fare, $4.65; and tips, $1.75.

Be consistent. Write *$6.15*, not *$6 and fifteen cents.*

In sums of money from one to ten dollars, ciphers are used when there are no fractional amounts. For sums above ten dollars, the ciphers should be omitted.

**Correct.** These were the prices: $7.00, $8.00, and $10.00.

**Correct.** We bought the desk for $95 and sold it a week later for $125.

### EXERCISE

In the following sentences, the numbers are all represented by figures. Which of them should be spelled out? Give reasons.

1. 30 years ago the population was approximately 3,000.

2. The frame was supported on 3 posts, each $7\frac{1}{2}$ inches in diameter.
3. If our expenses can be reduced 10 per cent, we should save about 2,500 dollars.
4. At 10 o'clock we were still waiting on 8th Avenue.
5. The round-trip fare is 90 cents.
6. Her address 2 years ago was 196 West 9th Street.
7. About 60 people answered the advertisement.
8. The 3rd and 4th grades are to have a spelling match.
9. The original drainage project consisted of about 200 miles of canals 60 feet wide. At the present time about 1,500,000 acres have been reclaimed.
10. He paid $80 for his new suit.
11. When I inserted 3 additional pages after page 28, the entire manuscript ran to 42 pages.
12. The antenna should be exactly 22 feet 4 inches long if one is to get best results on the 15 meter band.
13. When I lived at 2627 Channing Way, I had to walk about 8 blocks to my office.
14. The repairs to the porch cost two hundred fifteen dollars, but the bill for painting was only $27.50.
15. In a DC–7 the flying time to New York is about 8 hours.

# 48 ABBREVIATIONS

In ordinary, nontechnical writing, abbreviations should be avoided. Spell out Christian names, the words in addresses (*Street*, *Avenue*, *New York*, etc.), the months and days of the week, units of measurement (*ounces*, *pounds*, *feet*, *hour*, *gallon*, etc.). References to volumes, chapters, and pages should be spelled out in the text, but abbreviated in footnotes, parenthetical citations, and bibliographies.

**Correct.** Robert Wilson has lived at 245 West 51st Street, New York, since August 1, 1954.

**Correct.** The passage is on page 345 of the second edition.

**Correct.** For further information regarding abbreviations consult a dictionary (e.g., *Webster's Collegiate*, 5th ed., pp. 1175–1181.)

## 48a Standard Abbreviations

A few standard abbreviations are in general use in all kinds of writing: *i.e.* (that is), *e.g.* (for example), *etc.* (and so forth), *vs.* (versus), *A.D.*, *B.C.*, *a.m.*, *p.m.*, Washington, *D.C.* Names of some organizations and of many government agencies are commonly represented by their initials: DAR, GOP, NATO, CAA, TVA, etc.

Some abbreviations require periods (*Ph.D.*, *N.Y.*, *Sgt.*, *oz.*) but others are regularly written without periods (*FBI*, *Na*, *WAC*). The correct form of standard abbreviations can be found in your dictionary, either in regular alphabetical order or in a separate appendix.

### 48b Titles

Spell out all civil, religious, and military titles except the following:

(a) Preceding names: *Mr., Messrs., Mrs., Dr., St.* (for *Saint*). *Rev.* and *Hon.* are used only when the surname is preceded by a Christian name: *Rev. Henry Mitchell*, not *Rev. Mitchell.*

(b) Following names: *Esq., M.D., Sr., Jr., Ph.D., M.A., LL.D.*, etc. Do not duplicate a title before and after a name.

**Wrong.** Dr. Russell Williams, M.D.; Mr. Henry Smith, Esq.

**Correct.** Dr. Russell Williams, or Russell Williams, M.D.

For the correct forms of titles used in addressing officials of church and state, consult *Webster's New International Dictionary* (2nd ed., pp. 3012–14).

### 48c Technical Terms

In technical writing, directions, recipes, and the like, terms of measurement are often abbreviated when used with figures.

**Correct.** 32° F.; 2,000 rpm; 25 mph; ½ tsp. salt and 2 tsp. sugar; 12 ft. 9 in.; 5 cc.; 2 lb. 4 oz.

Abbreviations like *Co., Inc., Bros.*, should be used only when business organizations use them in their official titles. The ampersand (&) is used only when the company uses the symbol in its letterhead and signature.

**Wrong.** D. C. Heath & Co., D. C. Heath and Co., Harper and Bros.

**Correct.** D. C. Heath and Company, Harper & Brothers, McGraw-Hill Book Company, Inc., Brock & Co.

EXERCISE

Correct any errors in abbreviations in the following sentences:

1. Dr. Geo. C. Fryer lives on Sandy Blvd. near Walnut St.
2. I have worked for the Standard Oil Co. since Oct., '43.
3. Col. House was a personal friend of Pres. Wilson.
4. We expect to go to N.Y. for Xmas.
5. The date is b.c., not a.d.
6. The Acme Corp. ships mail-order goods C.O.D.
7. I was in Wash., D.C., on Aug. 10, 1950.
8. Mt. Whitney, which is 14,495 ft. high, is located in SE Calif.
9. Rev. Davis will read the psalm on p. 187.
10. The drive to Lexington, Ky., took us 3 hrs., 17 min.
11. I invested $200 dollars in American Tel. and Tel. stock.
12. A temperature of 32° F. is equivalent to zero on the cent. scale.
13. He bought three fl. oz. of aromatic spirits of amm.
14. Turn back to the 1st page of Ch. 3 and read pp. 18–22.
15. The feel of living in the USSR is different from that in the U.S.

## 49 USE OF ITALICS

Italics are used for titles, unnaturalized foreign words, and words used as such. To italicize a word in a manuscript draw one straight line below it, or use the special underlining key on the typewriter, thus: King Lear.

### 49a Italics in Titles

Italicize all words, including an initial *the*, *a*, or *an*, in the titles of separate publications, such as books, monographs, and pamphlets, but do not italicize the author's name. Titles of musical works are italicized, but titles of paintings and works of art are enclosed in quotation marks.

In the titles of newspapers, magazines, and periodicals only the distinctive words are italicized. Preceding articles and the name of the city in which a newspaper is published are usually printed in regular type.

**Correct.** *A Tale of Two Cities.* James Gould Cozzens' *The Just and the Unjust. Handbook of Common Commercial and Game Fishes of California.* The *Atlantic Monthly.* The San Francisco *Chronicle.* The *Yale Review.*

Titles of parts of published works and articles in magazines are enclosed in quotation marks.

**Correct.** The assignment is "Winter" from James Thomson's *The Seasons.*

**Correct.** She submitted her article, entitled "The Misinterpretation of Ezra Pound," to the *Saturday Review.*

## 49b Proper Names

Italicize the names of ships, trains, and aircraft, but not the names of the companies that own them.

**Correct.** The heavy cruiser *Bremerton* was in the harbor.

**Correct.** He went east on the Santa Fe *Chief* and returned on United Air Lines' *New Yorker*.

## 49c Foreign Words and Phrases

Italicize foreign words which have not yet become accepted in the English language. If you are not certain whether a foreign word has become naturalized, consult a dictionary. Foreign words which should be italicized are preceded in *Webster's New Collegiate Dictionary* by parallels (||) and in *Webster's New World Dictionary* by a double dagger (‡). If you use another dictionary, be sure to check the Explanatory Notes to see how foreign words are indicated. Latin abbreviations used in footnotes and scientific names for plants and animals are italicized.

**Correct.** Our painting class has graduated from water color to *gouache*.

**Correct.** *Ibid.*, *circa*, *op. cit.*, *passim*, *sic.*

**Correct.** The technical name of the May apple is *Podophyllum peltatum*.

## 49d Words and Letters as Such

When words, letters, or figures are spoken of as such, they are usually italicized. When a word is quoted, it is usually enclosed in quotation marks.

**Correct.** The misuse of *awful* and *nice* is a common fault.

**Correct.** "Intriguing" is now her favorite word.

**Correct.** The letter a̲ and the figure 2̲ on my typewriter are worn.

## 49e Italics for Emphasis

Words which require special stress in a sentence may be italicized. But the overuse of italics should be avoided. Do not italicize for the purpose of calling attention to humor or irony.

**Correct.** To speak French fluently and idiomatically and with a good accent — or with an idiom and accent which to other rough islanders *seemed* good — was a rather suspect accomplishment, being somehow deemed incompatible with civic worth.

— Max Beerbohm

### EXERCISE

Underline words that should be italicized in the following sentences. If quotation marks are necessary, supply them.

1. Harrison played the part of Shylock in The Merchant of Venice.
2. He quoted an editorial from the New York Times.
3. The Normandie was a beautiful ship.
4. Have you read Anthony Powell's Agents and Patients?
5. Our word liberty comes from the Latin libertas.
6. He explained what is meant by the laissez-faire system.
7. This little projection is called a lug.
8. Did you notice how he pronounced the a in Armada?
9. She always calls everyone darling.
10. I read the chapter entitled The Rise of Nationalism in Westbrook's History of Modern Europe.

# 50 SYLLABICATION

Dividing a word at the end of a line is mainly a printer's problem. In manuscripts it is not necessary to keep the right-hand margin absolutely even, and so it is seldom necessary to divide a word at the end of a line. If such a division is essential, observe the following principles, and mark the division with a hyphen at the end of the line.

## 50a Division between Syllables

Divide words only between syllables — that is, between the normal sound-divisions of a word. When in doubt as to where the division between syllables comes, consult a dictionary. One-syllable words, like *through* or *strength*, cannot be divided. Syllables of one letter should not be divided from the rest of the word. A division should never be made between two letters that indicate a single sound. For example, never divide *th* as in *another*, *sh* as in *cushion*, *ck* as in *ticket*, *oa* as in *approaching*, *ai* as in *attainment*. Such combinations of letters may be divided if they indicate two distinct sounds: *post-humous*, *dis-honest*, etc.

**Wrong.** go-ndola, illustr-ate, pun-ctuation, man-y, a-gainst.

**Correct.** gon-dola, illus-trate, punc-tuation, many, against.

## 50b Other Rules for Division of Words

The following rules should be followed when they do not distort the normal pronunciation of a word.

1. The division comes at the point where a prefix or suffix joins the root word, if pronunciation permits.

**Correct.** be-tween, pre-fix, ante-cedent, con-fine, de-light

**Correct.** lov-ing, love-ly, judg-ment, invit-ed, Jew-ish, punish-ment, strong-er, strong-est

**Exceptions because of pronunciation.** extraor-di-nary, prog-ress, prej-u-dice, proj-ect, hus-tling, twin-kling, bat-tling

2. When two consonants come between vowels, the division is between the consonants if pronunciation permits. If the consonant is doubled before a suffix, the second consonant goes with the suffix.

**Correct.** remem-ber, advan-tage, dip-lomat (*but* di-plomacy), impor-tant, rub-ber, ab-breviation, oc-casion, ad-dition, af-finity, Rus-sian, expres-sion, omis-sion, com-mit-tee, excel-lent, stop-ping, drop-ping, ship-ping, equip-ping

**But note.** knowl-edge

3. The division comes after a vowel if pronunciation permits.

**Correct.** sepa-rate, particu-lar, ele-mentary, criti-cism

## EXERCISE

Correct in the following sentences any errors in syllabication, abbreviations, numbers, capitals, and italics.

1. He made a survey of Athletics in the Universities and Colleges in the U. S.
2. When grandmother was a girl, she lived in Pittsburgh, Pa.
3. She always adds a P.S. to her letters.
4. Did he consult Edwardes' dictionary of nonclassical mythology?
5. He was traveling in the East last Winter.

6. I spent fifty cents for a pattern, $6.80 for my material, and a dollar and ten cents for trimming; so you see that my dress will cost only $8.40.
7. A 10-ton truck was loaded with *#1 common pine 2 × 4's*, 20 ft. long.
8. 1949 brought us good fortune.
9. "You will surely decide to go," he said, "For you will never have such a chance as this again."
10. After each war we resolve "That these dead shall not have died in vain."
11. Our country entered the second world war in nineteen hundred and forty-one.
12. You have a hard road ahead: There will be tedious hours of work under an exacting master, perhaps in unpleasant surroundings, and there will be little pay and less honor.
13. The use of the word like as a conjunction is a very common error.
14. My Chemistry and Math. grades were high, and my grade point average was 3.24.
15. The Harvard and Yale are good passenger boats.
16. To some southern democrats, all northerners are still black republicans.
17. They discussed the eighteenth amendment and the methods of repealing an amendment to the constitution.
18. The president of the United States rose to greet the president of our university.
19. Queen Elizabeth I tried to preserve the status quo.
20. Take either the Pennsylvania Railroad's Broadway Limited or the NYC's 20th Century Limited.

## The Library and the Research Paper

**51.** THE LIBRARY

**a.** The card catalog
**b.** Standard reference books and bibliographies
**c.** Finding information in periodicals

**52.** THE RESEARCH PAPER

**a.** Choosing a subject
**b.** Limiting the topic
**c.** The working bibliography
**d.** Bibliography cards
**e.** Choice of source material
**f.** Tentative plan
**g.** Taking notes
**h.** Writing the paper
**i.** Documenting the paper

# 51 THE LIBRARY

The library is the heart of a college or university, and all students should learn to use it effectively. The amount of knowledge one can carry in his head is small compared with the vast amount stored in books. A necessary part of a college education is learning to find, quickly and efficiently, any information needed on any subject. The process of digging out information is called research, and research of an elementary sort is required every time a student works on a term paper. To do research effectively, one must be able to use the card catalog, be familiar with important reference books, and know how to find and use bibliographies and periodical indexes.

## 51a The Card Catalog

The card catalog is the index of the library. Every book and bound periodical in the library is listed on 3 × 5 cards, which are filed alphabetically in drawers. A book is usually listed three times: under its author's name, under its title, and under its general subject. In some large libraries there are separate catalogs for the author cards, for the title cards, and for the subject cards, but usually they are combined in a single alphabetical listing.

Author cards are printed by the Library of Congress, so that they will be the same throughout the country, and the heading of each is the author's surname.

## Sample Author Card

PR
13
P9 **Hendren, Joseph William.**
v.14 . . . A study of ballad rhythm, with special reference to ballad music, by J. W. Hendren . . . Princeton, Princeton university press, 1936.

xii, 177 p. illus. (music) 22cm. (⌊Princeton university⌋ Princeton studies in English, ed. by G. H. Gerould. 14)

Thesis (PH. D.) — Princeton university, 1934.
Photoprinted.
Bibliography: p. 176-177.

1. Musical meter and rhythm. 2. Ballads, English. 3. English language — Rhythm. I. Title. II. Title: Ballad rhythm, A study of.

36—36411

Library of Congress ML3553.H4S8
——— Copy 2. PE1521.B35H4 1934
⌊42i2⌋ (820.8) 781.62

In the upper left-hand corner is typed the call number, which indicates where the book can be found on the library shelves. Next comes the author's name, last name first. On the lines below appear the title of the book, the author's name as he signs it, the place of publication, the publisher, and the date of publication. The lines that follow explain that the book contains 12 introductory pages (indicated by small Roman numerals) plus 177 pages of text and illustrations, and that the bound book is 22 centimeters high. Although an independent book, it is listed also as volume 14 in the *Princeton Studies in English*, edited by G. H. Gerould. In 1934 it was accepted as a Ph.D. thesis at Princeton. This edition is photoprinted from a typed manuscript. It contains a bibliography on pages 176–177.

The book may be cataloged under three subject headings: *Musical Meter and Rhythm; Ballads, English;* or *English Language — Rhythm.* In a title catalog it should appear as *A Study of Ballad Rhythm*, and perhaps also as *Ballad Rhythm, a Study of.* The rest of the information on the card is of special interest to librarians.

A title card for a book is the same, except that the title is typed in as a heading. Title cards are filed alphabetically according to the first important word of the title. (The articles *a*, *an*, and *the* at the beginning of a title are ignored in alphabetizing.) Bound periodicals are listed in the catalog only by their titles.

### Sample Title Card

PR 13 P9 v.14

A study of ballad rhythm.

**Hendren, Joseph William.**

. . . A study of ballad rhythm, with special reference to ballad music, by J. W. Hendren . . . Princeton, Princeton university press, 1936.

xii, 177 p. illus. (music) 22cm. ([Princeton university] Princeton studies in English, ed. by G. H. Gerould. 14)

Thesis (PH. D.) — Princeton university, 1934.
Photoprinted.
Bibliography: p. 176-177.

1. Musical meter and rhythm. 2. Ballads, English. 3. English language — Rhythm. I. Title. II. Title: Ballad rhythm, A study of.

36—36411

Library of Congress ML3553.H4S8
——— Copy 2. PE1521.B35H4 1934
[42i2] (820.8) 781.62

### Sample Subject Card

PR 13 P9 v.14

Ballads, English.

**Hendren, Joseph William.**

. . . A study of ballad rhythm, with special reference to ballad music, by J. W. Hendren . . . Princeton, Princeton university press, 1936.

xii, 177 p. illus. (music) 22cm. ([Princeton university] Princeton studies in English, ed. by G. H. Gerould. 14)

Thesis (PH. D.) — Princeton university, 1934.
Photoprinted.
Bibliography: p. 176-177.

1. Musical meter and rhythm. 2. Ballads, English. 3. English language — Rhythm. I. Title. II. Title: Ballad rhythm, A study of.

36—36411

Library of Congress ML3553.H4S8
——— Copy 2. PE1521.B35H4 1934
[42i2] (820.8) 781.62

Subject cards are intended to help a reader find books on a particular topic when he does not know authors or titles. They are usually the regular Library of Congress cards, with a subject heading typed in red. Note that the same book may be listed under several subject headings.

#### EXERCISE

1. By consulting the author cards, see if your library has the following books. If so, list the dates of publication.
   a. *The Triple Thinkers*, by Edmund Wilson
   b. *The Social Insects, Their Origin and Evolution*, by William Morton Wheeler
   c. *The Culture of Cities*, by Lewis Mumford
2. Find a title card for each book, and note any differences from the author card.
3. See if you can find subject cards for each book by looking under
   a. Literature, Modern — 19th Century — History and Criticism
   b. Insects
   c. Cities and Towns
4. List other subject headings under which these books are cataloged.
5. What other books by Wilson, Wheeler, and Mumford does your library contain?
6. Give the authors and titles of at least two other books on each of the three general subjects listed above.

### 51b Standard Reference Books and Bibliographies

If a search of the subject headings in the card catalog fails to produce any books on the subject you are investigating, do not assume that there is no material available. A great deal of information is probably hidden in books and periodicals to which you must be directed by special bibliographies and indexes. Most of these guidebooks will be in the Reference Room of your library, and it pays to get acquainted with the standard reference books early in your college career.

The lists which follow include reference books, bibliographies, and special indexes which should help you find material on almost any subject. (Since these are standard works, full bibliographic entries are not given. For the correct form of items in a formal bibliography, see page 426.)

### Guide to Reference Books

Winchell, C. M., and O. A. Johnson. *Guide to Reference Books.* 7th Edition. 1951. Supplements, 1952, 1954.

### General Encyclopedias

*Collier's Encyclopedia.* 20 vols. 1958. Vol. 20 contains bibliographies and an index.

*Columbia Encyclopedia.* 2nd Edition. 1950. Supplements, 1953, 1956.

*Encyclopaedia Britannica.* 24 vols. 1958. Vol. 24, Atlas and index.

*Encyclopedia Americana.* 30 vols. 1958.

*New International Encyclopaedia.* 27 vols. 1930.

### Gazetteers and Atlases

*Columbia Lippincott Gazetteer of the World.* 1952.

*Encyclopaedia Britannica World Atlas.* 1958.

*Hammond's Ambassador World Atlas.* 1954.

*Rand McNally's Commercial Atlas and Marketing Guide.* 1958.

Shepherd, William R. *Historical Atlas.* 1956.

*Webster's Geographical Dictionary.* 1955.

## Reference Books for Special Subjects

### Art and Architecture

Gardner, Helen. *Art through the Ages.* 3rd Edition. 1948.
Hamlin, T. F. *Architecture through the Ages.* 1953.
*Harper's Encyclopedia of Art.* 2 vols. 1937.
McColvin, Eric R. *Painting: A Guide to the Best Books.* 1934.
Robb, David M., and J. J. Garrison. *Art in the Western World.* 1953.

### Biography

*Biography Index.* 1946–.
*Current Biography.* 1940–.
*Dictionary of American Biography.* 20 vols. and index. 1928–1936. Supplement, 1944.
*Dictionary of National Biography* (British). 22 vols. 1885–1901. Supplements: 1901, 1912, 1927, 1937, 1949.
*Webster's Biographical Dictionary.* 1956.
*Who's Who, Who's Who in America, International Who's Who,* etc. Separate books containing brief accounts of living men and women. Issued more or less regularly.

### Classics

Harvey, Sir Paul. *Oxford Companion to Classical Literature.* 1937.
*Oxford Classical Dictionary.* 1949.
Sandys, Sir John. *Companion to Latin Studies.* 1925.
Whibley, L. *Companion to Greek Studies.* 1931.

### Current Events

*Americana Annual.* 1923–. An annual supplement to the *Encyclopedia Americana.*
*Britannica Book of the Year.* 1938–. An annual supplement to the *Encyclopaedia Britannica.*

*Facts on File.* 1940–. A weekly world news digest with a cumulative index.

*New York Times Index.* 1913–. A subject index to the *Times.*

*Public Affairs Information Service.* 1915–. A weekly subject and author index to books and articles in the field of economics and public affairs.

*Statesman's Year Book.* 1864–. A statistical and historical annual giving current information about the countries of the world.

*Times* (London) *Official Index.* 1906–.

*World Almanac.* 1868–.

ECONOMICS AND COMMERCE

Coman, E. T. *Sources of Business Information.* 1949.

*Encyclopedia of the Social Sciences.* 15 vols. 1930–1935.

Hauser, P. M., and W. R. Leonard. *Government Statistics for Business Use.* 1956.

Larson, H. M. *Guide to Business History.* 1948.

Manley, M. C. *Business Information: How to Find and Use It.* 1955.

Munn, G. G. *Encyclopedia of Banking and Finance.* 5th Edition. 1949.

*Statistical Abstract of the United States.* 1879–.

EDUCATION

Monroe, Paul. *Cyclopedia of Education.* 3 vols. 1926.

Monroe, Walter S. *Encyclopedia of Educational Research.* 1955.

HISTORY

Adams, J. T. *Dictionary of American History.* 5 vols. and index. 1940.

*Cambridge Ancient History.* 12 vols. 1923–1939.

*Cambridge Mediaeval History.* 8 vols. 1911–1936.

*Cambridge Modern History.* 14 vols. 2nd Edition. 1926. A new edition is in preparation.

Dutcher, G. M., and others. *Guide to Historical Literature.* 1949.
Handlin, Oscar, and others. *Harvard Guide to American History.* 1954.
Hockett, H. *Introduction to Research in American History.* 1948.
Langer, W. L. *Encyclopedia of World History.* Rev. 1952.
Ragatz, L. J. *A Bibliography for the Study of European History, 1815 to 1939.* 1942. Supplements, 1943, 1945.

## Literature

"American Bibliography." *PMLA.* (In March issue or supplement.) 1921–. Annual bibliography, classified by subject.
Baugh, A. C., and others. *A Literary History of England.* 1947.
*Cambridge Bibliography of English Literature.* 4 vols. 1941.
*Cassel's Encyclopedia of Literature.* 1953.
*Columbia Dictionary of Modern European Literature.* 1947.
Hart, J. D. *Oxford Companion to American Literature.* 3rd Edition. 1956.
Harvey, Sir Paul. *Oxford Companion to English Literature.* 3rd Edition. 1946.
Kunitz, S. J., and H. Haycraft. *Twentieth Century Authors.* 1942. Supplement, 1955.
Leary, Lewis. *Articles on American Literature, 1900–1950.* 1954.
Manly, J. M., Edith Rickert, and Fred B. Millett. *Contemporary British Literature.* 1935.
Millett, Fred B. *Contemporary American Authors.* 1940.
Modern Humanities Research Association. *Annual Bibliography of English Language and Literature.* 1921–.
Spiller, R. E., and others. *Literary History of the United States.* 3 vols. 1948. Volume 3 is a complete working bibliography of American literature.
Thrall, W. F., and A. A. Hibbard. *A Handbook to Literature.* 1936.

## Music

Apel, W. *Harvard Dictionary of Music.* 1949.

Grove, Sir George. *Grove's Dictionary of Music and Musicians.* 9 vols. 4th Edition. 1954.

*The Oxford History of Music.* 7 vols. 1929–1934.

Scholes, P. A. *Oxford Companion to Music.* 1950.

Thompson, O. *International Cyclopedia of Music and Musicians.* 5th Edition. 1949.

### Philosophy

Baldwin, J. M. *Dictionary of Philosophy and Psychology.* 3 vols. 1928.

*Bibliography of Philosophy.* 1934.

Copleston, Frederick. *A History of Philosophy.* 3 vols. 1950.

Hoffding, Harald. *A History of Modern Philosophy.* 2 vols. 1950.

### Political Science

Burchfield, L. *Student's Guide to Materials in Political Science.* 1935.

De Grazia, Alfred. *The Elements of Political Science.* 1952.

*Encyclopedia of the Social Sciences.* 15 vols. 1930–1935.

*Foreign Affairs Bibliography, 1919–1932. 1932–1942. 1942–1952.*

Wright, Quincy. *The Study of International Relations.* 1955.

See also references under "Current Events."

### Psychology

Guilford, J. P. *Fields of Psychology.* 1950.

*Psychological Abstracts.* 1927–.

### Religion

Case, S. J. *A Bibliographical Guide to the History of Christianity.* 1931.

Hastings, James. *Encyclopedia of Religion and Ethics.* 13 vols. 1911–1928.

*Index to Religious Periodical Literature.* 1949–1952. 1953–1954.

Latourette, Kenneth S. *History of Christianity.* 1953.

### Science

*Biological Abstracts.* 1926–.
*Chemical Abstracts.* 1907–. See "Annual Subject Index."
*Chronica Botanica.* 1935–.
*Current List of Medical Literature.* 1941–.
Hawkins, R. R. *Scientific, Medical, and Technical Books.* 1953.
*Physics Abstracts.* 1898–. (Section A of *Science Abstracts*)
*Van Nostrand's Scientific Encyclopedia.* 2nd Edition. 1947.
Whitford, R. H. *Physics Literature: a Reference Manual.* 1954.
*Zoological Record.* 1864–.

### Sociology and Anthropology

*American Anthropologist.* 1879–.
*American Sociological Review.* 1936–.
Broom, Leonard, and P. Selznick. *Sociology.* 1955.
*Encyclopedia of the Social Sciences.* 15 vols. 1930–1935.
Kroeber, A. L. *Anthropology Today: an Encyclopedic Inventory.* 1953.
Thomas, W. L., Jr. *Current Anthropology: a Supplement to Anthropology Today.* 1956.
*Social Work Year Book.* 1935–.

## 51c Finding Information in Periodicals

For subjects of current interest, magazines are the principal sources of information.

To find material in magazines and technical periodicals, you must use one or several of the periodical indexes. These list alphabetically every important article in all major periodicals, by author or subject, and generally both, and sometimes also by title. Most of the indexes appear monthly and are cumulated at frequent intervals; that is, all the items listed in the separate numbers are combined into one volume in a single alphabetical order. It may be necessary for you to look through a number of volumes — for those years during which your subject is most likely to have been discussed.

The most widely used periodical indexes are:

*Readers' Guide to Periodical Literature.* 1900–. Alphabetical list under author, title, and subject.
*International Index to Periodicals.* 1907–. Devoted chiefly to humanities and social science.
*Poole's Index to Periodical Literature.* 1802–1881; 1882–1906. Useful for earlier periods.
*Book Review Digest.* 1905–.
*New York Times Index.* 1913–.
*Monthly Catalog* (to U.S. Government Publications). 1895–.

Here are two sample entries from the *Readers' Guide*, the first a subject entry, the second an author entry.

**FOLK songs, American**

Country music; hillbilly music. E. Waldron. Reporter 12 : 35-7 My 19; 39-42 Je 2 '55

**IVES, Burl**

American folk songs. por Mus Am 71: 20+F '51

Notice that these entries are not in the form you will use in your own bibliography. An explanation of the abbreviations is given on the first pages of each volume of the *Guide*. The first reference given above is to an article by E. Waldron entitled "Country Music; Hillbilly Music." It appeared in Volume 12 of the *Reporter*, and extended over two issues: the first part appeared on pages 35–37 of the May 19 issue, and the article was concluded on pages 39–42 of the June 2 issue in 1955. The second reference is to an article by Burl Ives entitled "American Folk Songs." It appeared in the February, 1951, issue of *Musical America*, Volume 71. The article, which includes a portrait, begins on page 20 and is continued elsewhere in the magazine.

### Special Periodical Indexes

The general periodical indexes, like the *Readers' Guide*, index magazines of fairly general circulation. If you are investigating a technical subject, you may need to get information from the scientific and learned journals. To find relevant articles in these, use the following specialized periodical indexes.

*Agricultural Index*. 1916–.
*Art Index*. 1929–.
*Biography Index*. 1946–.
*Dramatic Index*. 1909–.
*Education Index*. 1929–.
*Engineering Index*. 1884–.
*Index to Legal Periodicals*. 1908–.
*Industrial Arts Index*. 1913–. In 1957, this index was divided into two parts: *Applied Science and Technology Index* and *Business Periodicals Index*.
*Music Index*. 1949–.
*Quarterly Cumulative Index Medicus*. 1927–.

See also the various *Abstracts* listed above under "Psychology" and "Science."

# 52 THE RESEARCH PAPER

In many college courses you will be required to write long papers, usually of several thousand words, based upon material that you will gather from various sources in the library. Such a paper ought to be an informed, original essay on a sharply defined topic. Before you can write at all, you will need to inform yourself adequately, if not fully, on the subject. Then you must do something of your own with the material you have found. A mere collection of quotations and paraphrases will not be satisfactory. You must organize the material into a pattern of your own; you must write it up in your own words. In many cases, especially on controversial topics, you will come to some conclusion of your own. Do not let a false modesty keep you from expressing your own opinion. If you have informed yourself thoroughly, your opinion is significant and worth setting down.

The principal steps in the process of writing the paper will be the following:

Choosing and Limiting the Subject
Making a Working Bibliography
Choice of Source Material
Tentative Plan
Taking Notes
Writing the Paper
Documenting the Research Paper
Making the Final Bibliography

## 52a Choosing a Subject

Choose a subject that interests you. It is true that almost any subject becomes interesting when you have gone into it, but for a term paper assignment you will do better to pick a field in which your interest is already aroused. You will be spending several weeks in reading on one subject. What would you like to know more about?

Your choice will be limited somewhat by the resources of your library. A small college library is not likely to have much material on recent developments in medicine, for example. Even a large library may not afford much information on the most recent events and discoveries. There is inevitably a lag between an event and printed accounts of it, and good books often take years to write. If the librarian or your instructor tells you that your library is inadequate for a subject you have proposed, choose another.

## 52b Limiting the Topic

Limit the topic so that it can be treated fully in the space assigned. (See Section **1a**.) A term paper should be more than a mere skimming of obvious sources; it should represent a real effort in research, and it should be narrow and deep rather than broad and shallow. If you start with an interest in a large subject — say, folklore — read a general article in an encyclopedia to acquaint yourself with the ramifications of the field. One encyclopedia lists three main headings under Folklore: Beliefs and Customs, Narratives and Sayings, and Art. One subdivision of the last heading is Folk Music, and this is further subdivided into Folk Songs and Ballads.

Suppose you decide to write on folk ballads. This narrowing of the subject is a start in the right direction, but as you begin to read you will find it necessary to limit your topic further: to English ballads, or to one particular ballad. The author of the sample term paper printed on pages 428–434 finally limited herself to one particular English ballad as it is found in this country. But she began reading about ballads in general, and she probably made her final limitation only after she had discovered how much material was available on the more general topic.

Here are some other examples of how a subject may be narrowed into a suitable topic. One student was interested in sailing. Before going to the library, he eliminated sailing ships (an enormous field, ranging from Spanish galleons to Yankee clippers), and decided to confine himself to racing sailboats. But a little investigation showed a bewildering variety of these, and since he wanted to do more than catalog the various types, he limited himself to a relatively new type of racing boat — the planing sailboat, which rises partially out of the water and thus attains remarkable speed.

Another student, from Oklahoma, was interested in the Indians of the former Indian Territory. This project involved getting some knowledge of Indian tribes and the history of our treatment of them. It was soon clear that this was too large a subject to be handled in one paper, and she decided to limit her investigation to one tribe, the Cherokees. Even this proved too large, and she eventually limited herself to one episode, the forced removal of the Cherokees from Tennessee to Oklahoma. This topic was small enough to permit a good deal of digging into eyewitness accounts and other original documents. The final paper gave a vivid picture of the migration as well as an explanation of why it happened and what came of it.

### EXERCISE

Suggest ways in which the following large subjects might be limited to topics which could be covered in about two thousand words. Give specific examples of limited topics.

1. The planets
2. Tragedy
3. The Soviet Union
4. Plastics
5. Costume
6. Antibiotics
7. The Roman Catholic Church
8. Modern architecture
9. The labor movement in the United States
10. Electronics

## 52c The Working Bibliography

The first step in informing yourself on a given subject is to make a working bibliography — a list of books, pamphlets, and articles which you will want to examine or read. In preparing a long paper, you should not limit yourself to one or two sources for your material. To insure covering all sides of the topic, you should consult as many sources as your library and your time permit.

Here are some suggestions for beginning your working bibliography:

(*a*) Start with an encyclopedia, reference book, or standard textbook in the general field you are investigating. These will contain selected lists of books and articles.

(*b*) Consult a specialized bibliography and one or more of the periodical indexes listed under the various headings in Section **51c.**

(*c*) Use the card catalog of your library. (1) Listed under subject headings you will find many books in your field. (2) At the end of the file on your subject you will often find a "see also" card, listing related subject headings that may lead you to additional books. (3) You should look under the subject headings listed at the bottom of library cards, since these may guide you to additional material. (4) Sometimes under a subject heading you will find a subdivision devoted to bibliographical cards; that is, cards listing books that are themselves lists of books on the subject.

For some topics, especially those which are recent, you will find relatively few references. Note all of these, since your library may not have all the books and periodicals referred to and you will need to use all the sources you can find. Ordinarily, however, you will find more articles than you can look up. In such cases, consult an encyclopedia or selected bibliography to find out the standard authoritative works on the subject, and select any others which seem particularly relevant. Fifteen or twenty sources should be adequate for a freshman research paper, but be sure that you have covered both sides of controversial topics.

### 52d Bibliography Cards

As soon as you find a reference to a book or article that you think will be of help to you, make a note of it. Each reference should be written down on a separate card or slip of paper (3 × 5 inches), so that you may quickly arrange your bibliography in alphabetical order and discard items that prove useless. Write down all the information you will need if you should use the book in your final bibliography. This will save time and trouble in the long run. As a rule, the following points should be included:

(*a*) Name of author in full, surname first.

(*b*) Title of book or article.

(*c*) For a book: edition, if other than the first; place of publication; publisher; date of publication; number of volumes, if more than one.

(*d*) For an article: title of periodical; volume number; page number; date of issue of the periodical (month, day, and year).

Additional information, not to be included in the final bibliography, may be noted on the card: library call number, scope of the book, bibliography included in the book, source of the reference, etc.

**Sample Bibliography Cards**

Scarborough, Dorothy

A Song Catcher in Southern Mountains

New York: Columbia University Press, 1937

M
1629
S29
Sc2

Gerould, Gordon H.

"The Making of Ballads"

Modern Philology, XXI (1923), 15-28.

## 52e Choice of Source Material

After you have made your tentative bibliography, you are ready to examine the books and periodicals themselves. You will probably not have time to read all of them. It is important, therefore, to learn (1) how to find out quickly if a book contains material you want, and (2) how to pick out the best of several books with relevant information.

(1) To find out the scope and contents of a book, look first at the Preface, which will usually indicate the author's intention and point of view, and the Table of Contents, which will list the chapter headings and may include a detailed analysis of the chapters. Many works contain introductory chapters which give a general survey of the subject. The index at the end of a work is an alphabetical list of topics, persons, places, events, etc., appearing in the book. From the index you can quickly find out whether a particular subject is treated in the work; from the Table of Contents you will get an outline of the whole work.

(2) As an aid in choosing between several books as sources consider the following questions:

(*a*) Is the book of recent date? (The date usually appears on the title page; if it is not there, look on the copyright page.) In many subjects, particularly the sciences, the value of the material depends directly upon the date. You should also note, in examining the card catalog, whether there is a "revised edition" or an "enlarged edition" of the book.

(*b*) Can the accuracy of the statements in the book be depended upon? Is it a popular book or a serious, scholarly treatise? (A popular book, aimed at holding the reader's interest rather than arriving at the truth, seldom indicates the sources on which it is based. A scholarly work is always documented.) Does the writer show signs of bias — political, religious, or national? Is the writer an authority on the subject? (If the title page indicates that the author is on the staff of a reputable college, university, or other institution, you can probably trust his work. Similarly, the imprint of a good publisher indicates that the editors and several experts in the field have confidence in the book. Additional information about the author may be found in biographical dictionaries, like *Who's Who*.)

## 52f Tentative Plan

Begin by reading some of the more general accounts of your subject, such as those found in encyclopedias and textbooks. Then go on to more specialized works. When you think you know the general outlines of the subject, make a tentative plan or outline of the points you want to cover. Remember the word *tentative;* you will probably change the plan several times as you read further in the subject. The advantage of making some kind of plan at an early stage is that you can read more selectively, using only those sources that are relevant to your purpose. But be ready to change the plan whenever you find abundant material that interests you, or when you find an absence or scarcity of material. It is still not too late to limit your subject further, if that seems desirable. No one can tell in advance what kind of material he will find, or what will interest him most. The plan for the paper should develop as your reading fills out or modifies your original ideas on the subject.

## 52g Taking Notes

As you read, take notes of information that seems relevant or significant. If you are uncertain whether a bit of information is relevant, take it down anyway. It is easier to discard an unnecessary note than to relocate a piece of information you remember having read somewhere.

Write your notes on cards at least $4 \times 6$ inches, or on half sheets of theme paper. Put each point upon a separate card or sheet. This is very important. You cannot readily organize your material for writing unless it is broken down into small units on separate cards. If more than one card is needed for one point, use the back, or note the subject and name of the book on a new card and continue. Number such cards and clip them together.

The notes may be in the form of a direct quotation or of a paraphrase or a summary in your own words. In the final written paper, quotations should be used only when the exact words are important, or when the point is very aptly phrased in your source. If the passages are not too long, exact quotations are useful in your notes, even though you paraphrase them later in writing the paper. Be very careful in your notes to enclose direct quotations in quotation marks; otherwise you may allow borrowed phrases to appear in your paper as your own. Remember that whether you are summarizing or quoting someone else's material, you must give credit to the author in footnotes.

The following suggestions on the form of notes may be helpful:

(*a*) State the topic in the upper left-hand corner.

(*b*) State on each card the exact source, noting the author, the work, and the page. It is not necessary to write the place of publication and the date on each card since your bibliography cards and the bibliography at the end of your paper will give fuller information regarding the source.

(*c*) Put quotation marks around material that is exactly quoted. If parts are omitted, ellipsis marks (. . .) should be used where the omission occurs. Brackets should enclose words that are not part of the quotation but that are written within the quotation marks. For example, "In this book [Cheever] demonstrates his fondness for eccentric people." Do not use quotation marks for paraphrases or summaries.

(*d*) Always quote exactly, even to the punctuation marks and the spelling. If there is an obvious error in the text, insert after it the word *sic* in brackets, which indicates that the quotation is exact even though not correct.

(*e*) If you use abbreviations in your notes, be consistent. As a rule, in a summarizing note omit the articles, copulas, and connectives.

## Sample Note Cards

DIRECT QUOTATION

Difference in tone—Eng. and Amer. ballads

"On the whole the English and Scottish ballads from the old world are prevailingly sorrowful and tragic. With the mountaineers all of this is slightly and subtly different. True, the same tragic themes are common enough. But they are handled with a lighter touch. There is a discernible _penchant_ among the Southern folk-songs toward the comic, even the burlesque.... To any one who knows at first hand the independent character and racy humor of the mountaineers---[this] is no matter for surprise."

J. W. Hendren, _A Study of Ballad Rhythm_, p. 48.

BRIEF SUMMARY

Difference in tone—Eng. and Amer. ballads

Tone of Eng. and Scot. ballads generally sad and tragic. Amer. treatment of same themes tends toward comic or burlesque, reflecting sturdy independence and earthy humor of mountaineer.

J. W. Hendren, _A Study of Ballad Rhythm_, p. 48.

PARAPHRASE AND DIRECT QUOTATION

Difference in tone - Eng. and Amer. ballads

Whereas the English and Scottish ballads are "prevailingly sorrowful and tragic," the same ballads found in America show a subtle but distinct tendency "toward the comic, even the burlesque." This difference in treatment probably reflects "the independent character and racy humor of the mountaineers."

J. W. Hendren, A Study of Ballad Rhythm, p. 48

## 52h Writing the Paper

By the time you have completed your reading and note-taking, you should have a pretty clear idea of the plan of your paper. Make an outline, or revise your tentative outline into final form, and sort and arrange your note cards accordingly. The topic headings which you have written in the left-hand corner of each card should be useful here.

Your paper will be written largely from your note cards, but it should be more than a collection of notes glued together with transitional phrases. Your own original contribution to the subject you are working on will be the assimilation and synthesizing of many separate sources.

The writing must also be your own. It is permissible to use exact quotations from your sources only if they are enclosed in quotation marks and identified by a footnote reference. But you will seldom need to quote exactly; the bulk of the paper will be your own interpretation of what you have read, and it must be in your own words.

Plagiarism, which may get professional writers into legal difficulties and students into difficulties with the Dean, means trying to pass off someone else's work as your own. There is an important distinction between the use of another investigator's results, properly acknowledged, and the unacknowledged borrowing of his words and phrasing. To change a word here and there in another writer's sentence or paragraph is to invite trouble. Since it is not an exact quotation, you cannot put such a sentence in quotation marks, but your trivial changes have not made it your own sentence. Even though you indicate the source, your instructor may justifiably object that you are plagiarizing.

There is a simple remedy. When you have read a note card, turn it over and write up the information in your own words, referring to the card only if you need specific facts (dates, figures, etc.) which you don't remember.

Here are three note cards, the first containing a direct quotation and the second and third paraphrased information.

> *Changes due to oral transmission*
>
> *"When songs are kept going by the mouth-to-ear method alone, curious things happen. Titles change, names of local characters and places are substituted for the remote originals, incidents may differ.... I found mountaineers in Virginia and North Carolina singing traditional English and Scottish ballads with a cheerful ignorance as to their origin."*
>
> *Dorothy Scarborough, A Song Catcher in Southern Mountains, p. 81.*

> *Change of names in American versions*
>
> *The hero of "Little Musgrove and Lady Barnard" has been changed in American versions to "Little Mose Groves" (p. 144) and "Little Mattie Grove" (p. 147).*
>
> *Scarborough, A Song Catcher, pp. 144, 147.*

> *Change of names in American versions*
>
> *The hero of "Lord Randall" appears in American versions as "Johnny Randall" and "Jimmy Randolph."*
>
> *Louise Pound, American Ballads and Songs, pp. 3, 4.*

In writing the paper, you might combine the information on these three cards as follows:

Ballads and songs which are handed down orally from generation to generation are bound to change in the course of time. This is particularly true of English ballads transplanted to America: "Titles change, names of local characters and places are substituted for the remote originals, incidents may differ." 1 For example, Little Musgrove, the ill-fated lover of Lady Barnard in the Scottish ballad, appears in American versions as "Little Mose Groves," or "Little Mattie Grove." 2 The

1 Dorothy Scarborough, A Song Catcher in Southern Mountains (New York, 1937), p. 81.

2 Ibid., pp. 144, 147.

```
well-known Scottish ballad "Lord Randall" becomes
"Johnny Randall" or "Jimmy Randolph." 3

     3 Louise Pound, American Ballads and Songs
(New York, 1922), pp. 3, 4.
```

## 52i Documenting the Research Paper

Since most of your material will be derived from books and articles, you must indicate the sources of your information in footnotes. Such footnote references serve four purposes: they give credit to the original authors, they enable the reader to check your use of source material, they indicate the authorities on whom you are relying, and they aid investigators working on related topics.

Whether you quote exactly, or whether you paraphrase or summarize in your own words, you must indicate the source of all direct quotations and of facts and opinions for which you personally are not a sufficient authority. It is not necessary to acknowledge the sources of proverbial expressions or familiar quotations, nor of facts and ideas that are common knowledge and about which there would be no difference of opinion. But any important fact which might be questioned or argued about should be documented. If the information contained in one of your paragraphs is all taken from one book, you can indicate the source by a footnote at the end of the paragraph.

Footnotes may also be used for additional explanatory material which would be undesirable in the text because it would interrupt the line of thought or because it is not strictly relevant to the text. Here is an example:

> Ballads sung by Appalachian mountaineers today are often accompanied by a guitar, banjo, or dulcimer,[1] although in earlier periods they seem to have been sung unaccompanied.
>
> ---
>
> [1] A stringed instrument, often home-made, which is a cross between a zither and a guitar.

### Position of Footnotes on the Page

Footnotes may be inserted in the manuscript in one of three ways:

1. At the bottom of each page, as they would appear if the paper were printed. The advantage of this method is that the reader can see the reference at a glance, without having to turn pages. A disadvantage is the difficulty of estimating the space the footnotes will require at the bottom of the page.
2. On a separate sheet at the end of the paper, double-spaced.
3. Between ruled lines as the footnotes occur in the text: for example,

trembling on the border of pure song."[1] Its plot is the only as-

---

[1] Francis B. Gummere, *The Popular Ballad* (Boston, 1907), p. 116.

---

pect of the ballad which has a fairly permanent form, and this

This form is common in theses and dissertations which are bound in manuscript. It has the advantage of keeping the footnote close to the index number.

### Numbering Footnotes

To indicate the reference of the footnote, numbers are preferred to asterisks (*) or other symbols. The index number should be placed at the end of the quotation, sentence, or paragraph to which the footnote refers. It is repeated at the beginning of the footnote. (See examples on page 420.)

Number the footnotes consecutively throughout the manuscript. This method has the disadvantage that additional footnotes cannot be inserted at the last minute without changing all the following numbers, but it is a guarantee against confusion if the paper should be printed.

### Content and Form of Footnotes

Despite minor variations in punctuation and style, most handbooks and journals agree on the following basic conventions for footnotes:

1. The author's name, in normal order, comes first.
2. The title of the book follows, underlined to indicate italic type. But if the reference is to an article in a periodical (or in a book), the author's name is followed by the title of the article, in quotation marks, and this is followed by the name of the periodical (or book), underlined.
3. Information regarding the place and date of publication follows. For books, this consists of the city in which the volume was published and the date, in parentheses; for articles in periodicals, volume number and (in parentheses) the date.
4. The last item in a footnote is the page number.

The form used in the following examples of footnotes is that recommended by *The MLA Style Sheet* (Revised Edition, compiled by William Riley Parker and published in 1954 by the Modern Language Association of America.) It is assumed that a research paper will include a bibliography of works consulted, that the first reference to a book or article will be a full footnote, and that subsequent references to the same book or article will be abbreviated. Normally, an abbreviated footnote reference consists of the author's surname and a page number, but if several books by the same author are referred to, it will be necessary to use a short title in addition to the author's name. The abbreviation *ibid.* (short for Latin *ibidem*, "in the same place") is used to refer to the work cited in the immediately preceding footnote. It is usually followed by a new page number. Note that *ibid.* is italicized since it comes from a Latin word; that it is followed by a period since it is an abbreviation; and that it is capitalized when it is the first word in the footnote.

### Sample Footnotes

REFERENCE TO A BOOK

[1] Dorothy Scarborough, *A Song Catcher in Southern Mountains* (New York, 1937), p. 33.

REFERENCE TO A PERIODICAL

[2] Gordon H. Gerould, "The Making of Ballads," *Modern Philology*, XXI (1923), 17.
[3] *Ibid.*, p. 24.

REFERENCE TO ANOTHER BOOK

[4] Dorothy Scarborough, *On the Trail of Negro Folk Songs* (Cambridge, Mass., 1925), p. 59.
[5] Gerould, p. 19.
[6] Scarborough, *Song Catcher*, p. 231.

Notice that the author's first name or initial is given first. (Bibliographies, which are arranged in alphabetical order, put the author's last name first.) If the author is unknown, the first item in a footnote is the title of the article or book. Commas are used between items, instead of the periods used in a bibliography. If you wish to include the name of the publisher, it is separated from the place of publication by a colon — "Boston: D. C. Heath and Company, 1956".

Volume numbers, for books of more than one volume and for periodicals, are in Roman numerals; page numbers are in Arabic numerals. When both volume and page numbers are given, the abbreviations *vol.* and *p.* may be omitted. When the page number stands alone, use *p.* for "page" and *pp.* for "pages."

As a general rule, reference information given in the text of the paper need not be repeated in the footnote. For example, if you say "T. S. Eliot [1] maintains that . . .," the footnote would begin with the title of the book, instead of the author's name. If you write "In his *Notes toward the*

*Definition of Culture,*[1] T. S. Eliot maintains that . . .," the footnote would begin "(New York, 1949). . . ."

The following additional words and abbreviations are sometimes used in footnotes, bibliographies, and references:

*c.* or *ca.* (*circa*), at or near a given date
cf. (*confer*), compare or consult
ed., edition, or editor, or edited by
f., *plural* ff., page(s) following
*id.* or *idem*, the same; usually, the same author
l., *plural* ll., line(s)
*loc. cit.* (*loco citato*), in the place already cited
ms., *plural* mss., manuscript(s)
n., *plural* nn., note(s)
*op. cit.* (*opere citato*), in the work cited. This abbreviation must be used with the author's name, to identify which work is being cited. If two works by the same author have been referred to, this abbreviation cannot be used. The general tendency today is to avoid such abbreviations altogether, and to use the author's name, plus a short title if one is needed. See footnote 6 on page 424.
*passim*, here and there
*sic*, so, thus
v., *plural* vv., verse(s)

### EXERCISE

Write footnotes for the following references. Write a full footnote when a work is first mentioned, but for subsequent references use abbreviations.

1. A reference to page 121 of a book entitled *Tristram Shandy's World*, written by John Traugott and published in 1954 by the University of California Press at Berkeley.
2. A reference to the Autumn, 1956, issue of the *Kenyon Review*, volume 18, page 566. The article, entitled "Johnson's Life of Boswell," was written by B. L. Reid.

3. A reference to page 547 of Reid's article.
4. A reference to page 243 of a book by Joseph Wood Krutch entitled *Samuel Johnson*, published in New York in 1954.
5. A reference to page 569 of Reid's article.
6. A reference to page 129 of Krutch's book.
7. A reference to page 216 of Krutch's book.
8. A reference to page 110 of a book entitled *Five Masters*, by Joseph Wood Krutch, published in 1930 in New York.
9. A reference to page 97 of Traugott's book.
10. A reference to page 119 of *Five Masters* by J. W. Krutch.

## Final Bibliography

At the end of the research paper, add an alphabetized list of the works you have consulted. Include in it all the books and articles you have referred to in your footnotes, plus any other books and articles which have furnished background material. Do not include books which you have merely glanced at and discarded. If an author's name is not known, the book or article is placed alphabetically according to the title.

The form of a bibliographical entry differs slightly from that of a footnote reference. Authors are listed with surname first, to make alphabetizing easy. The items of an entry are separated by periods instead of commas. The following models will illustrate correct form for various kinds of books and articles. Notice that they are not arranged in alphabetical order, as they would be if they were part of a final bibliography.

BOOKS

*1. By one author*

Trilling, Lionel. *The Opposing Self*. New York, 1955. (If it should be desirable to list the publisher, the form would be "New York: The Viking Press, 1955.") A second book by Mr. Trilling would be listed as follows:

———. *The Liberal Imagination*. New York, 1950.

2. *By two authors*

Dyson, H. V. D., and John Butt. *Augustans and Romantics.* London, 1940.

3. *By more than three authors*

Sizer, Theodore, and others. *Aspects of the Social History of America.* Chapel Hill, 1931.

4. *An edited text*

Wordsworth, William. *The Prelude*, ed. Ernest de Sélincourt. Oxford, 1926.

Pound, Louise, ed. *American Ballads and Songs.* New York, 1922.

5. *A translation*

Gregory of Tours. *The History of the Franks*, trans. O. W. Dalton. 2 vols. London, 1927.

6. *A book in a series*

Greene, Evarts Boutell. *Provincial America, 1690–1740.* New York, 1905. (The American Nation: A History, ed. Albert Bushnell Hart.)

ARTICLES

1. *Magazine article*

Sorenson, Lloyd R. "Historical Currents in America," *American Quarterly*, VII (1955), 234–246.

2. *Anonymous magazine article*

"Peasants on the March," *New Statesman and Nation*, XXXVIII (1949), 677.

3. *Essay in a collection*

Thompson, T. H. "The Bloody Wood," *T. S. Eliot: A Selected Critique*, ed. Leonard Unger. New York, 1948.

4. *Encyclopedia article*

Cole, G. D. H. "Socialism," *The Encyclopaedia Britannica*, 1954, XX, 877–887.

### Sample Freshman Research Paper

The following selections from a research paper written by Phyllis Grant will illustrate the methods of documentation just described. Title page, table of contents, and outline have been omitted, since individual instructors will want to specify their own requirements.

The Ballad "Barbara Allen" in America

Ordinary, everyday Americans are generally supposed to be indifferent to poetry, but most of them have more experience of poetry than they realize. They sing. When the latest novelty from Broadway or Hollywood has gone the way of all "popular" songs, people are still singing the familiar, inconsequential pieces that they never consciously learned: game songs, spirituals, cowboy songs, or, if they were born in the eastern mountains, perhaps a traditional ballad like "Barbara Allen." And what they will be singing, whether they know it or not, is a form of poetry, an honored and acknowledged branch of folk literature.

There are thousands of folk songs in America, but the number of true folk ballads is much smaller. Any song that has been transmitted orally is a folk song; the ballads are a specialized type -- anonymous narrative poems, completely impersonal.1 The singer relates the events simply, employing the most direct language but leaving much to the imagination of the listener. And it is a _listener_, not a reader. Folk ballads differ from art ballads in that they have no fixed, standardized form and are continually changing; in fact, they are apt to be changed somewhat by every individual singer.2

1 M. J. C. Hodgart, _The Ballads_ (London, 1950), pp. 10 f.

2 Louise Pound, ed., _American Ballads and Songs_ (New York, 1922), p. xii.

A fairly large number of traditional English ballads have been found, transplanted to a new country but thriving, in the United States. Strangely enough, they have often done better in America than in England; more variants exist here today than have been found in England. This is the more remarkable in that the chances against any ballad's surviving have always been great. To survive as living segments of folk literature, ballads must be sung and they must be taken seriously by the singer.3 When they cease to come from the mouths of singers who love them, they are as dead as fossils, even though they may be embalmed in books.

The old English ballad "Barbara Allen" lends itself particularly well to investigation. It has been described as "halting and trembling on the border of pure song."4 Its vitality is indicated by the fact that it is the most widely found of all the traditional ballads in America. Also, it furnishes an excellent example of a very common theme of the old ballads: dying for love.

Like other ballads in England and America, "Barbara Allen" has been, from time to time, printed on broadside sheets to be sold by hawkers and peddlers. These broadside versions, usually corrupted or vulgarized, did little to help preserve the ballad. It was the mountain people, isolated from printing presses, who kept Barbara Allen alive by singing about her. Sometimes her sad story was written out by hand, for the enjoyment of the singer's family and friends. These written versions, called "ballets" in the mountain country, have been very useful to ballad collectors.5

3 Hodgart, p. 138.

4 Francis B. Gummere, <u>The Popular Ballad</u> (Boston, 1907), p. 116.

5 Dorothy Scarborough, <u>A Song Catcher in Southern Mountains</u> (New York, 1937), p. 15.

Until fairly recent times ballad-collecting on a large scale was confined to the Old World. Then it was discovered that America furnished an even more fertile ground for their recovery, and that Professor Francis James Child, when he made his great collection of English ballads,6 might as well have stayed in America. At least 107 of the 305 Child ballads (of which "Barbara Allen" is No. 84) have been found in the United States, as against 85 in England.7 More than three fourths of these were recovered in the South, especially in Virginia.8

Brought across the Atlantic by early emigrants, sailors, or travelers, these ballads are led in geographical distribution and number of variants by "Barbara Allen." Under such titles as "Barbary Allen," "Barbara Ellen," "Barbara Allen's Cruelty," or "The Fate of Barberie Ellen," this ballad has been found in at least 92 versions, no two identical, in Virginia alone; its tune has been found in twelve quite different forms in that state. The song spread with the early settlers into the Midwest; Abe Lincoln is said to have sung it as a boy in Indiana.9 At least thirty main versions of it have been found in North and South Carolina, Georgia, the New England states, Ohio, Indiana, Michigan, Missouri, and Arkansas;10 there is even a Negro version in Virginia.11 John Jacob

6 <u>The English and Scottish Popular Ballads</u> (Boston, 1883–1898), 5 vols.

7 Horace Reynolds, "Balladry Still Flourishes," <u>Christian Science Monitor Magazine</u>, April 20, 1946, p. 7.

8 Vance Randolph, ed., <u>Ozark Folksongs</u> (Columbia, Missouri, 1946), I, 37.

9 Scarborough, p. 83.

10 Randolph, I, 126 f.

11 Dorothy Scarborough, <u>On the Trail of Negro Folk-Songs</u> (Cambridge, Mass., 1925), p. 59.

Niles, who has done much toward keeping the old ballads alive and toward finding new ones in the backwoods sections of the country, says that his singing career began when he was a nine-year-old in Louisville, Kentucky, and his father taught him seventeen verses of "Barbara Allen" so that he could sing in a school contest.12

..........................................................

In general, evolution of Old World ballads in America (and "Barbara Allen" is no exception) has led steadily downward; few real improvements, from a literary point of view, are found in American versions. In the seventeenth century, "Barbara Allen" could delight a true music-lover like Samuel Pepys,19 but in nineteenth-century New England the song had degenerated into a part of a game at play-parties. American ballad singers have tended toward increased simplicity and abridgement, perhaps because twentieth-century audiences lack the patience of their forefathers. In any case, American versions are usually poorer as literature than the earlier English versions.20

The Child ballads are quite frankly aristocratic, dealing almost exclusively with the high-born. Only those which could be easily adapted to the common-place, democratic American level were successful in this country. Thus "Barbara Allen," whose "Sir John Graeme of the West country" could be changed without noticeable difference in the plot to "Little Johnny Green," survived; while "Sir

12 Roger Butterfield, "Folk Singer: John Jacob Niles," Life, XV (September 6, 1943), 62.

..........................................................

19 In his Diary on January 2, 1666, Pepys wrote of going to Lord Brouncker's and meeting "my dear Mrs. Knipp, with whom I sang; and in perfect pleasure I was to hear her sing, and especially her little Scotch song of 'Barbary Allen.'"

20 Gordon H. Gerould, "The Making of Ballads," Modern Philology, XXI (1923), 26.

Patrick Spens," whose hero had to retain his nobility, did not.21

.................................................

In America, strange things have happened to some of the details of the song, although the central theme remains constant. In a variant from Missouri, the disappointed William's nose "gushed out a-bleedin'."25 In another,

> He reached out his pale, white hands
> Intending for to touch her.
> She jumped, she skipped all over the room,
> And says: Young man, I won't have you.26

A local reference, fortunately rhyming, is introduced in another variant:

> There once was a pretty fair maid,
> And she lived on Lake Vitallon,
> She'd be my own true bride, she said,
> And her name was Barbary Ellen.27

Occasionally William is most generous to Barbara, as in this West Virginia version:

> Look under my head, when I am dead,
> An' you'll find three rolls of money;
> Go share 'em wid those ladies 'round,
> An' don't slight Barbara Allen.28

And so it goes and so it goes. Perhaps people five centuries hence will still be singing of the sad fate of Sweet William, or of Young Belfry, or

21 Alan Lomax, "America Sings the Saga of America," New York Times Magazine, January 26, 1947, p. 16.

.................................................

25 Randolph, I, 135.

26 Olive A. Campbell and Cecil J. Sharp, eds., English Folk Songs from the Southern Appalachians (New York, 1917), p. 91.

27 Randolph, I, 129.

28 John H. Cox, Folk-Songs of the South (Cambridge, Mass., 1925), p. 104. See also Child, II, 276.

Little Jemmy Groves, or even of Sir John Graeme: they are all the same, for they all loved and lost the haughty young woman whose charms were so irresistible and whose name was Barbara Allen. But it will not be the wise, educated people who will carry on the ballad tradition; it will be the wise, illiterate ones, tucked away in cabins inaccessible even to the most hardy of modern educators, who will go on singing for their own enjoyment the fates of the two young people whose story began to be told so many centuries ago.

List of Works Consulted

Butterfield, Roger. "Folk Singer: John Jacob Niles," Life, XV (September 6, 1943), 57-64.

Campbell, Olive A., and Cecil J. Sharp, eds. English Folk Songs from the Southern Appalachians. New York, 1917.

Child, Francis James, ed. The English and Scottish Popular Ballads. 5 vols. Boston, 1883-1898.

Cox, John H. Folk-Songs of the South. Cambridge, Mass., 1925.

Gerould, Gordon H. "The Making of Ballads," Modern Philology, XXI (1923), 15-28.

Gummere, Francis B. The Popular Ballad. Boston, 1907.

Hendren, J. W. A Study of Ballad Rhythm. Princeton, 1936.

Hodgart, M. J. C. The Ballad. London, 1950.

Lomax, Alan. "America Sings the Saga of America," New York Times Magazine, January 26, 1947, pp. 16 and 41.

Pound, Louise, ed. American Ballads and Songs. New York, 1922.

Randolph, Vance, ed. _Ozark Folksongs_. (British Ballads and Songs, Vol. I.) Columbia, Missouri, 1946.

Reynolds, Horace. "Balladry Still Flourishes," _Christian Science Monitor Magazine_, April 20, 1946, p. 7.

Scarborough, Dorothy. _A Song Catcher in Southern Mountains_. New York, 1937.

------. _On the Trail of Negro Folk-Songs_. Cambridge, Mass., 1925.

Wimberly, L. C. _Folklore in the English and Scottish Ballads_. Chicago, 1928.

# Correspondence

**53.** CORRESPONDENCE

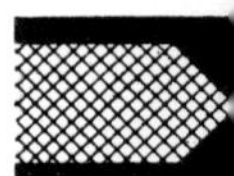

# 53 CORRESPONDENCE

A letter is equivalent to paying a call in person. Just as, in a personal interview, you are judged by your dress, manners, and attitude, so you will be judged by the appearance, form, and tone of a letter. No matter how persuasive and forcible the content of your letter may be, a bad first impression caused by carelessness in form or pompousness of tone will be hard to overcome.

Attention to form, style, and tone is particularly important in a business letter. Personal letters — those written to friends and intimates — should be easy and natural. No hard and fast rules for personal letters can be prescribed, beyond those that are applicable to every kind of good writing. Business letters, on the other hand, should follow strictly the conventional forms. They should be courteous and direct in tone, without being stiff or abrupt. Conspicuous familiarity or jocularity is as much out of place as back-slapping or elbow-nudging would be in a personal call. Business letters should be concise and to the point. Wordiness in such a letter is just as annoying as long-windedness in conversation.

### Business Letters

Business letters should be written on one side only of bond paper, $8\frac{1}{2} \times 11$ inches in size, and of good quality. If possible, they should be typewritten, single-spaced, with double-spacing between paragraphs.

The sample letters which follow illustrate the correct form for business letters.

**Heading**

320 Fifth Street
Santa Cruz, California
August 2, 1956

**Inside Address**

World Travel Bureau
274 Alvarado Street
Monterey, California

**Salutation** Gentlemen:

Please try to make a reservation for me on American Airlines Flight 671, from New York to Los Angeles, on September 21, 1956. I will also need a reservation for a connecting flight, preferably Coach, from Boston to New York on the same day.

**Body**

American Airlines has an early morning Coach flight from Boston to New York, but it lands at La Guardia Field, and Flight 671 leaves from Idlewild. I doubt that there would be time to transfer from one airport to the other. Some airline, however, must have a flight to Idlewild in time to make the connection.

**Close** Very truly yours,

**Signature** Edwin Frazer

Edwin Frazer

# WORLD TRAVEL BUREAU

**Printed Heading** 274 Alvarado Street Monterey, California

August 10, 1956

**Inside Address**
Mr. Edwin Frazer
320 Fifth Street
Santa Cruz, California

**Salutation** Dear Mr. Frazer:

This will confirm the following reservations for you:

**Body**

| | |
|---|---|
| Leave Boston, Sept. 21, American Airlines Flight 393 | 7:50 a.m. |
| Arrive Idlewild | 9:00 a.m. |
| Leave Idlewild, Sept. 21, American Airlines Flight 671 | 9:30 a.m. |
| Arrive Los Angeles | 3:00 p.m. |

The flight from Boston to New York is First Class, but it is the only flight on any airline that will make this connection. Thank you very much for the opportunity to be of service.

**Close** Yours truly,

WORLD TRAVEL BUREAU

**Signature** Robert A. Southwell

Robert A. Southwell
Manager

RAS:KB

### The Heading

The heading gives the address of the writer and the date, in that order. Avoid abbreviations. The heading is typed in the upper right-hand corner of the first page; printed or engraved letterheads are usually centered on the page, and the date is typed in at the right. Block style is preferred, but if indented style is used in the heading, it should be used consistently throughout the letter.

**Block style.**

```
5743 Dorchester Avenue
Chicago, Illinois
October 21, 1956
```

**Indented style.**

```
5743 Dorchester Avenue
   Chicago, Illinois
      October 21, 1956
```

Punctuation at the end of the lines is usually omitted, but if it is used, there should be a comma at the end of the first two lines and a period after the date. In any case, there should be punctuation within the lines: a comma after the city and after the day of the month.

**Without end punctuation.**

```
2684 Webster Avenue
Atlanta, Georgia
March 15, 1957
```

**With end punctuation.**

```
2684 Webster Avenue,
Atlanta, Georgia,
March 15, 1957.
```

### The Inside Address

The inside address should contain the name and the full postal address of the person written to. It should be placed at the left-hand side of the page, flush with the margin and at least three or four lines below the heading. The usual form is block style without punctuation, but it should be consistent with the heading. Avoid the use of abbreviations, except that names of firms should be written exactly as they appear on the letterhead of the firm. Abbreviate only the following titles: *Mr.*, *Esq.*, *Messrs.*, *Mrs.*, *Mmes.*, *Dr.*, *Rev.*, *Hon.* The proper titles to be used in addressing high officials and dignitaries may be found in *Webster's New International Dictionary*, pages 3012–14.

**Correct.**
E. P. Dutton & Company, Inc.
300 Fourth Avenue
New York 10, New York

**Correct.**
Dr. E. A. Addington
415 Cobb Building
Seattle, Washington

**Correct.**
Mr. John R. Walden
D. C. Heath and Company
285 Columbus Avenue
Boston 16, Massachusetts

### The Salutation

The salutation should be written flush with the left-hand margin, two spaces below the inside address. In formal business letters it is followed by a colon. The following salutations are used when the name of the person addressed is not known, or when a personal tone is not especially desired:

**Correct.** Dear Sir: (*My dear Sir* is more formal; *Sir* is extremely formal.)
Dear Madam:
Gentlemen:
Ladies: (*Mesdames* is correct, but old-fashioned.)

When a person is addressed by name, the following salutations are used:

**Correct.** Dear Mr. (or Mrs.) Harper:
Dear Dr. Addington:
Dear Professor Linforth:

When the sex of the person addressed is not known, the masculine salutation is used. When the marital status of a woman addressed is not known, use *Dear Madam.*

### The Body

The body of the letter begins two lines below the salutation. Paragraphing may follow either the block style (see sample letter, page 438) or the indented style (sample letter, page 437); but if the heading and inside address are indented, the paragraphs in the body should be indented. Typewritten letters are usually single-spaced, with double-spacing between paragraphs. The length of the letter determines the width of the margins. Try to center the letter attractively on the page. In a short letter use double-spacing, if necessary.

Say what you mean in ordinary, idiomatic English. Do not omit pronouns, articles, or prepositions, and avoid trite formulas like *your favor of the 17th inst.*, *would beg to state*, etc.

**Pompous and old-fashioned.** Yours of the 17th inst. at hand, and in reply would beg to state. . . . Will try to carry out instructions in same. . . . Please find enclosed check for three dollars.

**Improved.** I have received your letter of April 17. . . . I will try to carry out your instructions. . . . A check for three dollars is enclosed.

### The Complimentary Close

The complimentary close should be written two lines below the last line of the body of the letter. It should begin near the middle of the page and should be followed by a comma. Only the first word is capitalized.

The complimentary close, like the salutation, should be appropriate to the person or persons addressed and to the tone of the letter.

**Impersonal, frequently used.**

Yours truly,
Yours very truly,
Very truly yours,

**Formal, used for persons superior in rank.**

Yours respectfully,
Respectfully yours,
Very respectfully yours,

**Informal, friendly, personal.**

Yours sincerely,
Sincerely yours,
Cordially yours,

### The Signature

The signature is usually placed about two spaces below the complimentary close, and either directly beneath it or two spaces or so to the right. The signature should always be written by hand. In a typewritten letter in which the name of the writer does not appear on the letterhead, the name may be typewritten beneath the written signature. Sometimes the writer's official capacity is indicated.

A married woman should sign, not her husband's name preceded by *Mrs.*, but her own married name. If she wishes to be addressed in reply as *Mrs.*, she should precede her name by *Mrs.* in parentheses, or write her husband's name preceded by *Mrs.*, all in parentheses, on the line below her signature. The usual custom is to address a woman as *Dear Madam* if her married status is not indicated.

**Correct.**

Very truly yours,
(Mrs.) Mary Osborn Williams

**Correct.**

Very truly yours,
Mary Osborn Williams
(Mrs. John R. Williams)

**Correct but usually unnecessary.**

Very truly yours,
(Miss) Elizabeth Elliot

### Mechanical Directions

Envelopes should match the paper in color and quality, and should hold the paper easily when it is properly folded. For a business letter written on sheets of full commercial size (approximately $8\frac{1}{2} \times 11$ inches) use

1. an envelope of commercial size (approximately $3\frac{1}{2} \times 6\frac{1}{2}$ inches). Fold the letter in half, with a horizontal crease slightly below the center, and then fold the half-sheet into three equal sections.

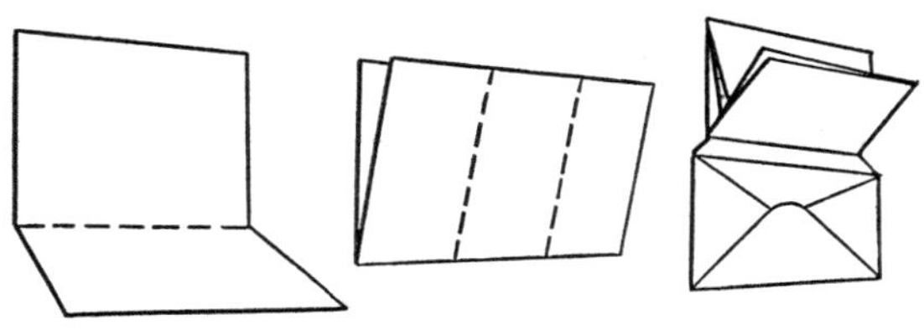

2. an envelope of official size (approximately $4 \times 10$ inches). Fold the letter from bottom and top into three equal sections.

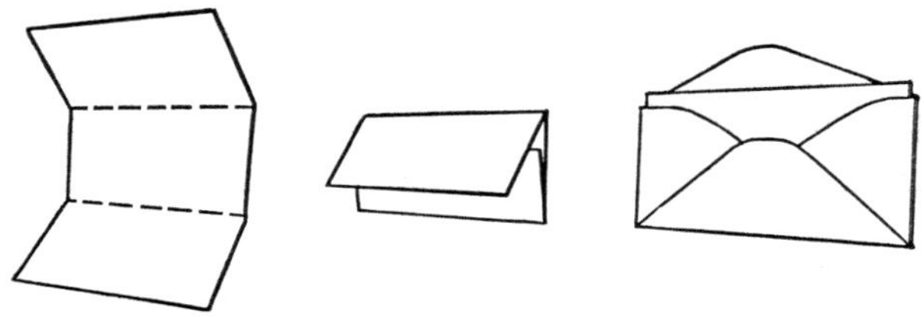

The form of the address on the envelope is the same as that of the inside address. The return address should be placed on the front of the envelope in the upper left-hand corner.

James Swift
463 Ninth Street
Davenport, Iowa

Mr. Thomas Howe
1802 Wendell Drive
Bridgeport
Connecticut

### Formal Notes

A formal note should be written by hand, not typed, and should have no salutation, no complimentary close, and no signature. An inside address is written in the lower left-hand corner. The third person should be used consistently throughout: the writer should not refer to himself as *I*, nor to the addressee as *you*. No abbreviations except *Mr.*, *Mrs.*, and *Dr.* should be used, and the numbers in dates should — unlike those in ordinary letters — be spelled out. The present tense should be used throughout the note.

Mr. and Mrs. James Burton request the pleasure of Miss Helen Irwin's company at dinner on Friday, May the twenty-second, at seven o'clock.

935 Webster Street
May the third

Miss Helen Irwin accepts with pleasure the kind invitation of Mr. and Mrs. James Burton to dinner on Friday, May the twenty-second, at seven o'clock.

1720 Princeton Avenue
May the fourth

Miss Helen Irwin regrets that because of another engagement she is unable to accept the kind invitation of Mr. and Mrs. James Burton to dinner on Friday, May the twenty-second, at seven o'clock.

1720 Princeton Avenue
May the fourth

# INDEX